This Must Be the Place

This Must Be the Place

DISPATCHES & FOOD FROM THE HOME FRONT

Rachael Ray

FOOD PHOTOGRAPHY BY KATE MATHIS

Ballantine Books · New York

Published in the United States by Ballantine Books, an imprint of
Random House, a division of Penguin Random House LLC, New York.

BALLANTINE and the HOUSE colophon are registered trademarks of
Penguin Random House LLC.

Additional photograph credits and permissions appear on page 331.

Hardback ISBN 978-0-593-35721-7
Ebook ISBN 978-0-593-35722-4

Printed in China on acid-free paper

randomhousebooks.com

9 8 7 6 5 4 3 2 1

First Edition

Book design by Phoebe Flynn Rich

This book is for those we've lost during this terrible pandemic. And to our beloved Isaboo.

Additionally, I dedicate this to all of the frontline workers in the battle against the deadly global pandemic—to the nurses, doctors, therapists, EMTs, police and firefighters, grocery and delivery workers, and anyone who answered the call across the country and the world, who put their own lives at risk to save us before they knew what they were even saving us from. When I think about the heroism they've shown, it washes over me and leaves me filled with awe and love, and the deepest of gratitude to those who tried to keep us safe as best they could.

Contents

This Must Be the Place

On March 12, 2020, as I walked into my home in Upstate New York with my husband, John, and my fifteen-year-old dog, Isaboo, all I felt was dread. A pandemic was upon us. Our in-studio production had halted with dozens of shows left to shoot in our season. Izzy was battling cancer and the challenges of advanced age. My mom, who is eighty-six, lives across the way from our rural home, and we were concerned for her health and her ability to see her doctors. John's folks would be farther away from us, in New Jersey. They also have issues and conditions that put them at increased risk of infection. How could we help them from a distance? Then there was the looming fact that to continue my work, to do my job, I'd have to give up my safe place. I'd have to cross a line that I had never crossed before, let the

world into my most private space, and record our show from <u>my home</u>. The prospect of this made me feel like an anxious child again, frightened to let someone into my room for fear they might break my things or make fun of them, or haunt me like the bogeyman.

My spring began with crossing that line and turning my home into my workspace. My summer began with the death of my dog in my arms. My home wouldn't survive the summer either. It caught fire and burned on August 9.

My cabin in the woods had always made me feel safe and free. It was where I could <u>feel</u>, period. It's where I had the time to create and to be my fullest and best self. It's where I could write and develop ideas, where I could read and learn and grow and play. The house came to life by my own hand: I literally drew the layout myself. There was a great room with a kitchen at one end looking straight through the living space to slab windows facing into the forest at the far end. In the center sat a hearth and a huge fireplace with glass on either side, and stone benches. It was the heart of my home and in a few months it would also be the cause of the demise of my home.

As I write this, I've been living and working from upstate for eight months, two of them in the small but cozy guesthouse where we've become the most grateful of semi-permanent guests. We are making our way and rebuilding our lives. I'm writing in my new office, which used to be our garage.

After hundreds of days up here, distanced from the people and city and life I love, I feel that I'm closer to the world—to viewers, readers, colleagues, and friends—than ever before. In the long months of 2020, I would come to know them all in a much deeper and in a more substantive way. It was during these days that I also had to watch as the charred and damaged remains of my home were torn down and the ashes of all of my things were carted away, down the hill. And while this was going on outside my guesthouse window, I was required to conduct interviews and conversations where I'd have to act upbeat. Thankfully, I've also watched trucks go _up_ that same hill on the side of our little almost-mountain every day, framing the rebuild of my house and my life.

The year 2020 was a paradox. Nearly every human on the planet was touched by not just one thing, but multiple core-shaking events—the pandemic, civil unrest, a new understanding of racial suffering, a socioeconomic uprising. And yet, we came together in ways we wouldn't have done otherwise. I wanted to sit down and write this book, focusing on what this year meant to me, because despite the social distancing we were all doing (few more passionately than my germophobic husband and me in our quiet little forest), I felt more attached to the world around me than ever before.

Everybody did more home cooking. Grocery sales—online and in-store—saw huge spikes. Most of us in food media had record ratings and audience levels. Ask anyone who writes recipes for a living and they'll tell you it was a tough reality to swallow, the idea that we might be benefitting from a catastrophe—especially as many of our colleagues in the restaurant industry were in deep distress. It was a conundrum. And for me it was also a line to walk. How do I get people to want to learn new things to cook while they're going through what may be the hardest period of their lives?

When I started recording the show

from home, we led off with pantry staples, because everyone was worried about supply chains, and it was all about using up what we had on hand. What can you do with canned tuna or beans? (The answer is, lots and lots!) No one knew how long this was going to last, and several months later I felt free to come up with recipes for almost anything I wanted, since we all got familiar with ordering groceries and learned we could buy whatever we wanted with competitive pricing that allowed us to cook anything we could afford. And as restaurants tragically shuttered, we learned to fulfill more of our cravings at

home. I began with Chinese and Thai, making more Make Your Own Takeout (MYOTO) than ever before. Conversely, when the holidays arrived, we scaled way back. It was not the year to host large groups. Over the year, I coached readers, viewers, fans, and followers on the TV show, in the magazine, on Instagram TV, and on TikTok through recipes and techniques reflecting the moment. The arc of my cooking in 2020 is a chronicle of the year—the ups and downs, losses and gains, emotions and experiences that we were all going through.

This book offers dispatches from what felt like the edge of reality. It's a scrapbook in recipes and words, offering a year in the life. It includes many of the recipes I prepared over this weird time, but more important, it's a record of my thoughts, emotions, voice, and food. I am a very private person (I know, kinda strange for someone on TV every day), but after this year I wanted to share. And now, with this book and the shows I recorded from my home, I've shared more than ever before.

I tried to write recipes for food that would make people happy, and also comfort them, especially during this difficult time. Over the year, I cooked well over four hundred meals, between feeding content to my audiences and feeding my family. I always say, you can't make everybody happy at the same time on the same day, but maybe you can make them all happy within a year. I sure tried. This book is the chronicle of the year that was, and the recipes I cooked.

"This Must Be the Place" is one of my favorite songs. David Byrne's lyrics and the Talking Heads melody bring the feeling of home, the warm feeling of the familiar. What I've learned this year is that home is a state of mind and heart. We've lost a lot, my husband John and I, but we have each other, we have a new loving dog to care for, and our parents remain safe. I can feel at home again. This is the place. This must be the place. We are home.

The food I created for those first few shows focused on what to make from pantry items. Americans at that moment felt like we were all on a short, unknown adventure, and we were concerned about stocking up on staples that would last however long quarantine would.

GREEK SHEET PAN CHICKEN WITH FETA AND PEPPERONCINI

EASY FLORENTINE PASTA WITH ITALIAN TUNA

TUSCAN MEAT SAUCE LASAGNA

POPCORN CHICKEN WITH WHITE CHEDDAR POPCORN

ONE-POT CHICKPEA PASTA

5-MINUTE EASTER: HAM WITH ORANGE BALSAMIC GLAZE OR
SMOKED LEG OF LAMB, LEMONY SMASHED POTATOES,
AND SPRING VEGETABLE MEDLEY

OLD BAY SHRIMP QUESADILLAS

Coming Home

5-SPICE CHILI-TOPPED BAKED POTATO SKINS

EVERYTHING CHILI WITH TORTILLA TOPS

PORK CHOPS WITH APPLES, POTATOES, AND ONIONS

LINGUINE ALLE VONGOLE

BOMBAY GRILLED CHEESE

JOHN'S MUMBAI MULE

Crossing that Line

I'm a homemaker by nature and by nurture. When I was growing up, my mom always had a way, often with limited funds, to turn rooms into magical living, breathing spaces. She still has a unique eye for design, and I love her style.

When I was a girl, my family lived in a Yankee Barn on Cape Cod—a beam, peg, and groove house with sliding wooden barn doors. I remember as a child drifting off on many nights, nestled under a cozy throw on the sofa, not wanting to go to bed. I preferred falling asleep there in the living room, near the glow of a fire, looking at all the magical shapes and forms that surrounded me. Mom has always loved to layer a room with both shape and texture: statues and sea glass, an old lobster trap, weathered leather and nubby fabrics, wood and metal accents. The natural materials made the room feel real, like it had a personality and a life force of its own.

My room in the barn was a hayloft with a small balcony and a ladder that dropped down into the living room. I put a lot of effort into keeping it cozy and nice, just the way my mom did with the rest of the house. I arranged my stuffed animals and dolls in animated poses at a tea set and around the shelves and room—Raggedy Ann and Andy swinging from their ragdoll knees on the ladder. In the morning, I'd leave the art paper on my easel either clean, calling me to paint or draw after school, or with a completed work, art to decorate the space until I felt the need for a change. I rarely left it with a work-in-progress, and the same was true with my weaving loom and Erector set. I arranged my books by height and color before that was a thing, and placed some favorites around the room on side tables and my worktable, as if my toys would come to life and read them while I was away. I took pride in making my bed and would organize the pillows in an inviting way, and I always wanted the corner turned down, an invitation to climb in and take comfort there. My room was loved as if it were a member of the family, and that's the way I feel about where I live to this day. The house I grew up in and the comfort it provided became the inspiration for the design of the home that my husband and I built in the Adirondacks.

In cooking, you gather elements or surprising ingredients in new combinations and right before your eyes it all comes together, like magic. Home design is like that, too: some science, but also that magic that makes something surprising just <u>work.</u> I've lived in houses small and large, apartments cramped to sprawling, and rarely have I been able to sleep if there was a dish in the sink or a mess to pick up or a pillow on the floor. I don't want to live in a "perfect" or precious space, but I do want the space to reflect that it is loved and that its purpose is care and comfort. I want my home to feel welcoming to human and animal guests, a space where they instantly feel love and warmth.

I've also always thought of my home upstate as a refuge, a safe place away from my career in the public eye. Over the years I've been asked dozens of times to be photographed or filmed here and I have always, with very rare exceptions, said no. I wanted to keep our secret garden, our crazy fort, our treehouse/clubhouse to ourselves, to be shared with only our closest friends and family. This is one reason why—knowing I would have to start recording my show from here, and let the world into my safe space—that I looked at my homecoming in March with fear and dread. Trucking upstate each week after recording shows, taking meetings, reviewing magazine spreads, and talking about new recipes was always a joyful and regular reprieve for me, one that I looked forward to throughout the week after a run of hard workdays in the city. Now that time that I used to look forward to was laced with panic. The idea of filming at home during the pandemic would mean showing viewers my private space, something I'd resisted doing for fifteen years.

Another concern was that I would have to do my own hair and makeup. The counterpoint to my love for homemaking is my hives-inducing dislike of "self-care"—including applying makeup and looking at myself in a mirror for long stretches to do it. But because it wasn't safe to have another person touching my face during this time, I'd have to do it myself. Each day of filming at home I would put on the bare minimum of makeup—a few swipes of my Milk blur stick—and groom my eyebrows. Sharing a stripped-down version of myself meant people would judge me for who I was underneath the warpaint. In terms of wardrobe, while I was used to having people pull and prepare my clothes in advance of each show, I was now pulling on-air clothes from whatever stuff I kept in my upstate closet—mostly comfy tees and pull-on pants. And I'm not sure if it was my Sorel slippers or sneakers that first day, but it for sure wasn't the heels I'd wear in the studio in New York. Though I'd always prided myself on being authentic on the show, this was a whole new level of "real."

I was also worried, like everyone, about staying healthy and safe during the pandemic. And I was terrified about letting people into my home virtually, to see me in this new, intimate way. Still, this was the best plan we could come up with, so John and I got ready to shoot an episode of our show from our kitchen upstate. When the iPhone camera that John was manning rolled at last, and I said that first sentence, "Hey everybody, it's Rachael here. Welcome to our home!" my eyes welled up a bit. I'd jumped into uncharted waters with those

words. I flashed on my first swimming lesson at the YMCA when I was in grade school, when everyone made fun of my bathing suit and I sank like a stone. Would people make fun of me?

They didn't. My team called to say that ratings held and viewers responded really positively (I never watch myself on TV or check the ratings). We shot those first shows on an iPhone and Mac. The content was just us, Rach 'n' John, cooking, making cocktails, and answering questions from viewers. The food was focused mostly on what to make with pantry staples. Americans at that moment felt like we were all on a short, unknown adventure, and we were concerned about stocking up on staples that would last however long quarantine would. What can we cook from canned tuna and beans that would taste really good so we don't feel deprived? John made our show very meta in that you'd hear a voice from behind the camera shouting out comments and inquiries (and _a lot_ of direction). "Why do you do that?" Or "Slide to the center counter so we can

see you better." And the ever-popular "Tell us more about that." The funny thing was, it was _good_ television—it felt intimate and real in ways a studio show never quite could.

And after taping that first show I felt . . . great! There was relief and catharsis in letting it all hang out. And this new radical transparency felt like a good and much needed kick in the pants. I'd been feeling so trapped and boxed in by circumstance, panicked that I had no choice but to tape from my home if I wanted to keep the show going, keep people working. Then, on the other side, I found fresh purpose. It was liberating.

As with all things, this has been a huge learning process. It felt so good making the shows together, John and me, and we'd be so proud when we completed two per week. Our interviews were very limited, as it took us a while just to figure out how to optimize Zoom. I got overly industrious with the food in one show, a pizza special. I started at 5 A.M. lighting the oven and finished cleaning up at 11 that night. Still, we made our way, very slowly, and we were eventually shooting seven shows per week. When we started, the system involved a skeleton crew over the phone and computer, and round-the-clock editing; as I write this we just got another upgrade on our microphone and a computer that can be controlled by our friends and colleagues in the show's control room in NYC. The quality has improved with cables and wires that run all around us and have turned taping into a strange game of Double Dutch from the ends of my kitchen countertops.

I miss the studio. I miss our great circus and our team and crew so much, all of our habits and rituals. I miss my daily routine: coffee, gym, hair, car, studio, check food in kitchen, "good morning everyone!" Try on clothes, makeup, show, show, show, home, make dinner, bed, do it all again. Now I get up at 4 A.M. most days and we never catch up to the work that needs to be done before we collapse at night. These are strange and strained days, and I am so curious what our new vibe and life will become when we go back to rebuild the show and ourselves, all together again in the same place.

Greek Sheet Pan Chicken

WITH FETA AND PEPPERONCINI

SERVES 4

2 bulbs garlic (16 to 18 cloves), peeled and trimmed of root end

About ½ cup EVOO

8 pieces bone-in, skin-on chicken, or 12 skinless chicken thighs, or 6 boneless, skinless chicken breasts, halved across

3 tablespoons fresh oregano, chopped (or 1 tablespoon dried), plus more to finish

2 halved lemons, plus ⅓ cup lemon juice

Kosher salt and freshly ground black pepper

1½ to 2 pounds fingerling or small thin-skinned potatoes

12 to 16 ounces feta cheese, cut into large cubes

½ cup chopped flat-leaf parsley, to finish

1 cup Greek pepperoncini peppers

■ In a small pot, combine the garlic cloves and oil to cover. Heat over medium heat until hot, then reduce the heat to low and gently cook until the garlic is light tan or caramel in color, 20 to 25 minutes. Remove the garlic from the oil and mash with a fork into paste. Let the oil and garlic cool.

■ Position a rack in the center of the oven and preheat the oven to 425°F. Line a sheet pan with foil.

■ In a bowl, pour the cooled oil over the chicken and add the mashed garlic. Add the oregano, halved lemons, lemon juice, salt, and pepper.

■ In a large pot, combine the potatoes with water to cover. Bring to a boil and cook at a full boil for 5 to 6 minutes. Drain, cool, halve, add to the chicken, and toss gently so you don't destroy the potatoes.

■ Arrange everything on the lined pan, with all the chicken pieces skin-side up and the potatoes a mix of skin- and cut-side up. Tuck the feta all around it.

■ Transfer to the oven and roast until the potatoes are crisp, the chicken reads 160°F on a meat thermometer, and the feta chunks are browned, 45 minutes to 1 hour.

■ Top with parsley and oregano. Douse the potatoes with the juice of the roasted lemon halves. Top the chicken with chopped or whole pepperoncini.

Use the leftovers from this easy meal for a big Greek-style salad for lunch. Just toss with red wine vinaigrette, sweet peppers, onions, celery, cucumbers, tomatoes, and Kalamata olives.

Easy Florentine Pasta

WITH ITALIAN TUNA

SERVES 4

1½ to 2 pounds spinach or 2 (16-ounce) packages frozen spinach, thawed

¼ cup EVOO

1 large shallot or small onion, finely chopped

Salt

4 large cloves garlic, finely chopped

1 teaspoon crushed red pepper flakes

1 tablespoon grated lemon zest

¼ teaspoon freshly grated nutmeg

2 tablespoons lemon juice

1 (14-ounce) can Italian cherry tomatoes, 1½ cups semi-dried tomatoes (lightly drained and chopped), or 2 cups halved fresh cherry tomatoes

½ cup dry vermouth or white wine

2 (5-ounce or so) jars or cans Italian tuna in oil, drained and flaked, or 2 cups pulled/shredded cooked chicken

1 pound spaghetti, chitarra (square spaghetti), or bucatini pasta

1 cup freshly grated Parmigiano-Reggiano or Romano cheese (optional)

Bring a large pot of water to a boil for the pasta.

If using fresh spinach, bring another pot of water to a boil. Add the spinach and blanch briefly, then drain, squeeze dry, and chop. If using thawed frozen spinach, squeeze it dry in a kitchen towel, then chop.

In a large skillet, heat the EVOO (four turns of the pan) over medium heat. Add the shallot and a couple pinches of salt and stir for 2 minutes. Add the garlic, pepper flakes, and lemon zest. Add the spinach, loosen it up, and season with nutmeg. Add the lemon juice and tomatoes and break them up. Add the vermouth and simmer at a good bubble for 5 minutes. Add the tuna to heat through.

Salt the boiling water and cook the pasta 1 minute less than the package directions for al dente. Before draining, ladle out about a cup of the starchy pasta cooking water. Drain the pasta and toss with the sauce and Parmigiano (if using), adding cooking water as needed to merge and add gloss to the pasta. Serve.

I make this dish with fresh or frozen spinach and pantry staples like tuna and canned cherry tomatoes or semi-dried tomatoes. You can also swap pulled/shredded rotisserie or poached chicken for the fish.

Tuscan Meat Sauce Lasagna

SERVES 6 TO 8

MEAT SAUCE

3 tablespoons EVOO

1 medium onion, finely chopped

1 rib celery with leafy tops, finely chopped

1 carrot, finely chopped

2 large cloves garlic, chopped

Salt

1 pound ground beef, pork, and veal blend, or beef and veal blend

2 chicken livers, trimmed and finely chopped (optional, but recommended)

Finely ground black pepper and/or white pepper

3 or 4 fresh sage leaves, finely chopped (1½ to 2 teaspoons)

2 small sprigs fresh rosemary, leaves stripped and finely chopped (1½ to 2 teaspoons)

1 small fresh bay leaf

1 cup white wine

3 tablespoons tomato paste

3 cups chicken stock (see Note)

1 cup whole milk

BESCIAMELLA (WHITE SAUCE)

3 tablespoons butter

3 tablespoons AP flour

3 cups whole milk

Salt and ground white pepper

⅛ teaspoon freshly grated nutmeg

ASSEMBLY

1 (16-ounce) package square or rectangular lasagna sheets

1 (24-ounce) jar passata or 3 cups canned tomato sauce

1½ to 2 cups freshly grated Parmigiano-Reggiano cheese

1 small ball (6 ounces) fresh mozzarella cheese, very thinly sliced, or 1½ cups shredded mozzarella

1 small handful of fresh flat-leaf parsley, finely chopped

■ Make the meat sauce: In a Dutch oven or other sturdy saucepot, heat the EVOO (three turns of the pan) over medium to medium-high heat. Add the onion, celery, carrot, and garlic. Season with salt. Cook, stirring often, until the vegetables soften, 4 to 5 minutes. Add the meat and chicken livers (if using). Cook until the meat is no longer pink, about 6 minutes. Season with salt and pepper. Stir in the herbs, then the wine. Cook, stirring occasionally, until the wine is absorbed, 8 to 10 minutes. Add the tomato paste and stir for 1 minute. Add the stock and milk and bring to a bubble. Reduce the heat to low and simmer, stirring occasionally, until the sauce thickens and the vegetables and meat are well combined, 1 hour to 1 hour 30 minutes. Remove the sauce from the heat and discard the bay leaf.

■ Make the besciamella: In a large skillet or saucepan, melt the butter over medium to medium-high heat. When the butter foams, whisk in the flour, then whisk in the milk. Season the sauce with salt, white pepper, and the nutmeg. Cook the sauce, stirring often, until it thickens enough to coat the back of a spoon, about 10 minutes. Remove the sauce from the heat.

(CONTINUED)

(CONTINUED)

Bring a large pot of water to a boil for the pasta. Salt the water, add the pasta, and cook for 5 minutes. Drain the pasta and arrange the noodles in a single layer on a kitchen towel. Top with another kitchen towel.

Position a rack in the center of the oven and preheat the oven to 375°F.

Pour half of the passata into a 9 × 13-inch baking dish and spread evenly in the bottom of the dish. Add a layer of noodles (3 noodles per layer) and one-third of the meat sauce. Add another layer of noodles, one-third of the white sauce, and a handful of Parmesan. Repeat the process two more times. Top with a final layer of noodles and the remaining passata, then top with the mozzarella and the remaining Parm. Cover with foil.

Transfer to the oven and bake for 40 minutes. Uncover and bake until browned and bubbling, 20 to 30 minutes more. Let stand until set, 20 to 30 minutes. Slice and serve in shallow bowls. Garnish with the parsley.

Note: If you have a chunk of Parm rind, add it to the chicken stock and warm for 30 minutes to develop a nice rich flavor.

Popcorn Chicken

WITH WHITE CHEDDAR POPCORN

SERVES 4 TO 6

This is also great with shrimp.

2 pounds chicken tenders

Canola oil, for deep-frying

1 cup AP flour

½ cup cornmeal

3 tablespoons Old Bay Seasoning

1 tablespoon sugar

2 teaspoons dried lemon peel or finely grated lemon zest

1 teaspoon cayenne pepper or other ground chiles

1 tablespoon kosher salt

2 large eggs

¼ cup whole milk

1 teaspoon hot sauce, preferably Frank's RedHot

White Cheddar Dill Popcorn (recipe follows)

½ cup finely chopped fresh dill and chives, for garnish

Buffalo Ranch Dipping Sauce (recipe follows)

■ Cut each chicken tender crosswise into three pieces.

■ Heat 3½ to 4 inches oil in a Dutch oven or deep-fryer to 350°F (medium to medium-high heat).

■ In a medium bowl, whisk the flour, cornmeal, Old Bay, sugar, lemon peel, cayenne, and salt. Pour half of the flour mixture into a large resealable plastic bag. Add the chicken and shake to coat.

■ In another medium bowl, whisk the eggs, milk, and hot sauce. Shake excess flour off the chicken. Dip the chicken in the egg mixture, then coat in the flour mixture left in the bowl. Working in batches, fry the chicken until the outside is deep golden brown and the meat is cooked through, about 5 minutes.

■ Add the chicken nuggets to a bowl of the cheddar dill popcorn and toss. Top with the dill and chives. Serve with Buffalo sauce.

(CONTINUED)

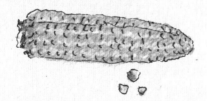

WHITE CHEDDAR DILL POPCORN

SERVES 4 TO 6

1 (8.5-ounce) bag white cheddar popcorn

1 tablespoon dried dill

1 tablespoon granulated garlic

1 tablespoon granulated onion

1 teaspoon celery seeds

■ In a large bowl, toss the popcorn with the dill and spices.

BUFFALO RANCH DIPPING SAUCE

MAKES ABOUT 1¼ CUPS

1 cup sour cream or whole-milk Greek yogurt

½ cup mixed finely chopped fresh leafy herbs: dill, flat-leaf parsley, and chives

¼ cup hot sauce, preferably Frank's RedHot

2 teaspoons Worcestershire sauce, or to taste

1 clove garlic, grated

Salt and freshly ground black pepper

■ In a small bowl, mix all the ingredients until combined.

Note: I'm kind of famous for my flavored popcorns. This one's got a shortcut and I am here to tell you: There is no shame in the shortcut!

One-Pot Chickpea Pasta

There are a million different recipes for pasta e ceci—it's a very classic Italian recipe. Every family has its own way of doing things, including ours. If you're vegetarian, leave out the pancetta and use vegetable stock.

3 tablespoons EVOO

¼ pound pancetta, diced (optional)

1 small onion, chopped

½ bulb fennel, finely chopped, plus chopped fronds (optional) for garnish

2 to 3 cloves garlic, minced

2 tablespoons chopped fresh rosemary or 2 teaspoons dried

Salt

1 teaspoon crushed red pepper flakes

2 cups vegetable stock or chicken bone broth

1 (15-ounce) can chickpeas, drained, half the can very finely chopped or mashed

1 (14-ounce) can crushed, diced, or cherry tomatoes

1½ cups any short pasta (about ½ pound)

4 to 5 cups chopped escarole, stemmed lacinato kale, or green Swiss chard

Freshly grated pecorino or Parmigiano-Reggiano cheese

In a deep skillet, heat the EVOO (three turns of the pan) over medium-high heat. Add the pancetta (if using) and render 3 minutes. Add the onion, fennel, garlic, rosemary, salt to taste, and pepper flakes. Cover and sweat a couple of minutes. Add the stock and 2 cups water and bring to a boil. Add the whole and finely chopped chickpeas and tomatoes and return to a full rolling boil. Add the pasta, reduce to a simmer, and cook the pasta to al dente. Add the greens and let wilt. Stir in a big handful of pecorino. Top with the fennel fronds (if using) and more cheese and serve.

HAM WITH ORANGE BALSAMIC GLAZE

SERVES 4 TO 8 (WITH LEFTOVERS)

1 small boneless smoked ham (7 to 10 pounds) or 1 spiral-cut half ham (about 10 pounds)

1 cup chicken stock or bone broth

½ cup orange or lemon marmalade

¼ cup balsamic vinegar

½ cup grainy Dijon mustard

1 tablespoon fresh rosemary, chopped

1 tablespoon fresh thyme, chopped

- Preheat the oven to 325°F.

- Place the ham in a baking dish or pan and pour the stock into the bottom of the pan.

- In a small saucepan, combine the marmalade, vinegar, mustard, rosemary, and thyme and heat over medium heat until loose and brushable.

- Use a pastry brush to brush a generous amount of the glaze over the ham (if using a spiral cut ham, make sure you get in all the nooks and crannies between the cuts). Reserve the remaining glaze.

- Cover the whole pan with foil and transfer to the oven. Heat the ham until heated all the way through, about 1 hour or 6 to 7 minutes per pound.

- Remove the ham from the oven and remove the foil. Brush another generous round of the glaze over the top of the ham and return the ham to the oven and bake for another 15 minutes.

- Serve the ham with any leftover glaze.

SMOKED LEG OF LAMB WITH FRESH MINT SAUCE

SERVES 4 TO 8 (WITH LEFTOVERS)

1 large boneless smoked leg of lamb (7 to 10 pounds)

1 cup chicken or beef stock

FRESH MINT SAUCE

1 bunch parsley, washed and leaves picked

1 bunch mint, washed and leaves picked

2 cloves garlic, peeled

2 small or 1 large shallot, coarsely chopped

1 tablespoon kosher salt

Freshly ground black pepper

¼ cup white wine vinegar

¼ cup sugar

- Preheat the oven to 325°F.

- Place the lamb in a roasting pan and pour the stock into the bottom of the pan. Cover the pan with foil and transfer to the oven. Cook until the lamb is heated all the way through, about 1 hour or 5 to 6 minutes per pound. Remove the foil and bake for 10 more minutes.

- Meanwhile, make the fresh mint sauce: In a food processor, combine the parsley, mint, garlic, shallots, salt, and pepper to taste and pulse until finely chopped. Remove the mixture to a bowl.

- In a small saucepot, combine ¼ cup water, the vinegar, and the sugar and bring to a boil over medium-high heat, stirring to dissolve the sugar. Remove from the heat and let stand for 2 minutes to cool very slightly. Pour over the herb mixture and stir to combine.

- Serve the lamb with the mint sauce on the side.

This was a hit on IGTV. Warning: It does *not* take five minutes—that's just how long the video was. But it *is* super-easy. I also did a 5-Minute Passover video, using the brisket recipe from page 296. That whole menu works for Passover, too!

LEMONY SMASHED POTATOES

SERVES 4

2 pounds small potatoes, such as baby Yukon Golds (but you could use any small potato here—rule of thumb is ½ pound per person)

Salt

EVOO

Freshly ground black pepper

1 lemon, halved and charred in a small skillet over medium-high heat

■ In a medium saucepot, combine the potatoes with cold water to cover. Season the water with a generous pinch of salt. Bring to a boil over high heat, then reduce the heat to a simmer and cook until the potatoes are tender all the way through, 30 to 40 minutes depending on the size of the potatoes.

■ Meanwhile, preheat the oven to 450°F. Line a sheet pan with parchment paper.

■ Drain the potatoes and transfer them to the lined sheet pan. Using the bottom of a drinking glass or measuring cup, carefully smash each potato down so that it is about ½ inch in height. Slather with a generous amount of EVOO and season with salt and pepper.

■ Transfer to the oven and roast until nicely browned and very crispy, 35 to 40 minutes.

■ Squeeze the charred lemon halves over the potatoes to serve.

SPRING VEGETABLE MEDLEY

SERVES 4

1 large or 2 medium leeks (white and light-green parts)

Salt

3 medium carrots, sliced crosswise on an angle

½ pound haricots verts, stem ends snipped

1 tablespoon unsalted butter

2 tablespoons EVOO

½ pound sugar snap peas

Freshly ground black pepper

¼ to ½ cup chicken stock

Chopped fresh herbs: dill, chive, or tarragon

■ Trim the tough parts off the leeks, then clean thoroughly and slice crosswise ½ inch thick.

■ Set up a bowl of ice and water. In a saucepot of boiling salted water, blanch the carrots for 2 to 3 minutes, then scoop out and plunge into the ice bath. Add the green beans to the boiling water and blanch 2 to 3 minutes, then plunge into the ice bath.

■ In a large skillet, melt the butter and EVOO (two turns of the pan) over medium-high heat. When the butter foams, add the leeks and season with a pinch of salt. Allow to sweat a few minutes and soften. Add the sugar snap peas and sauté for another minute or two. Add the carrots and haricots verts and stir to combine everything. Season with another pinch of salt and pepper. Sauté another 4 to 5 minutes and add a splash of stock. Allow stock to cook off.

■ Toss with the fresh herbs to finish.

The New Rules

When we decided to turn our home into a studio, with no production crew in sight to help us, John and I had to learn all new rules for ourselves and for our home.

Pre-COVID, I would make wildly long grocery lists based on fantasy foods, new disciplines I wanted to try, big-project cooking ideas, and anything special for family. I'd get up an hour before work on Wednesday and head to the Union Square Green Market, near my apartment in New York City, to find something new I could play with when I went upstate on Thursday night.

Once our home became a working studio, I had to start managing it like a business. I had done this kind of work for many decades. I'd run markets. I'd worked in restaurants since I was twelve years old.

But I'd never run my <u>home</u> like a business. Turning my happy place into a working production kitchen was daunting, a total sea change. Instead of fun and play, my usual recess on the weekends, I now had to operate it as the studio and back office of a daily TV show, a full-service content-making business, a <u>job</u>.

So I got to work. I cleaned out the freezer. Reorganized everything. Relabeled. Started master lists. Like everyone else in the early days of the pandemic, I was worried about how and where and when I'd be able to get great produce. So when I could get it, I'd order extra and blanch and freeze it. I cleaned the entire pantry and alphabetized every herb and spice. I arranged dried pastas by the dates on the packages. I'll admit, I went pretty cuckoo-pants. But I wanted to achieve the order and organization of a professional operation. Doing all this made me feel like we were accomplishing something, that we had control over something, as we created order in a world that seemed very precarious.

Then there was the procurement. If I'm taping multiple shows per week, I need products coming in on a regular basis. To do that when everyone is panicking and hoarding, you have to build an efficient system. So my sister, who lives nearby, and helpers who do work for my mom and for us became an enlisted brigade, a little army of helpers. The team scoped out and catalogued items that could be found at every shop between Lake George and Albany. Purveyors in the city who didn't usually ship outside of it agreed to send some things to me. I made friends with online suppliers. Fish from War Shore Oyster Company, Lobster Place Chelsea Market, and Fulton Fish; unusual finds from Goldbelly and random food sites. We were creating a landscape of how to get our hands on food for the show in order to tape it from home. It was challenging, but thanks to friends helping on the ground in New York City, and my pilot in command and communications director, Michelle Boxer, we shared our needs with the network each week and established a working system. Like many home cooks during this time, I learned how to get access to food and just about any ingredient, which got first harder than usual, and then easier and more and more accessible as we explored different grocers in our areas, and stayed up late to claim slots with delivery services we never knew existed before. Many of us became product and pantry management experts.

Who knew that this would happen twice in the same year? When our home that we had lived in for fifteen years, the one where we were now taping all of our daily shows and Instagram videos, burned down five months later, what didn't go up in flames in my kitchen suffered water and chemical damage. I had to start fresh in the guesthouse, with a new kitchen and a pantry half the size of what I'd had. It was time to create new rules yet again, but this time instead of adapting our pantry into a professional kitchen, we had to build one from scratch.

And in very little time. Three days after the fire, I had a message from my producers: We need pictures of the guesthouse and your plan for how to proceed.

I had absolutely no plan. But work is work; you gotta put your pants on and figure it out. I quickly made laundry lists of every spice from A to Z, and every ingredient I could think of, recalling what had been a staple in my recently formed and thoughtfully adjusted work-from-home pantry. I'd kept my lists from March on, but this was different because that house had been pretty well stocked for my playing and testing. So I tried to recapture as much as possible of the work I'd already done and build on it.

By August, when we started taping for the new season of our show, our fifteenth, the culinary team, under the direction of my friend and colleague of twenty years Emily Rieger, had created a safe packaging system to provide portioned ingredients for the recipes that I'd be shooting on air each week. These were all based on highlighted grocery lists I would create as I came up with my recipes. I'm a super-specific person with my ingredients and way too bossy about where and how I want a product sourced. So after doing it all myself for several months, it was hard for me to let go enough to allow others to help me improve my system. But I did, and the procurement team expanded, and it's amazing how we all pulled this off week after week. The unboxing of orders alone was an hours-long process that John and I managed, like everything else in our "home studio," by ourselves.

As the months spent working and living from home passed, the food I made for our show became more sophisticated. When I started, it was all pantry staples because we (me, my team, the audience, the country) were all worried about getting our hands on fresh ingredients. Eventually I went back to creating recipes around what I wanted to eat, based on almost any ingredient I could dream up, because I knew that most everyone could once again get their hands on it. I now love shopping for food online. The pricing is surprisingly competitive and I

can source (almost) anything. Even locally, here in Upstate New York, I'm amazed at the finds from local small grocers, including things like tamarind paste, Thai basil, fresh turmeric root, and curry leaves.

The year 2020 brought so many of us back home and into the kitchen. We learned so much. Many friends shared their stories of self-discovery with me, and of the payoff in spending more time at their kitchen counter and stovetop. So many people hadn't really understood it before—the emotional component of devoting time to cooking for yourself, the ones you love, and your family. The beauty of getting into a routine, and the skills you can develop simply by cooking every day, often multiple times. For me and for many people across the country, preparing food for or with our families became the discipline, diversion, and devotion that got us through.

Roasted Sausages with Fennel & Moondrop Grapes

1 large bulb fennel
2 onions · 1 bulb garlic
1 pound moon drop or
black seedless grapes
EVOO ~ Salt & Pepper
4 sprigs rosemary, stripped
2 pounds Italian Sausage hot or sweet
Aged Balsamic vinegar to drizzle

Preheat oven to 425.
Slice the fennel and the onions into thin wedges. Peel & crush garlic.
Remove grapes from stems, leaving a small bunch or two attached for garnishing serving platter.
Drizzle a few tablespoons of EVOO over the mixture on a parchment lined baking sheet.
Add rosemary, toss and nest the sausages into the fennel & grapes.
Roast the sausages & grapes about 30 minutes & drizzle with Aged Balsamic Vinegar.

Old Bay Shrimp Quesadillas

SERVES 4

1 tablespoon extra-virgin olive oil

1 tablespoon butter

½ onion, finely chopped (½ to ¾ cup)

2 ribs celery, finely chopped (½ to ¾ cup)

1 green bell pepper, finely chopped (½ to ¾ cup)

1 tablespoon chopped fresh thyme or 1 teaspoon dried

Salt

2 to 3 cloves garlic, peeled

¾ to 1 pound shrimp, peeled and deveined, tails off, chopped

2 tablespoons Old Bay Seasoning

Ground cumin

Ground coriander

Freshly ground black pepper

Hot sauce

¼ cup silver/white tequila

1 lemon, halved

Nonaerosol cooking spray

4 (8- to 10-inch) flour tortillas or 8 (6-inch) soft corn tortillas

2 cups shredded Monterey Jack, Colby, and/or cheddar cheese

Guacamole, for topping

Cilantro, for topping

Sliced scallions, for topping

■ In a large skillet, heat the EVOO (one turn of the pan) and butter over medium-high heat. Add the onion, celery, and bell pepper and stir 2 to 3 minutes. Add the thyme and salt to taste and cook until tender, 2 to 3 minutes. Grate in the garlic, then add the shrimp, Old Bay, a large pinch each of ground cumin and coriander, and salt and black pepper to taste. Stir and cook until the shrimp are just opaque and barely cooked through, 1 to 2 minutes, flipping halfway. Add a few dashes of hot sauce. Add the tequila and shake the pan for 1 to 2 minutes to let the tequila evaporate or burn off. Squeeze in the juice of the lemon and remove from the heat.

■ Heat a cast-iron or nonstick skillet over medium heat and lightly mist with cooking spray. Add a tortilla, char one side, and remove. Repeat with the remaining tortillas.

■ To assemble, add a tortilla to the pan, charred-side up, top with cheese and shrimp and more cheese. Fold in half if using larger tortillas, or stack another tortilla on top, charred-side in, if using smaller 6-inch ones. Keep flipping to brown and melt the cheese.

■ Top the quesadillas with guacamole, sprinkle with cilantro and scallions, and serve.

Old Bay Seasoning and the trinity of bell peppers, celery, and onions give these shrimp quesadillas an extra-flavorful and festive kick. Serve them with guac and a batch of black beans.

5-Spice Chili-Topped Baked Potato Skins

MAKES 8 TO 12 LARGE SKINS

POTATOES

4 to 6 large russet potatoes, scrubbed clean

Nonaerosol cooking spray

Salt and freshly ground black pepper

5-SPICE BLEND

1½ tablespoons chili powder

2 teaspoons ground cumin

2 teaspoons ground coriander

2 teaspoons smoked paprika (pimentón)

1 teaspoon dried oregano

You'll be really happy with this comfort food classic reinvented for a healthier generation and time.

CHILI FILLING

Nonaerosol cooking spray

1 pound lean ground sirloin or plant-based meat

1 small onion, finely chopped

1 jalapeño or Fresno chile, seeded and finely chopped

Salt and freshly ground black pepper

3 fat cloves garlic, peeled

¾ cup beef stock (if using sirloin) or vegetable stock or water (if making vegetarian)

1 (14-ounce) can fire-roasted crushed tomatoes

ASSEMBLY

2 cups shredded easy-melting cheese, such as pepper Jack, cheddar, or vegan cheese

Pickled jalapeño slices

Chopped fresh cilantro

Scallions, thinly sliced on an angle

■ Bake the potatoes: Preheat the oven to 400°F. Prick each potato with a fork 4 or 5 times. Place the potatoes directly on an oven rack and bake until tender and just cooked through, about 45 minutes. Remove from the oven, but leave it on and increase the temperature to 450°F.

■ Line a baking sheet with parchment paper. When the potatoes are cool enough to handle, halve them lengthwise. Using a spoon, scoop out the middle, leaving about a ⅓-inch border of potato. Lightly mist the skins on both sides with cooking spray and season with salt and pepper. Arrange on the lined baking sheet and roast until crispy and lightly browned, about 20 minutes.

■ Meanwhile, make the 5-spice blend: In a bowl, toss together the spices.

■ Make the chili filling: Heat a large nonstick skillet over medium-high heat and mist with cooking spray. Brown the sirloin or plant-based meat. Stir in the onion, jalapeño, 5-spice blend, and salt and pepper to taste. Grate in the garlic. Add the stock and let it cook out. Stir in the canned tomatoes to combine, reduce heat to low, and simmer to absorb.

■ To assemble, fill the skins with chili and top with cheese. Bake to brown and melt the cheese. Serve with jalapeños, cilantro, and scallions.

Everything Chili with Tortilla Tops

SERVES 4 TO 6

CHILI SPICE BLEND

2 teaspoons smoked paprika (⅔ palmful)

2 teaspoons ancho or other mild chile powder (⅔ palmful)

2 teaspoons ground cumin (⅔ palmful)

2 teaspoons ground coriander (⅔ palmful)

CHILI

2 tablespoons olive or vegetable oil

1 pound ground sirloin or 1 (12-ounce) package plant-based meat

Salt and freshly ground black pepper

1 large onion, finely chopped

4 cloves garlic, chopped

2 (4-ounce) cans green chiles or ¾ to 1 cup jarred or thawed frozen Hatch chile peppers

2 tablespoons chipotle paste from a tube (see Note)

2 tablespoons Worcestershire sauce or vegetarian Worcestershire sauce

1 tablespoon soy sauce

1 (28-ounce) can fire-roasted tomatoes, chopped, crushed, or whole

1 (8-ounce) can tomato sauce or taco sauce

2 (15-ounce) cans beans, such as black, red kidney, or pinto (get 2 different colors)

2 cups beef or vegetable stock

TORTILLA TOPS

6 flour or corn tortillas, cut into wedges, or 5 to 6 taco shells, broken into large pieces

Nonaerosol cooking spray, to toast soft tortillas (skip if using hard shell tacos)

1 (8-ounce) brick cheddar, pepper Jack, Monterey Jack, or Colby Jack cheese, shredded

OPTIONAL TOPPINGS

Pickled jalapeño peppers

Scallions and/or cilantro

Sour cream

Hot sauce

Note: If you can't find chipotle paste in a tube, puree canned chipotle peppers in adobo sauce.

■ Make the chili spice blend: In a small bowl, stir together all the spices.

■ Make the chili: In a Dutch oven or chili pot, heat the oil over medium-high heat. Add the meat or plant-based meat, season with salt and pepper, and cook until browned. Add the onion, garlic, and chili spice blend and stir a few minutes to soften. Add the chiles, chipotle paste, Worcestershire, soy sauce, fire-roasted tomatoes, tomato sauce, beans, and stock and cook to thicken a bit.

■ Make the tortilla tops: Preheat the oven to 350°F. Line a baking sheet with parchment paper. If using soft tortillas, scatter the tortilla wedges on it and mist with cooking spray. If using taco shells, scatter the pieces on the baking sheet. Bake until golden and crisp, 4 to 5 minutes for taco shells or 10 to 15 for soft corn or flour tortillas. Remove from the oven (but leave the oven on). Top toasted tortilla wedges or taco shell pieces with cheese and bake until the cheese is melted.

■ Serve the chili with cheesy tortilla tops and toppings of choice.

Pork Chops
WITH APPLES, POTATOES, AND ONIONS

SERVES 4

4 center-cut pork loin chops (about 1½ inches thick)

Salt and freshly ground black pepper

1 teaspoon granulated garlic

1 teaspoon granulated onion

2 tablespoons EVOO

2 tablespoons butter

6 small or baby potatoes (about 1 pound), thinly sliced

2 sweet-tart apples, such as Gala or Honeycrisp—quartered, cored, and thinly sliced (with peels or without)

1 small red onion or 2 small shallots, thinly sliced

½ cup chopped mixed fresh herbs: sage, rosemary, and thyme

½ cup chicken stock

Juice of ½ lemon

1 tablespoon grainy mustard

▪ Bring the pork chops to room temperature. Pat the meat dry, then sprinkle both sides with salt and pepper and the granulated garlic and granulated onion.

▪ Heat a very large cast-iron skillet (13 to 14 inches) or Dutch oven over medium-high heat. Add the EVOO (two turns of the pan). When the oil shimmers, add the chops and cook until browned, 3 minutes per side. Transfer to a plate.

▪ In the same skillet, melt the butter. Add the potatoes, apples, onion, and herbs. Season with salt and pepper. Cover and cook, stirring occasionally, until the vegetables and apples soften a bit, 4 to 5 minutes.

▪ Stir in the stock, lemon juice, and mustard. Slide the chops back into the skillet. Cover partially and cook until a meat thermometer inserted horizontally into the chops registers 140°F, about 5 minutes. Serve the chops directly from the skillet.

Linguine alle Vongole

SERVES 4 TO 6

2 pounds fresh cockles or littleneck clams, scrubbed clean (or 2 cans baby clams)

3 tablespoons EVOO

3 to 4 anchovy fillets

5 to 6 large cloves garlic, chopped

2 tablespoons fresh thyme, chopped, or 2 teaspoons dried

1 lemon, zested and halved

Chile paste or crushed red pepper flakes

1 cup white wine or dry vermouth

Kosher salt

4 tablespoons (½ stick) butter

1 big handful of fresh parsley (about 1 cup), chopped

1 pound linguine

1 handful of micro celery or celery tops, chopped

■ If using fresh clams or cockles, put them in a bowl of iced salted water and let sit for 30 minutes. Drain.

■ Bring a large pot of water to a boil for the pasta.

■ Put the clams in a large pot over medium heat. Add about ½ cup water, cover, and steam until the shells open and release their clam juice (liquor, as it's called), 3 to 5 minutes, then turn off the heat.

■ In a large pan, heat EVOO (three turns of the pan) over medium-low heat. Add anchovies and gently stir until they melt. Add garlic, thyme, lemon zest, and chile paste or pepper flakes and stir. Add wine, turn up the heat to medium, and simmer until sauce is reduced by half.

■ Salt the pot of boiling water and add pasta.

■ Working over a bowl to catch the clam liquor, remove about three-quarters of the clam meats from their shells. Transfer the remaining clams in their shells to a plate.

■ Squeeze both lemon halves into the sauce. Add the butter and half the parsley. Add the reserved clam liquor and shelled clams to the pan sauce.

■ Cook the pasta just shy of the package directions for al dente, then drain, add to the sauce, and finish cooking. Add the micro celery and garnish with the reserved clams in the shell. Finish with the remaining parsley.

Anchovies are the secret ingredient in this sauce. Once you melt them, they just taste like natural salt. You can omit them if you like, but I strongly recommend you try as is!

Bombay Grilled Cheese

SERVES 4

12 ounces baby potatoes

Salt

1 cup mixed fresh mint and cilantro leaves

1 jalapeño, seeded and coarsely chopped

1 fat clove garlic, smashed and peeled

Juice of 1 lime

8 slices whole wheat bread, crusts trimmed

Softened butter, for spreading

1½ teaspoons Goan masala, garam masala, or other curry spice blend

1 tomato, very thinly sliced

Half of 1 seedless cucumber or 2 Persian (mini) cucumbers, thinly sliced

1 small white, red, or yellow onion, thinly sliced

8 slices sharp yellow cheddar cheese

Pickled Indian vegetables, giardiniera, or pickled cauliflower, for serving

Chips, for serving

■ Set up a bowl of ice and water. In a medium pot, combine the potatoes and cold water to cover. Bring to a rapid boil over high heat, then reduce the heat to medium-high, salt the water, and cook until the potatoes are tender but not falling apart, 10 to 12 minutes. Using a slotted spoon, transfer the potatoes to the ice bath. When the potatoes are cool enough to handle, drain them, pat them dry, then thinly slice.

■ Meanwhile, in a blender or mini food processor, pulse the mint/cilantro mixture, jalapeño, garlic, and lime juice and process to a thick paste. Season the mint chutney with salt.

■ Arrange 4 slices of bread on a work surface. Spread with some butter to coat evenly but lightly on both sides. Spread a liberal layer of the chutney on top of one side. Toss the potatoes with the Goan masala, then arrange on top of the chutney in an even layer. Top with the tomato, cucumber, and onion, then the cheese. (Make sure to arrange all of the ingredients in an even layer so you get a little bit of everything in every bite.) Spread butter thinly on remaining bread slices, then top sandwiches with them, butter side up.

■ Preheat a panini press or heat a large cast-iron skillet over medium-low heat. If using the panini press, press the sandwiches until the bread is toasted and the cheese melts. If using the skillet, add the sandwiches, working in batches if needed. Using another heavy skillet, press the sandwiches, turning once, until the bread is toasted and the cheese melts, about 3 minutes per side.

■ Slice each sandwich diagonally and serve with the pickled vegetables and chips.

This creamy, crunchy, tangy, spicy sandwich was inspired by classic Indian street food. I researched it and there are a million interpretations, so I made up my own based on what I like and don't like!

COCKTAIL BY JOHN

John's Mumbai Mule

MAKES TWO COCKTAILS

- ½ cup sugar
- 2 teaspoons grated peeled fresh ginger
- 1 teaspoon grated peeled fresh turmeric
- 3 ounces vodka
- 2 ounces fresh lime juice
- 6 to 8 ounces ginger beer
- 2 lime wheels, for garnish

In a small saucepan, stir the sugar and ¼ cup water over medium heat until the sugar dissolves, 3 to 5 minutes. Stir in the ginger and turmeric. Remove from the heat and let cool about 1 hour. Strain the ginger/turmeric syrup. Into each of two ice-filled copper mugs, pour 1½ ounces vodka, 1 ounce lime juice, and ½ ounce of the ginger/turmeric syrup. Top with ginger beer. Garnish with lime wheels.

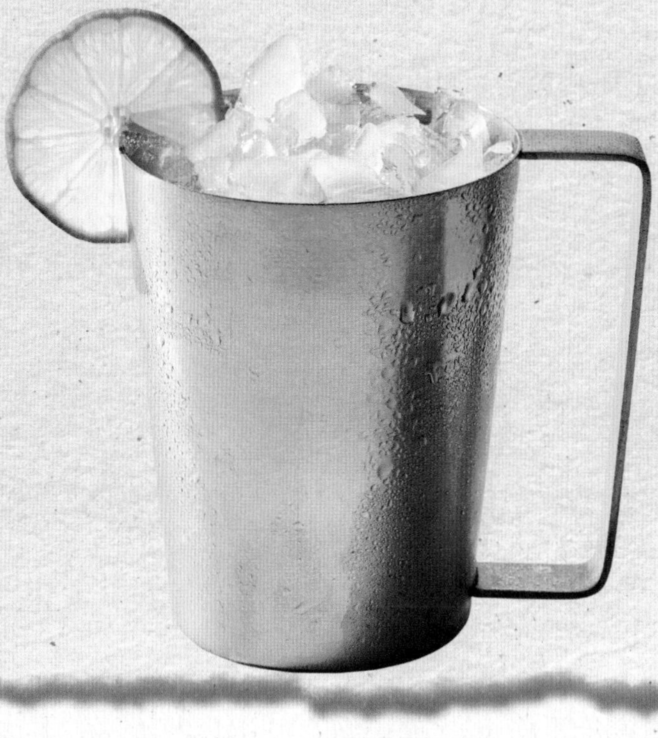

We started simple, believing it was a short-term situation, trying to use up what we had and get our hands on what we could. But we soon realized that to be in a good state of mind and stay healthy over the long term, we needed less processed food. We broadened our horizons and our diets, to be healthier and happier.

SAUSAGE, FENNEL, AND GREENS WITH WHITE BEANS

SHRIMP AND CHORIZO PAELLA

ONE-PAN SEAFOOD BAKE WITH GARLIC BREAD

STEAK NIÇOISE

EGGPLANT SCHNITZEL WITH WHIPPED HONEY AND SCHUG

SPINACH SALAD WITH WARM BACON-MAPLE DRESSING

Making Adjustments

BUTTERNUT SQUASH CARBONARA

BUCATINI ALL'AMATRICIANA WITH SPRING PEAS

SPRING SALAD WITH PISTACHIOS AND BURRATA TOAST

CHICKEN AND APPLE CURRY DINNER: CHICKEN AND APPLE CURRY, ALMOND RICE PILAF, MINT-CHILE RAITA, AND NAAN

HALIBUT WITH CREOLE SAUCE

STUPID GOOD, SILLY EASY TRAY BAKE: SAUSAGE, APPLES, FENNEL, ONION, AND FINGERLING POTATOES

JOHN'S FILTHY DIRTY MARTINI

The Director's Chair

During the past year, whenever we would shoot video for the shows at home, my husband, John, would spend Monday through Thursday sitting above me in his black director's chair. The chair came into play fairly late in the game. He'd been recording us (me and him) for several months, for our daily show and for my Cook-Alongs on Instagram TV, and he decided he needed a director's chair, so he ordered one. The day the chair arrived, it went straight to his head. Scorsese? Not so much. But he worked hard at overseeing the shoots. And he loved sitting up in that chair.

John is a lawyer by day and a musician by night . . . and at heart. With the pandemic, he was forced to wear additional hats, those of on-site director, producer, and crew for our daily show, not to mention being my one-man tech department. Prior to March 2020, his interest in technology manifested itself in preordering the new iPhone before the old one became obsolete, but that was about it. Still, over the last year John has raised the bar for demonstrating patience (not a strong suit for either of us) as he faced a steep learning curve for TV show production and production equipment.

Many people will tell you it's a mistake to work with your romantic partner, husband, or wife. (The expression "Don't sh*t where you eat" comes to mind. Or my mother's warning: "Two large rats in a small cage will eat each other.") John works for our holding company, Watch Entertainment, but the offices are across town from the studio I record in, so usually we work on the same team but in different stadiums. After installing ourselves permanently upstate, we worked right on top of each other. Some of our days stretched over eighteen hours. Others consisted of two hours being lost just in processing food deliveries. I cleaned the stove four to five times a day between takes and shows. John ran loads and loads of dishes in the dishwasher, and we both vacuumed and swept often. (COVID protocols and John's fear of contamination meant no cleaning person.) There were always laundry buzzers going off and more ironing to do. The work was never done, and most nights we'd just pass out eventually for a few hours of sleep. It's no wonder that we snapped at each other or became impatient. If familiarity breeds contempt, we should've been full of it. Thankfully, we are tough, thick-skinned, and able to laugh at ourselves and at each other. Having a sense of humor got us through as a couple and as co-workers.

The key was to use some of what little free time we had to work on things separately, to keep our independence and pursue our own interests. I studied Italian for a few hours a week and wrote for the show and magazine and this book, and tried to make time to draw. John had his music studio, which was separate from the house and needed a deep cleaning after the fire, but survived. He wrote a new song each week, and he and his band recorded a fantastic rock album remotely over the summer as well.

We also made time to share things together as a couple that weren't work. We Zoomed with friends and hosted cook-alongs and cocktail hours. We watched the news together, sometimes for several hours a day depending on what was going on. We felt it kept us attached to the world, which was going through so much, and united us in empathy. We of course ate together as well, and made time to enjoy our dinner, even if we'd already cooked several for the show that day. What we produced on camera was afterward often packaged and given to friends and family nearby.

Once we became permanent guests in our guesthouse, space was tight and the setup was intense. There was one closet for both of us, one queen-size bed for us and Bella, our pit bull/Weimaraner puppy who is sixty pounds as I write this, on her way to ninety by the vet's estimate. We had wires, lights, cords, and equipment stuffed any- and

everywhere, so to find room for John's very tall, large director's chair (sadly not collapsible) was a problem. I found a niche in the corner of our closet next to a cool David Bowie poster and it actually looked good in there. Each day we carried it onto the set, aka our kitchen.

Our first day having that chair on set, nothing went well. We had a glitchy Zoom connection that kept freezing. Turns out Herr Director had forgotten to plug into the ethernet, a necessity to get the bandwidth you need for steady, reliable recording. We had to begin the interview over again. The guest was Gloria Estefan. Luckily she's an old friend and laughed with us over our technical difficulties.

That said, I have to give John major credit. He researched his multiple jobs tirelessly in order to do them well, and enlisted tutorials and support from his techie bandmate Andrew Meskin, as well as our crew and producers, editors, engineers, and control room director. On top of all of his work behind the scenes (literally), John was a great and frequent cohost (he hid his blotting papers in the kitchen drawer under the hammer) and the show's resident (also literally) mixologist. The point is, he may have let the chair go to his head, but he was crushing the work. I loved seeing him in that chair at the end of the day, with a double Scotch on ice in his hand, feeling proud of himself. I'm proud of him, too. He earned that chair and we're gonna keep it even when taping from home is over. It suits him.

Sausage, Fennel, and Greens

WITH WHITE BEANS

SERVES 4

2 tablespoons EVOO

1 pound sweet Italian fennel sausage, casings removed

1 bulb fennel, quartered and chopped

2 ribs celery with leafy tops, chopped

1 onion, chopped

4 cloves garlic, sliced

1 teaspoon crushed red pepper flakes

Salt and freshly ground black pepper

1 head escarole, trimmed and coarsely chopped

2 quarts chicken stock

1 (15- to 19-ounce) can cannellini beans, rinsed and drained

1 chunk of Parmigiano-Reggiano rind

¼ teaspoon freshly grated nutmeg

■ Heat a large soup pot or Dutch oven over medium-high heat. Add the EVOO (two turns of the pan). When the oil shimmers, add the sausage and cook, stirring often, breaking up the sausage with a spoon, until the meat is browned, about 8 minutes. Add the fennel, celery, onion, garlic, and pepper flakes. Season with salt and black pepper. Partially cover the pot and cook, stirring often, until the onion and fennel soften, 5 to 6 minutes. Add the escarole and stir until it wilts, about 1 minute. Stir in the stock, beans, Parm rind, and nutmeg. Let the soup simmer until slightly thickened, about 10 minutes. Remove the Parm rind before serving.

I'm not a snob about most things, but you want real cheese in your food. Buy a chunk of Parmigiano-Reggiano and shred it yourself (or make your partner do it!). And when you're down to the rind, save it for cooking.

Shrimp and Chorizo Paella

SERVES 4

PAELLA SPICE

1 tablespoon smoked paprika (pimentón)

2 teaspoons chili powder

1 teaspoon cayenne pepper

1 teaspoon ground turmeric

½ teaspoon saffron threads

PAELLA

1 pound shell-on large shrimp

1 quart vegetable or chicken stock

2 tablespoons EVOO

Salt and freshly ground black pepper

½ pound hard cured chorizo or plant-based chorizo, peeled and diced

1 small white or yellow onion, finely chopped

1 cup short-grain rice, such as bomba or Arborio

2 cloves garlic, peeled

Scant 1 tablespoon tomato paste

½ cup dry sherry or white wine

¾ cup fresh or frozen green peas

¼ cup diced pimientos or piquillo peppers

Juice of 1 lemon

Chopped flat-leaf parsley

▪ Make the paella spice: In a small bowl, combine the spices.

▪ Make the paella: Peel the shrimp and save the shells. Devein the shrimp, then rinse and drain.

▪ In a saucepan, toast the shrimp shells over medium-high heat until pink, bright, and fragrant. Add the stock and bring to a boil, then reduce to a low boil and cook until reduced to 3 cups. Strain the stock and set aside.

▪ In a large skillet, heat 1 tablespoon of the EVOO (one turn of the pan) over medium-high heat. Add the shrimp, season with salt and black pepper, and cook for 2 minutes, turning halfway, just to take the color off and get them going. Transfer the shrimp to a plate. Add the remaining 1 tablespoon EVOO (one turn of the pan) and cook the chorizo 1 to 2 minutes to render out some of the fat. Transfer the chorizo to the plate with the shrimp.

▪ Reduce the heat just a touch. Add the onion and rice and toast for 2 minutes. Stir in the paella spice and grate in the garlic. Stir in the tomato paste. Add the sherry, increase the heat, and scrape up the browned bits using a wooden spoon. Stir in about three-quarters of the stock, bring to a boil over medium-high heat, and cook, stirring occasionally, until most of the liquid is absorbed but not dry, about 10 minutes.

▪ Reduce the heat to medium-low. Stir in the peas, then the pimientos. Return the shrimp and chorizo to the pan, press into the rice, and add the remaining stock. Cook until the rice is tender and flavors are melded, 8 minutes more. Douse the pan with lemon juice and top with parsley to serve.

One-Pan Seafood Bake

WITH GARLIC BREAD

SERVES 4

- 4 medium thin-skinned potatoes, gold or white, thinly sliced on a mandoline or by hand
- 1 large or 2 medium bulbs fennel, thinly sliced on a mandoline or by hand (fronds reserved)
- 1 large or 2 medium onions, thinly sliced
- Salt and freshly ground black pepper
- ⅓ cup EVOO
- 3 cups chicken stock, vegetable stock, bone broth, or fortified stock (see Note)
- 3 anchovy fillets, chopped (optional)
- 4 sustainable white fish fillets, such as halibut (1 inch thick, 6 to 8 ounces each), patted dry
- 1 pound large shrimp, peeled (shells reserved for fortified stock, if making; see Note)
- 2 to 3 cloves garlic, shaved
- 1 handful of thyme leaves, plus another handful for garnishing
- 2 bay leaves
- 1 lemon, zest grated and reserved, halved
- ¾ cup white vermouth or white wine
- 1 cup chopped mixed fresh celery tops, parsley, and fennel fronds

GARLIC BREAD

- 1 baguette, split lengthwise, then halved crosswise and lightly toasted
- Butter or olive oil
- Dried chives
- Dried parsley
- Dried dill
- Fresh garlic slivers
- Crushed red pepper flakes, for sprinkling
- Grated Parmigiano-Reggiano cheese

- Position a rack in the center of the oven and preheat the oven to 450°F.

- Arrange the potatoes, fennel, and onions in a roasting pan. Season with salt and pepper, drizzle with the EVOO, and toss to coat. Roast for 15 minutes.

To make a fortified stock, reserve shells when peeling the shrimp. Then, in a skillet, toast the shells. Add 1 leek, a handful each of parsley and thyme sprigs, 4 lemon slices, and 5 cloves peeled garlic. Add stock to cover, bring to a bubble, then cook on low about 20 minutes. Strain.

- Meanwhile, in a saucepan, cook the stock over medium-low heat until reduced a bit, about 8 minutes. Stir in the anchovies, if using.

- Remove the roasting pan from the oven (leave the oven on). Arrange the fish and shrimp on top of the potatoes in the pan and season with salt and pepper. Drizzle the reduced stock on top, add the shaved garlic, thyme, bay leaves, and lemon zest. Douse with the vermouth and cover the pan with foil.

- Roast until the fish is flaky and lightly browned and the shrimp are opaque, 7 to 8 minutes. Uncover and bake for 2 to 3 minutes more. Remove the pan from the oven, and turn the oven temperature to broil. Spoon the pan juices over the top, then sprinkle with fresh herbs and squeeze the lemon halves over everything.

- Make the garlic bread: Put bread on a foil-lined baking sheet. In a small saucepan, melt butter or heat olive oil, and add dried herbs (about a ½ palmful of each) and garlic. Brush mixture onto bread and sprinkle with red pepper flakes and grated Parm. Broil until crisp and golden.

Steak Niçoise

SERVES 4

This is my way of doing meat and potatoes, lightened up.

2 boneless sirloin steaks
  (10 to 12 ounces each)

4 large eggs

12 ounces haricots verts or
  trimmed green beans

1 pound baby potatoes

Kosher salt

Nonaerosol cooking spray

Coarsely ground black
  pepper

DRESSING

2 anchovy fillets, finely
  pasted or minced, or salt

2 cloves garlic, grated or
  pasted

1 shallot, grated or minced

Juice of ½ lemon

2 tablespoons Dijon
  mustard

3 tablespoons white wine
  vinegar

2 teaspoons herbes de
  Provence (⅔ palmful)

½ cup EVOO

ASSEMBLY

8 cups chopped greens
  (romaine or leaf lettuces,
  cook's choice)

1 cup Niçoise olives

1 pint cherry tomatoes,
  halved (see Note)

■ Allow the steaks to come to room temperature and pat dry.

■ Set up a bowl of ice and water. Place the eggs in a saucepan of cold water and bring to a boil. Boil the eggs for 8 minutes. Drain and cold-shock in the ice bath. Peel and halve the eggs.

■ Set up another bowl of ice and water. Bring a pot of water to a boil for the beans and potatoes. Add the beans and cook for 3 minutes, then scoop out with a spider and cold-shock in the ice bath. Drain well. Meanwhile, add the potatoes to the boiling water, salt the water, and boil until firm-tender, 10 to 12 minutes. Drain and when cool enough to handle, quarter them.

■ Heat a large cast-iron skillet over medium-high heat and mist with cooking spray. Season the steaks with salt and pepper. Add the steaks to the hot pan and cook for 3 minutes on each side and 1 minute on each edge for medium-rare; cook 1 minute longer on the sides and a bit longer on the edge for medium to medium-well. Let the meat rest a few minutes, then slice against the grain, portioning 4 to 5 ounces per salad.

■ Make the dressing: In a bowl, combine the anchovies (or a pinch of salt), garlic, shallot, and lemon juice. Let stand a few minutes. Whisk in the mustard, vinegar, and herbes de Provence. Then, while whisking, slowly stream in the EVOO.

■ To assemble, toss the greens with three-quarters of the dressing and arrange on plates. Top with the beans, potatoes, olives, tomatoes, halved eggs, and sliced steak. Drizzle the remaining dressing over the top.

Note: Use my trick to halve cherry tomatoes in bulk: Place the tomatoes snugly, 1 cup at a time, between two deli cup lids, both facing up, and press firmly to hold the tomatoes in place. Slice horizontally with a sharp knife across the tomatoes between the lids to halve them.

Eggplant Schnitzel

WITH WHIPPED HONEY AND SCHUG

SERVES 4 TO 6

2 to 3 firm eggplants

2 cups AP flour

Salt and freshly ground black pepper

4 large eggs

2 teaspoons Dijon mustard

2 cups dried breadcrumbs

1 cup panko breadcrumbs

2 tablespoons Peppery Cumin and Caraway Spice Blend (recipe follows)

¼ teaspoon freshly grated nutmeg

Safflower or canola oil, for frying

Whipped honey (available at some markets and online)

3 tablespoons EVOO

¼ cup drained capers

Schug (recipe follows)

■ Slice the eggplants lengthwise into planks ¼ to ½ inch thick. Salt generously on both sides and transfer to paper towels to drain for 30 minutes.

■ Set up a dredging station: In one shallow dish, season the flour with some salt and pepper. In a second shallow dish, whisk the eggs and mustard. In a third dish, mix the breadcrumbs, panko, cumin and caraway blend, and nutmeg.

■ In a large cast-iron skillet, heat ½ inch safflower oil over medium to medium-high heat. Line a large sheet pan with foil and top with a wire rack. Preheat the oven to 275°F.

■ Pat the eggplant planks dry. Coat the eggplant first in the flour, then in the egg, and finally the breadcrumbs. Working in batches, fry until deep golden brown, about 3 minutes on each side. Transfer to the wire rack to drain. While they're warm, spread a thin layer of honey on the eggplant. Transfer to the oven to keep warm while you fry the rest.

■ In a small skillet, heat the EVOO over medium-high to high heat. Add the capers and fry until crispy, 3 to 4 minutes. Transfer to paper towels to drain.

■ Arrange the eggplant on a platter. Top with the fried capers and schug.

Even if you're a carnivore, eggplant schnitzel is pretty magical—and surprisingly meaty—if you take the time to salt the eggplant.

PEPPERY CUMIN AND CARAWAY SPICE BLEND

MAKES ABOUT ½ CUP

3 tablespoons cumin seeds

3 tablespoons caraway seeds

2 tablespoons white peppercorns

■ Heat a medium skillet over medium heat. Add the spices and toast, tossing frequently, until fragrant, 4 to 5 minutes. Let the spices cool, then transfer them to a spice grinder and pulse until powdery.

SPICY GREEN HERB SAUCE (SCHUG OR ZHUG)

MAKES 1½ TO 2 CUPS

This fresh hot sauce traces its origins to Yemen but is used all over the Middle East. Stash leftovers in the fridge and use as a sandwich spread.

2 cups cilantro tops

1 cup packed fresh flat-leaf parsley tops

½ cup packed fresh mint leaves

1 teaspoon salt

1 teaspoon freshly ground black pepper

4 cloves garlic, smashed and peeled

2 jalapeños, seeded and coarsely chopped

4 or 5 fresh red bird's eye chiles, stemmed

1½ teaspoons Peppery Cumin and Caraway Spice Blend (recipe above)

Scant 1 teaspoon ground cardamom

Juice of 2 limes or 1 lemon

½ cup EVOO

■ In a food processor, pulse all of the ingredients except the EVOO until the herbs are finely chopped. With the machine running, slowly stream in the EVOO, mixing until the sauce is smooth.

Spinach Salad

WITH WARM BACON-MAPLE DRESSING

SERVES 1

This was one of my three-minute meals for the magazine, but it's so good I make it even when I have all the time in the world. Double everything to serve as a side dish, and add dressing to taste.

BACON-MAPLE DRESSING

2 tablespoons olive oil

1 slice meaty bacon, finely chopped

1 small shallot, chopped

2 cloves garlic, grated or chopped

2 tablespoons apple cider vinegar or sherry vinegar

1 tablespoon maple syrup

1 rounded teaspoon Dijon or grainy Dijon mustard

1 tablespoon fresh thyme or 1 teaspoon dried

Salt and freshly ground black pepper

SALAD

3 cups packed baby or medium spinach

Salt and freshly ground black pepper

1 to 2 radishes, thinly sliced

2 tablespoons drained marinated mushrooms

1 handful of fried onions or potato sticks (from a can or pouch)

1 hard-boiled egg, quartered

■ Make the bacon-maple dressing: In a medium skillet, heat the EVOO (two turns of the pan) over medium-high heat. Add the bacon and cook, stirring, until crispy. Add the shallot and garlic and stir for a minute. Add the vinegar and maple syrup. Swirl the skillet, then remove it from the heat. Off the heat, whisk in the mustard and thyme. Season the dressing with salt and pepper.

■ Assemble the salad: In a large bowl, toss the spinach with some of the warm dressing. Season with salt and pepper. Top with the radishes, mushrooms, fried onions, and egg. Add additional dressing if desired.

Carbonara with Nduja & Spring Garlic

6 egg yolks
1 cup grated Pecorino Romano
Salt ~ 1 lb 500g spaghetti
3 T EVOO ~ 4 oz 250g 'nduja
1 bulb spring garlic, finely chopped
½ c Italian white wine ~ pepper

Whisk up eggs & cheese.
∴ Bring water to a boil. Season it with salt, cook pasta 1 minute less than package directions. Reserve 1 cup of boiling water, whisk into egg yolks. Meanwhile, heat EVOO in a large skillet, melt 'nduja into it, stir in garlic, add wine.
∴ Add pasta to 'nduja, toss and remove pan from heat, add tempered eggs & cheese, toss a minute more. Top pasta with black pepper. Pass extra cheese & EVOO at table.

PASTAI
GRAGNANESI
No. 42
SPAGHETTI
CON CURVA
500 g

Butternut Squash Carbonara

3 tablespoons EVOO

⅓ pound meaty pancetta, finely chopped

1 large shallot or 1 small onion, very finely chopped

4 large cloves garlic, chopped

1 handful of sage leaves, stacked and very thinly sliced

Salt and freshly ground black pepper

½ cup dry Italian white wine or dry vermouth

1½ cups (about 12 ounces) thawed butternut squash puree

4 large egg yolks

¼ teaspoon freshly grated nutmeg

1 pound spaghetti or chitarra (square spaghetti)

1 cup freshly grated Pecorino Romano cheese

1 cup freshly grated Parmigiano-Reggiano cheese

■ Bring a large pot of water to a boil for the pasta.

■ In a large skillet, heat the EVOO (three turns of the pan) over medium-high heat. Add the pancetta and cook until the fat renders, 3 to 4 minutes. Add the shallot, garlic, sage, and salt and pepper to taste. Stir for another 3 to 4 minutes, then add the wine and let the liquid reduce for a minute or so. Reduce the heat to low to keep warm.

■ In a medium bowl, whisk the squash puree and egg yolks. Season with the nutmeg and salt and pepper to taste.

■ Salt the boiling water and cook the pasta 1 minute less than the package directions for al dente. Before draining, ladle out about a cup of the starchy pasta cooking water. Drain the pasta.

■ Slowly whisk the cooking water into the squash and yolks to temper the eggs. Toss the pasta in the skillet with the pancetta, add the squash mixture and both cheeses, and toss to coat. Stir until the sauce thickens slightly, about 2 minutes. Season with salt and pepper.

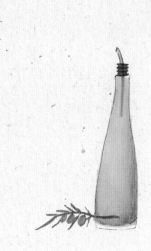

Bucatini all'Amatriciana

WITH SPRING PEAS

SERVES 4

2 tablespoons EVOO

⅓ to ½ pound pancetta, finely chopped

2 medium onions, finely chopped

1 large fresh bay leaf

1 cup fresh shelled green peas

4 cloves garlic, chopped

Salt and freshly ground black pepper or crushed red pepper flakes

½ cup white vermouth or white wine

2 cups passata or tomato sauce

1 pound bucatini

1 cup grated pecorino or Parmigiano-Reggiano cheese

Fresh basil or tarragon leaves, for garnish

■ Bring a large pot of water to a boil for the pasta.

■ In a large skillet, heat the EVOO (two turns of the pan) over medium heat. Add the pancetta and render for 3 minutes. Add the onions and bay leaf and soften for 5 minutes. Add ½ cup water and let it absorb. Add the peas, garlic, and salt and pepper to taste and cook for 3 to 4 minutes more. Add the vermouth and let it absorb. Add the passata and reduce the heat to low. Remove bay leaf.

■ Salt the boiling water and cook the pasta 1 minute less than the package directions for al dente. Before draining, ladle out about a cup of the starchy pasta cooking water. Drain the pasta and toss it with the sauce and cheese for a full minute, using some of the cooking water if the sauce and pasta get too dry.

■ Top with the herb of choice and serve on a platter or in shallow bowls.

Spring Salad

WITH PISTACHIOS AND BURRATA TOAST

SERVES 4

SALAD AND DRESSING

1 cup shelled fava beans

1 bunch asparagus, tough ends trimmed

1 small bulb spring fennel, thinly sliced on a mandoline or by hand

3 cups medium to large arugula or baby lacinato kale

½ white or red onion, thinly sliced on a mandoline or by hand

1 cup mint sprigs, leaves picked and coarsely chopped

¼ cup tarragon leaves, coarsely chopped

¼ cup chopped chives and chive flowers, for garnish

Juice of 1 small lemon

Salt

1 small shallot, grated or finely chopped

2 tablespoons white wine vinegar or champagne vinegar

⅓ cup EVOO

Crushed red pepper flakes

½ cup raw pistachio nuts (I use Sicilian), lightly toasted in a skillet or the oven

BURRATA TOAST

4 large or 8 small slices sesame Italian bread

1 large clove garlic, halved

EVOO, for drizzling

2 balls burrata (about 8 ounces each)

A sprinkle of flaky salt

■ Make the salad and dressing: Set up a bowl of ice and water. Bring a medium pot of water to a boil for the favas.

■ Add the favas to the boiling water and cook for 5 minutes. Drain and cold-shock in the ice bath. Drain again and peel off the skins.

■ Use a vegetable peeler and thinly shred the asparagus spears into ribbons. Place in a bowl and add the fennel, favas, arugula, onion, and herbs.

■ In a small bowl, combine the lemon juice, salt to taste, the shallot, and vinegar. Whisk in the EVOO. Dress the salad and season with pepper flakes to taste. Top with toasted pistachio nuts.

■ Make the burrata toast: Char or toast the bread and rub with the garlic. Drizzle with some EVOO, spread with the burrata and season with flaky salt.

■ Serve the salad on platters or plates with toasts.

My family loves shaved asparagus salads. I serve them up often with chicken Milanese, sliced steaks, or, as here, with bread and cheese!

Chicken and Apple Curry Dinner

SERVES 4 TO 6

CHICKEN AND APPLE CURRY

SERVES 4 TO 6

POACHED CHICKEN

1 leek, halved lengthwise, well washed, then quartered

2 large carrots, scrubbed and cut into large pieces on an angle

1 onion, peeled and quartered

4 large cloves garlic, smashed and peeled

2 large bay leaves

1-inch piece fresh ginger, sliced

1 small piece fresh turmeric root, sliced (optional)

1 whole chicken (3½ pounds)

Salt

1½ teaspoons black peppercorns (½ palmful)

SPICE BLEND

2 tablespoons cumin seeds

1 tablespoon mustard seeds

1 tablespoon black peppercorns

1½ teaspoons fenugreek seeds (½ palmful)

1½ teaspoons fenugreek leaves (½ palmful)

1½ teaspoons coriander seeds (½ palmful)

1 teaspoon caraway seeds (⅓ palmful)

1 teaspoon fennel seeds (⅓ palmful)

1-inch piece cinnamon stick

2 cardamom pods

CURRY

5 tablespoons butter

1 large or 2 medium onions, chopped

2-inch piece fresh ginger, peeled, sliced into thin planks, then into long thin sticks, then into short matchsticks

1 small fresh turmeric root (see Note), peeled and cut into small thin matchsticks

3 large cloves garlic, chopped or thinly sliced

2 to 3 chiles, halved lengthwise, seeded, stemmed, and thinly sliced

Salt and freshly ground black pepper

2 green apples, peeled and chopped, tossed with the juice of ½ lemon

½ cup picked fresh curry leaves (optional), available online

4 tablespoons AP flour

½ cup mango chutney

Fresh cilantro, for garnish

NAAN

4 store-bought garlic naan breads

2 tablespoons butter

■ Poach the chicken: In a large pot, combine all the ingredients and add about 4 quarts water. Bring to a boil, then reduce to a simmer and cook 1 hour to 1 hour 15 minutes, turning occasionally, until meat is cooked through.

■ Let the chicken cool in the broth. Transfer the chicken to a shallow dish and remove the skin and bones. Pull the meat into bite-size or smaller pieces with your hands. Strain the broth, which will have reduced to about 2½ quarts. Measure out 1 quart to use in the curry and store the remainder.

■ Make the spice blend: In a small skillet, toast the spices 2 to 3 minutes over medium heat. Grind in an electric spice mill, then transfer to a small bowl or container.

(CONTINUED)

Note: If you don't have fresh turmeric root, just add 1½ teaspoons ground turmeric to the curry spice blend.

Serve this curry with the fixings on the side and plenty of naan to sop up the sauce!

■ Make the curry: In a large deep skillet, heat the butter over medium to medium-high heat, When the butter foams, add onions, ginger, turmeric, garlic, chiles, and salt to taste and cook, stirring occasionally, for 4 to 5 minutes to soften. Add the apples, curry spice blend, and curry leaves (if using). Cover and let soften but do not brown. Add the flour and stir a minute. Add the reserved stock and cook until the sauce is thick enough to coat a spoon. Add the shredded chicken and chutney and reduce the heat to a low simmer. Garnish with cilantro.

■ Prepare the naan: Heat a griddle over medium to medium-high heat. Sprinkle bread with a little water, like ¼ cup, and place 2 naans on the griddle. Blister and then flip.

■ Melt the butter in the microwave 40 seconds. Brush the charred bread with melted butter, cut into quarters, and serve with the curry.

ALMOND RICE PILAF

SERVES 4 TO 6

2 tablespoons butter

½ cup broken spaghetti (1-inch pieces)

½ cup chopped blanched almonds

Salt and freshly ground black pepper

1 clove garlic, chopped

1-inch piece fresh ginger, grated or finely chopped

1-inch piece fresh turmeric root, grated and finely chopped or ½ teaspoon ground turmeric

1 handful of curry leaves (optional; see Notes)

1½ cups long-grained white rice

2½ cups chicken stock (see Notes) or half stock and half water

■ In a saucepot, heat the butter over medium to medium-high heat. When the butter foams, add the spaghetti and almonds and toast them. Season with salt and pepper and add the garlic, ginger, turmeric, and curry leaves (if using) and keep toasting. Once everything is golden and toasted, add the rice and stir for a minute. Add the stock and bring to a boil, then reduce to a low simmer, cover, and cook for 15 minutes. Remove from the heat and let stand covered for 10 minutes. Fluff the rice and serve.

Notes: If you bought curry leaves for the Chicken and Apple Curry (page 58), you can use any left over here. And if you made the poached chicken and broth, use that for the chicken stock here.

MINT-CHILE RAITA

SERVES 4 TO 6

1½ cups Greek yogurt

1 large clove garlic, grated or pasted

1 tablespoon grated peeled fresh ginger

1 green or red chile pepper, seeded and finely chopped

1 teaspoon ground cumin (⅓ palmful)

½ cup mixed finely chopped fresh herbs: mint, dill, and cilantro

Juice of 1 small lime

Salt

■ In a small bowl, mix together the yogurt, garlic, ginger, chile, cumin, herbs, lime juice, and salt to taste.

Halibut

WITH CREOLE SAUCE

SERVES 4 TO 6

- 4 tablespoons EVOO
- 2 tablespoons butter
- 1 small bell pepper, finely chopped
- 1 small onion, finely chopped
- 2 small ribs celery with leafy tops, finely chopped
- 4 cloves garlic, thinly sliced
- 1 large bay leaf
- 2 tablespoons fresh thyme, chopped
- Salt and freshly ground black pepper
- 1 tablespoon Worcestershire sauce
- About ¼ cup hot sauce (to taste), preferably Frank's RedHot
- ½ cup chicken stock or vegetable stock
- 1 (8-ounce) can tomato sauce
- 1 (14- to 14.5-ounce) can diced fire-roasted tomatoes or crushed tomatoes
- 4 scallions, chopped
- 4 to 6 halibut fillets (4 to 6 ounces each)
- 2 tablespoons Old Bay Seasoning
- Baguette, for serving

■ In a large saucepan or skillet, heat 2 tablespoons EVOO (two turns of the pan) over medium-high heat. Add the butter and melt it into the oil. When the butter foams, add the bell pepper, onion, celery, garlic, bay leaf, and thyme. Season with salt and black pepper. Cover and cook, stirring occasionally, until the vegetables soften, about 5 minutes. Add the Worcestershire, hot sauce, stock, tomato sauce, and tomatoes. Simmer until the sauce thickens, 10 to 15 minutes. Stir in the scallions.

■ Season the fish with salt and black pepper and the Old Bay. In a large nonstick skillet, heat the remaining 2 tablespoons EVOO (two turns of the pan) over medium-high heat. Add the fish, and cook, turning occasionally, until opaque in the center, 7 to 8 minutes.

■ Transfer the fish to shallow bowls. Top with lots of sauce. Serve with the baguette.

Stupid Good, Silly Easy Tray Bake:

SAUSAGE, APPLES, FENNEL, ONION, AND FINGERLING POTATOES

SERVES 4

2 crisp apples, cut into ½-inch wedges or bite-size chunks

1 bulb fennel, cut into thin wedges

1 large or 2 medium onions, peeled and root attached, cut into thin wedges

1 pound fingerling potatoes, halved

Juice of 1 lemon

1 tablespoon honey, preferably acacia

3 sprigs rosemary, stripped and chopped (about 2 tablespoons)

10 to 12 leaves sage, stacked and very thinly sliced or chopped (about 2 tablespoons)

2 tablespoons fresh thyme, chopped

¼ cup EVOO

Salt and freshly ground black pepper

6 links Italian sausage (pork, chicken, or plant-based), skins pricked with the tines of a fork

■ Preheat the oven to 425°F. Line a large sheet pan with parchment paper.

■ In a large bowl, toss together the apples, fennel, onions, potatoes, lemon juice, honey, herbs, olive oil, and salt and pepper to taste. Spread them on the prepared sheet pan and nestle in the sausages.

■ Roast until the sausage juices run clear and the potatoes are tender, about 45 minutes.

■ To plate, halve 2 sausages to allow 1½ sausages per adult portion and about one-quarter of the apples, fennel, onions, and potatoes.

John's Filthy Dirty Martini

MAKES TWO COCKTAILS

3 ounces gin

1½ ounces vermouth

2 dashes orange bitters

About 1 ounce olive, cornichon, or cocktail onion brine, to taste

Olives, cornichons, and cocktail onions, for garnish

Combine the gin, vermouth, bitters, and brine. Add ice and stir to chill. Strain into two chilled martini glasses. Garnish with olives, cornichons, and cocktail onions.

May

During this year, we were all cooking more meals than we ever had before. For many people it became their entertainment, the thing they looked forward to after a hard day's work. And as restaurants tragically shuttered, we fulfilled more of our cravings at home. I cooked pub grub and steakhouse specials, Chinese and Thai, and more Make Your Own Takeout than ever before.

BIG SMACK BURGERS WITH SWISS-HORSERADISH
SPECIAL SAUCE AND SKILLET BARBECUE BEANS

PIZZAFEST: "THE RACHAEL" PIZZA, "THE JOHN" PIZZA, POTATO
AND ROASTED GARLIC PIZZA, ZUCCHINI AND RAMP PIZZA

CHICKEN MARSALA

BBQ CHICKEN NACHOS

Diversions

WHISKEY WINGS ON THE GRILL

CARNITAS WITH BLACK BEANS, SOFRITO RICE, AND
HATCH PEPPER SALSA

CRAB AND CHEDDAR STUFFED MUSHROOMS AND
PINWHEEL STEAKS

JOHN'S HIBISCUS MARGARITA

RR Catering Company

From the time I was a little girl to just a few years ago, going for a ride in the car with my mom could mean anything from errands with a specific purpose, made in record time, to a true adventure of any duration. If we were on a mission, like picking up a prescription for one of us kids, Mom would speed to the pharmacy. If she were pulled over for speeding, as often happened, Mom would argue with sympathetic officers to <u>give</u> her the ticket rather than <u>forgive</u> her for it because that was the right thing to do. That, and just her love of speed itself, led to mandatory driving courses and temporary suspensions of her license over the years.

However, if there was no actual rush, Mom would take us out for a drive and make a left when she was supposed to take a right, just to discover something new for herself and for her children. And that's when the adventure would begin, and we would end up in countless special places she had discovered by sheer force of serendipity. This ever-present sense of discovery had an indelible effect on my life.

One winter, my mom took us to an inn, and as we pulled up we caught a glimpse of the bright, warm, gentle light spilling over the snow-covered bushes surrounding the path to the entrance and covered overhang of the large, old main house. Once inside the doors, it was as if we had stepped into a snow globe, but it was warm and cozy with the faint crackle of a fire from a hearth in the next room. The air was thick with pleasant aromas and sounds, giggles and hearty laughs, carols being played, some guests humming or singing along. The room was tinted with

orange and gold and I felt as if I were wearing sunglasses. As we waited for our table, the hostess came over and asked if I'd like to take one wrapped gift from their holiday chest, full of toys waiting for young guests to take them home. I started to cry, maybe the first time I'd ever done so from being overwhelmed with beauty, kindness, and wonder.

So many little things made me cry like that over this past year. Small kindnesses, like the delivery men bringing dog treats again for Bella, after giving condolences when Isaboo passed. Or the UPS guy wearing funny masks from <u>Shrek</u> or <u>Star Wars</u>, and changing them to get a laugh. It was dozens and dozens of cards and long letters from old friends and total strangers, bonding over loss and getting through these strange days with hope and a positive attitude. It was flowers and blankets and food baskets. It was care and love for one another and

the absolute belief that each stone cast with love skips and ripples, and those meet other ripples to return in a wake that buoys us.

When people come to my home, I want them to know what kind of person raised me, and to go with me to that kind of magical place. I want every day to be special and warm and anything but lonely or forgotten. Basically, I want every day to be Christmas, especially when it comes to feeding people.

During most holiday seasons, I'm making grand plans and a schedule for five to six families to stay at our home over the course of the holiday break, and for my own family to have very special holidays, too. I make charts and lists and more lists for seven or eight Chanukah, Christmas, and New Year's meals. Throughout the year when friends visit, they joke about it feeling more like booking time at an inn than dropping by at a friend's house. I cook everything we eat, taking requests from guests and following all dietary guidelines, and getting their menu approval (seriously). If they have kids, there has to be a plan for what will please or excite them, too. I live for the feeling, the tingle and hairs standing up on your neck when you can see the spark as you surprise someone with a dish that truly delights them. It's the look a child gets when she opens a gift that was not on her list, but she adores so much.

This last year, I couldn't always do the things I was used to doing—giving time and energy to my friends and loved ones as I and they have grown accustomed to—but the days felt better when we found a way to share. That's the primary force behind what we record for the show, what I write, the music John makes, and the food I cook.

So if I used to run an inn, I'm now a caterer. Most days I made multiple meals, far more than John and I could ever eat ourselves. At our show, when we're in the studio, our excess food goes to Food Bank and City Harvest to feed New Yorkers in need. While recording upstate, our food went to my mom, my sister, and some close friends who helped us out on a regular basis and improved the quality of our lives immeasurably. There's Peter and Susan, who have many talents, but to us they're florists and designers, artists of all living things. They eat everything, so they get everything the picky eaters won't touch, including the really awful stuff like mushrooms, truffles, and caviar. (That was sarcasm, if you were wondering.) Then there's Steve Colletti, who built our house and is now <u>re</u>building our house. He's a

contractor, yes, but he's also an all-around, everything man. He has held, or knows enough of, just about every job. Steve is a vegetarian and occasional pescatarian. Mom has been eating mostly plant-based for a few years now, but last year she strayed occasionally—I think, being next door to us 24-7, the aroma of chicken or sausages occasionally broke her usually steadfast will. My sister eats no mushrooms, no seafood, only overcooked beef or eggs, and no sausage or pork as a main ingredient (but she will accept pancetta in a soup for flavor). My brother, who lives nearby, follows a careful diet that's pretty restrictive, but he tried to walk a line and join in special meals, and his daughter, my niece, Viv, eats almost everything, but not too spicy. John is my captive audience and I'm sure he'd eat anything I set in front of him to save me time and effort, but I like for him to be happy and surprised, too, and to know it's not just about the shows or what I do for other people. Many meals I shared around were recipes in development or special meals for an occasion, or when our friend Tommy Crudup, an executive producer on the show and its talent booker, came upstate for a backyard visit or a golf game with John. He's family to us, and I cook for him like I do for John. Anything goes, but I want to make it special.

I tailored the packaging and disbursement of food to each person's dietary needs and sometimes added wine or chocolates or John's mixed cocktails and sweet treats for fun. If nothing in the day's cycle and schedule of food preparation suited my mom or my sister—who became our doggy sitter, the school bus who drove Bella to puppy kindergarten each day, and our pipeline to the outside world—then I'd plan for and prepare another meal for that evening. Each meal I packaged, I would try and garnish with flowers or herbs and give a note on how to reheat along with a description of how the dish is prepared or main ingredients. For my family, I tried to plate on real dishes and platters, color coded by recipient.

I would text people when the deliveries were ready to be picked up, then I'd package the food, wipe it down, and place it on a garden workbench outside the back door with a table and a few shelves and hooks. It became our "bird feeder for humans," where they'd swing in and grab their dinner. Once the frost came and winter weather was upon us, I had a shelter built for it. The feeder got a roof and some walls. RR's Catering remained open for business, even though there were no vacancies at the inn.

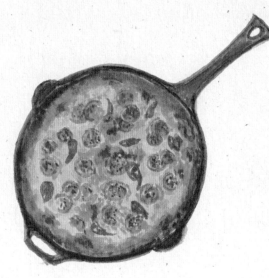

Big Smack Burgers

WITH SWISS-HORSERADISH SPECIAL SAUCE AND SKILLET BARBECUE BEANS

SERVES 6

BIG SMACK BURGERS

SERVES 6

2¼ to 3 pounds ground beef sirloin (80% lean) or 1½ pounds plant-based meat

Salt and freshly ground black pepper

12 slices yellow American cheese

6 soft sesame seed buns

1 small Vidalia or white onion, finely chopped

½ head iceberg lettuce, cored and chopped

Dill pickle chips

Swiss-Horseradish Special Sauce (recipe follows)

■ For beef sirloin, form 6- to 8-ounce patties thinner at the center than the edges for even cooking. For plant-based meat, form 4- to 5-ounce thin patties. Season with salt and pepper.

■ Preheat a cast-iron skillet over medium-high heat. Add the patties and cook for 7 to 8 minutes, turning occasionally. Add 2 slices cheese to each patty in the last 1 to 2 minutes.

■ To build the burgers: bun bottom, onions, chopped iceberg lettuce, dill pickle slices to cover surface, cheese-topped patty, horseradish-ranch sauce, and bun top.

(CONTINUED)

I call them that because they are lip-smackingly delicious and they clearly have nothing to do with the flagship burger from a major national fast food chain.

(CONTINUED)

SWISS-HORSERADISH SPECIAL SAUCE

MAKES ABOUT 1½ CUPS

1 cup sour cream or whole-milk Greek yogurt

3 rounded tablespoons prepared horseradish

2 tablespoons Worcestershire sauce

1 clove garlic, grated or pasted

¼ cup packed chopped mixed fresh herbs: dill, parsley, and chives

Salt and freshly ground black pepper

■ In a small bowl, combine all the ingredients.

SKILLET BARBECUE BEANS

SERVES 6

1 or 2 tablespoons olive or canola oil (use the smaller amount if using bacon)

¼ pound meaty bacon, finely chopped (optional)

1 Vidalia or white onion, finely chopped

Salt and coarsely ground black pepper

2 large cloves garlic, grated or chopped

3 tablespoons apple cider vinegar

3 tablespoons Worcestershire sauce

3 tablespoons light brown sugar

1 cup tomato sauce

1½ tablespoons mustard powder or 3 tablespoons prepared yellow mustard

1 tablespoon smoked paprika (pimentón)

1 (29-ounce) can or 2 (15-ounce) cans pinto or black beans, rinsed and drained

A couple of scallions, chopped, for topping

■ In a large skillet, heat the oil over medium-high heat. If using bacon, add it and render 2 to 3 minutes. Add the onion and season lightly with salt and heavily with pepper and soften a few minutes. Add the garlic and stir a minute. Stir in the vinegar, Worcestershire, brown sugar, tomato sauce, mustard, and smoked paprika. Add the beans and simmer at a low bubble for 20 minutes to thicken and reduce the sauce. Cover to keep warm and reheat to serve. Garnish the beans with scallions.

THE "RACHAEL" PIZZA

MAKES ONE 10-INCH PIZZA

These are four different pizzas created from the same batch of dough. All delicious, and all made in one day of taping. I lit the oven at 5 A.M. and we were done at 11 P.M., when we collapsed into bed. It was one of the longest days of my career.

1 portion Same-Day Pizza Dough (recipe follows)

About ½ cup Easy Pizza Sauce (recipe follows)

1½ cups mixed shredded mozzarella and provolone cheese

¼ cup hot cherry pepper rings

1 green or red bell pepper or frying/cubanelle pepper, thinly sliced

½ red onion, very thinly sliced

■ Preheat the oven to 550°F (or as high as it can go) and preheat a large pizza stone.

■ Roll the dough out to a 10-inch round. Top the dough with a thin layer of sauce. Add most of the cheese, then arrange the hot peppers, bell pepper, and onion on top. Sprinkle with a little more cheese.

■ Slide the pizza onto the hot stone and bake for 5 minutes, then broil 3 to 5 minutes more, until crisp, browned, and bubbling.

THE "JOHN" PIZZA

MAKES ONE 10-INCH PIZZA

1 portion Same-Day Pizza Dough (recipe follows)

About ½ cup Easy Pizza Sauce (recipe follows)

8 to 10 slices hot soppressata

1½ cups shredded smoked mozzarella cheese

3 tablespoons grated pecorino cheese

Torn fresh basil, for serving

Crushed red pepper flakes, for serving

EVOO, for drizzling

■ Preheat the oven to 550°F (or as high as it can go) and preheat a large pizza stone.

■ Roll the dough out to a 10-inch round. Top with a thin layer of sauce. Arrange the hot soppressata on top, then some smoked mozzarella and more soppressata. Top with pecorino and smoked mozzarella.

■ Slide the pizza onto the hot stone and bake for 5 minutes, then broil 3 to 5 minutes more, until crisp, browned, and bubbling. Top with basil and pepper flakes, drizzle with EVOO, and serve.

(CONTINUED)

POTATO AND ROASTED GARLIC PIZZA

MAKES ONE 10-INCH PIZZA

5 baby potatoes

3 tablespoons EVOO

2 bulbs garlic, peeled

About 3 tablespoons sliced fresh sage, plus torn leaves, for topping

1 portion Same-Day Pizza Dough (recipe follows)

1½ cups shredded Fontina Val d'Aosta, Gruyère, or mozzarella cheese

Grated Parmigiano-Reggiano cheese, for topping

Truffle oil (optional)

■ Preheat the oven to 550°F (or as high as it can go) and preheat a large pizza stone.

■ In a pot of boiling water, parboil the potatoes for 5 minutes. Drain, cool, and very thinly slice. At the same time, in a separate pot, combine the EVOO and garlic and simmer over low heat until the garlic turns to mush. Stir in the sliced sage.

■ Roll the dough out to a 10-inch round. Slather the dough gently with the garlic/sage paste and top with a thin layer of potatoes. Top the potatoes with Fontina, then sprinkle with Parm.

■ Slide the pizza onto the hot stone and bake for 5 minutes, then broil 3 to 5 minutes more, until bubbling and browned. Top with truffle oil (if using) and torn sage leaves.

ZUCCHINI AND RAMP PIZZA

MAKES ONE 10-INCH PIZZA

2 tablespoons EVOO

4 to 5 ramps, spring onions, or scallions, chopped, whites and greens separated

Salt

1 cup ricotta cheese

½ cup grated pecorino cheese, plus more for topping

Generous pinch of fennel pollen (optional)

1 portion Same-Day Pizza Dough (recipe follows)

Zucchini blossoms, stamens removed, or 1 small zucchini, thinly sliced

½ cup sliced or shredded fresh mozzarella cheese

Crushed red pepper flakes

Honey, for drizzling

■ Preheat the oven to 550°F (or as high as it can go) and preheat a large pizza stone.

■ In a skillet, heat the EVOO (two turns of the pan) over medium heat. Add the whites of ramps, season with salt, and sauté until just softened. Scrape the ramp whites into a bowl and stir in the ricotta, pecorino, and fennel pollen (if using).

■ Roll the dough out to a 10-inch round. Top the dough with the ramp/ricotta mixture and spread gently and evenly. Top with zucchini blossoms or sliced zucchini in a big sun pattern. Scatter the mozzarella on top, followed by the ramp greens, more mozzarella, and a few more blossoms. Sprinkle everything with pecorino.

■ Slide the pizza onto the hot stone and bake for 5 minutes, then broil 3 to 5 minutes more, until browned and bubbling. Top with pepper flakes and a drizzle of honey to serve.

SAME-DAY PIZZA DOUGH

MAKES ENOUGH FOR FOUR 10-INCH PIZZAS

- 2¼ teaspoons or 1 envelope active dry yeast
- ¾ cup hot water (115°F)
- 2 tablespoons EVOO, plus more to oil the bowl
- 1½ cups "00" flour, plus more for dusting
- 1 cup AP flour
- 1½ teaspoons sugar
- 1½ teaspoons kosher salt

- In a stand mixer with the dough hook or in a food processor, combine the yeast, hot water, and oil and let stand for 10 minutes.

- In a bowl, combine both flours, the sugar, and salt. With the machine running, slowly add the flour mixture to combine and form a dough.

- Oil a bowl and add the dough. Cover with a towel and let stand for 1 hour.

- Divide the dough into 4 equal portions and knead each portion a few times on a lightly floured work surface. Wrap and store until ready to roll out.

EASY PIZZA SAUCE

MAKES ENOUGH FOR FOUR 10-INCH PIZZAS

- 1 (14.5-ounce) can fire-roasted or diced San Marzano tomatoes
- 5 to 6 leaves basil, torn
- 1 tablespoon fresh oregano or 1 teaspoon dried
- 1 large clove garlic, peeled
- 1 teaspoon salt
- 2 tablespoons EVOO

- In a food processor, combine all the ingredients and process until smooth.

Chicken Marsala

- 3 cups chicken bone broth or stock
- 1 cup dried porcini mushrooms (about 1 ounce)
- 4 to 6 boneless, skinless chicken breasts (6 to 8 ounces each)
- 1 to 1½ cups AP flour (use the smaller amount if making 4 breasts)
- 1 tablespoon ground sage
- 1 teaspoon granulated garlic
- ⅛ teaspoon freshly grated nutmeg
- Salt and freshly ground black pepper
- 4 tablespoons EVOO
- 5 tablespoons butter
- 1 pound fresh cremini mushrooms, sliced, or fresh hen of the woods (maitake) mushrooms, pulled into bite-size pieces
- 2 large shallots, thinly sliced
- 4 cloves garlic, chopped
- 2 tablespoons fresh thyme, finely chopped
- 1 cup dry Marsala (Sicilian fortified wine)
- ¾ cup heavy cream or half-and-half
- 1 pound tagliatelle or fettuccine
- 1 cup shredded Parmigiano-Reggiano cheese (about 4 ounces), plus more for serving
- 1 handful of fresh flat-leaf parsley leaves, for topping

▪ Bring a large pot of water to a boil for the pasta.

▪ In a small saucepan, bring the broth and porcinis to a simmer over medium heat. Keep the broth at a low simmer until the mushrooms soften, about 10 minutes. Using a slotted spoon, transfer the porcinis to a cutting board and chop. Reserve the mushroom broth.

▪ Meanwhile, butterfly the chicken breasts. Starting on the fat side of a chicken breast, cut horizontally across the breast but not all the way through. Open it up like a book. Pound the chicken to about ¼ inch thick. (To make smaller cutlets, halve the breasts horizontally as described, but cut all the way through for a total of 8 to 12 cutlets. Pound the chicken as directed.)

▪ Place the flour in a shallow bowl and mix in the sage, granulated garlic, and nutmeg. Season the chicken with salt and pepper.

Then dredge the chicken in the flour on both sides, shaking off the excess.

▪ In a large skillet, heat 2 tablespoons of the EVOO (two turns of the pan) over medium to medium-high heat. Add 2 tablespoons of the butter to the oil. Add half of the chicken and cook, turning once, until golden, about 6 minutes. Transfer the chicken to a platter and tent with foil to keep warm. Repeat with the remaining chicken, remaining 2 tablespoons EVOO, and 2 tablespoons of the butter.

▪ Add the remaining 1 tablespoon butter to the skillet. Add the fresh mushrooms and cook, stirring often, until browned, about 5 minutes.

▪ Add the shallots, garlic, and thyme. Cook, stirring often, until the shallots soften, about 2 minutes more. Add the Marsala

and cook, stirring often, until the liquid reduces by half, about 5 minutes. Season with salt and pepper. Carefully pour in the porcini broth, leaving behind any grit that may have settled in the pan. Stir in the cream and chopped porcinis. Let the sauce reduce while you cook the pasta.

■ Salt the boiling water and cook the pasta 1 minute less than the package directions for al dente.

Before draining, ladle out about 1 cup of the starchy cooking water, then drain the pasta.

■ Spoon half of the sauce over the chicken. In the skillet, toss the rest of the sauce with the pasta, pasta cooking water, and 1 cup Parm until the pasta is coated.

■ Serve the pasta alongside the chicken. Sprinkle everything with parsley and Parm.

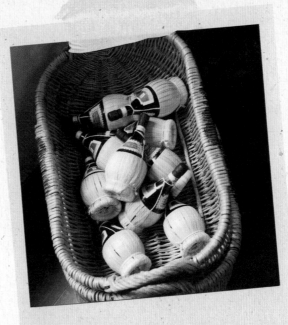

Serve the barbecued chicken mixture as nachos (as here), as a taco salad on chopped lettuce with salsa, or on soft sandwich rolls with pickles and chopped onions.

POACHED CHICKEN

1 to 1½ pounds boneless, skinless chicken breasts or thighs

Salt

1 bay leaf

1 onion, halved

Parsley and/or thyme sprigs

BARBECUE SAUCE

1 tablespoon EVOO or vegetable oil

4 slices meaty bacon, finely chopped (optional)

1 onion (yellow, white, or red), finely chopped

1 sweet/mild pepper, such as bell pepper, finely chopped

2 small hot chile peppers, such as jalapeño, serrano, or red finger peppers, seeded and finely chopped

Salt and freshly ground black pepper

2 cloves garlic, peeled

Splash of apple cider vinegar or wine vinegar

2 to 3 tablespoons Worcestershire sauce

½ cup ketchup or tomato sauce

2 tablespoons light brown sugar

1 to 2 tablespoons (mild to hot) cayenne pepper sauce, such as Frank's RedHot

1 tablespoon smoked paprika (pimentón)

Ground cumin (optional)

Ground coriander (optional)

NACHOS

1 bag (11 to 13 ounces) tortilla chips

About 2 cups shredded Monterey Jack, pepper Jack, or cheddar, or a combination

Guacamole, homemade (see Note) or store-bought, or diced avocado

----

■ Make the poached chicken: In a large skillet, combine the chicken, salt, bay leaf, onion halves, and herbs and add water to cover the top of the chicken (about 1 quart). Bring to a low boil, then reduce to a low simmer to cook through, 20 to 30 minutes, turning occasionally. Remove from the heat and let stand 10 minutes to cool. Drain the chicken through a sieve set over a bowl. Reserve the poaching liquid and thinly shred the chicken with forks or fingers.

■ Make the barbecue sauce: In a large skillet, heat the EVOO (one turn of the pan) over medium heat. Add the bacon (if using) and render 2 to 3 minutes. Add the onion, sweet pepper, chiles, and salt and black pepper to taste. Cook, stirring, for a few minutes. Grate in the garlic. Add the vinegar, Worcestershire, ketchup, brown sugar, hot sauce, smoked paprika, and a dash each of cumin and coriander (if using). Stir in 1 cup of the reserved poaching liquid and bring to a bubble. Stir in the shredded chicken, cover, and simmer for 10 minutes to reduce and combine flavors.

■ Assemble the nachos: Preheat the broiler.

■ Warm the chips in a broilerproof skillet or in a sheet pan. Remove from oven and top with the chicken and cheese. Slide under the broiler and broil to bubble and brown. Top with guacamole to serve.

Note: Make a simple guacamole with jalapeño, onion, garlic, lime, salt, avocado, and optional cilantro.

Whiskey Wings

ON THE GRILL

SERVES 6 TO 8

WINGS

24 to 36 chicken drumettes

¼ cup bourbon, whiskey, or rye

¼ cup Worcestershire sauce

¼ cup hot sauce, preferably Frank's RedHot

¼ cup apple cider vinegar

3 or 4 cloves garlic, smashed

Kosher salt and coarsely ground black pepper

Wood chips, for smoking (optional)

WHISKEY SAUCE

4 tablespoons (½ stick) butter

4 large cloves garlic, grated, chopped, or pasted

1 tablespoon coarsely ground black pepper

3 shots bourbon, whiskey, or rye

½ cup hot sauce, preferably Frank's RedHot (optional)

¼ cup Worcestershire sauce

2 tablespoons soy sauce

½ cup chicken stock or bone broth

FOR SERVING

Celery sticks

Carrots

Scallions

Crumbled smoked or regular blue cheese

■ Prepare the wings: Up to 2 days before grilling, double-bag the wings in two resealable plastic bags. Add the bourbon, Worcestershire, hot sauce, vinegar, garlic, and about 1 tablespoon each salt and pepper. Press the air out of the inner bag, seal, then give it a good massage to work the marinade into the chicken. Once evenly coated, press out excess air from the second bag, then set in the lowest part of your refrigerator for 12 to 48 hours.

■ Prepare a smoker or charcoal grill for indirect heat and preheat to 325°F or up to 350°F. If using wood chips in the charcoal grill, scatter a handful of them over the coals for flavor.

■ Drain the wings and put on a plastic cutting board lined with a paper towel. Roll the wings off the paper towel and directly onto the cutting board. Discard the paper towel and pat the wings dry with more paper towels.

■ Oil the grill grates. Arrange the wings on the grate, cover, and grill over indirect heat until the skins are tight and crispy, 60 to 75 minutes.

■ Make the whiskey sauce: In a small pot, melt the butter over medium heat. Add the garlic, black pepper, and bourbon. Cook off the alcohol and let the sauce reduce by half to concentrate the flavors. Add the hot sauce (if using), Worcestershire, soy sauce, and chicken stock and let it bubble over low heat to reduce and thicken up, 15 to 20 minutes.

■ Meanwhile, set the celery, carrots, and scallions in a baking dish with icy cold water to crisp up.

■ Remove the cooked wings to a large bowl, pour in the whiskey sauce, and toss to coat. Serve on a platter with the chilled fresh veggies and sprinkled with blue cheese.

Carnitas

CARNITAS

SERVES 6

3 pounds pork shoulder (butt)

1 tablespoon (scant palmful) each of ancho chile powder or chili powder blend, ground cumin, ground coriander, and dried oregano

¼ teaspoon ground cloves

Kosher salt and coarsely ground black pepper

3 to 4 tablespoons neutral oil, such as safflower or canola

1 large onion, sliced

1 large bay leaf

½ cinnamon stick

Juice of 1 large orange

Juice of 2 limes

¾ cup lager beer (light in color and flavor)

1 bulb garlic, peeled and smashed

2 jalapeños, sliced

FOR SERVING

Lime wedges

Soft corn or flour tortillas, charred over an open flame or in a cast-iron skillet

3 to 4 radishes, thinly sliced

Chopped white, sweet, or red onions, tossed with lime juice, salt, and black pepper

Cilantro tops

Pickled sliced jalapeños

■ Cut the pork into large pieces, 2½- to 3-inch chunks. In a small bowl, combine the ancho powder, cumin, coriander, oregano, and cloves. Season the meat liberally with salt and pepper and the spice blend.

■ In a large Dutch oven, heat 3 tablespoons of the oil (three turns of the pan) over medium-high heat. Add the pork and brown the meat (light to medium brown in color) evenly all over. Remove, add the remaining 1 tablespoon oil if needed (one turn of the pan) and the onion, bay leaf, cinnamon stick, and salt and pepper to taste. Cook to soften the onions. Add the pork, orange juice, lime juice, beer, garlic, and jalapeños, cover, and cook for 2 hours.

I've made carnitas a bunch of times over the years, but this particular version was for Tommy, a friend who's basically family. To serve, put out the taco shells, pork, toppings, and salsa and let folks build their own perfect bite—especially if your Hatch peppers are spicy! Rice and beans go on the side.

■ Uncover and cook at lowest simmer until pork is tender and will shred easily, about 1 hour more. Remove the bay leaf.

■ Position a rack in the center of the oven and preheat the broiler. Line a sheet pan with parchment paper or foil.

■ Remove the pork from the sauce and shred. Strain or whisk the sauce (depending on how smooth you prefer it to be) and toss the pork in the sauce. Arrange the pork on the lined pan and broil to crisp the meat a bit on top and at the edges.

■ Serve the pork in a large shallow dish with wedges of lime. Wrap the charred tortillas in a cloth napkin to keep them warm. Set out the sliced radishes, onions, cilantro, and jalapeños.

(CONTINUED)

BLACK BEANS

SERVES 6

1 tablespoon EVOO

1 small onion, chopped

1 large jalapeño, seeded and chopped

2 large cloves garlic, chopped

1 teaspoon ground cumin (⅓ palmful)

1 teaspoon smoked paprika (pimentón)

1 teaspoon dried oregano (⅓ palmful)

Salt

2 (15-ounce) cans black beans (see Note)

▪ In a medium skillet, heat the EVOO (one turn of the pan) over medium heat. Add the onion, jalapeño, garlic, cumin, smoked paprika, oregano, and salt to taste and soften for a few minutes while stirring frequently. Add ½ to ⅔ cup water and let it absorb, then add the beans and heat through. Keep warm over lowest heat.

Note: If you have time, soak 1½ cups dried black beans overnight and cook in salted boiling water with 1 halved onion and a bay leaf.

SOFRITO RICE

SERVES 6

1 tablespoon olive oil or canola oil

1 small sweet pepper (bell or cubanelle/frying pepper), seeded and chopped

1 small fresh chile pepper (optional), seeded and chopped

1 onion, chopped

2 to 3 cloves garlic, chopped

1 carrot, finely chopped (optional)

Salt and freshly ground black pepper

2 teaspoons chili powder

1 teaspoon ground cumin

1½ cups long-grain white rice

2 cups chicken broth, stock, or bone broth

1 cup fresh green peas

1 (8-ounce) can tomato sauce

Juice of 1 lime

1 handful of chopped fresh cilantro or parsley

▪ In a pot, heat the oil (one turn of the pan) over medium to medium-high heat. Add the peppers, onion, garlic, and carrot (if using). Season with salt and black pepper, the chili powder, and cumin and soften a couple of minutes. Add the rice and stir a minute more. Add the broth and bring to a boil. Reduce the heat to low, cover, and cook for 10 minutes, shaking the pan occasionally. Stir in the peas and tomato sauce and cook until the rice is tender, 5 to 8 minutes more. Remove from the heat and let stand for 5 minutes. Stir in the lime juice and cilantro.

HATCH PEPPER SALSA

SERVES 6

6 fresh tomatillos, husked, or 1 (15-ounce) can tomatillos

1 small onion, peeled and cut into quarters

3 to 4 cloves garlic, unpeeled

2 cups thawed frozen Hatch chiles (see Note), mild, medium, or hot

½ cup fresh cilantro or flat-leaf parsley

1 teaspoon dried oregano or 1 tablespoon fresh

1 teaspoon ground cumin

1 teaspoon light agave or mild-flavored honey

Salt

Juice of 1 lime

■ Position a rack one rung above the center and preheat the broiler to high. Line a baking sheet with foil. Arrange the tomatillos, onion, and garlic on the baking sheet. Slide under the broiler and char and blister them, flipping them halfway. The total time under the broiler will be 10 to 12 minutes. When cool enough to handle, peel the garlic.

■ Meanwhile, if the thawed whole Hatch chiles have skins and seeds, discard the skins and seeds.

■ In a food processor, combine the tomatillos, onion, garlic, Hatch chiles, cilantro, oregano, cumin, agave, salt to taste, and lime juice. Pulse-process into a thick salsa. Serve alongside tacos.

Note: Hatch chiles are available online in jars or frozen pouches.

Crab and Cheddar Stuffed Mushrooms and Pinwheel Steaks

CRAB AND CHEDDAR STUFFED MUSHROOMS

SERVES 6

- 18 extra-large stuffing mushrooms (or 30 to 36 medium stuffing mushrooms), wiped clean and stemmed
- Nonaerosol cooking spray
- Salt and freshly ground black pepper
- 4 tablespoons (½ stick) butter
- 2 small ribs celery with leafy tops, finely chopped
- 4 cloves garlic, grated or finely chopped
- 2 large shallots, finely chopped
- 2 tablespoons thyme leaves, chopped
- 1 rounded tablespoon prepared horseradish (optional)
- 1 bay leaf
- ½ cup dry sherry
- 1 pound crabmeat, lump or king leg meat, picked through for any bits of shell or tendon
- 1 English muffin, toasted to deep golden and ground into panko-like crumbs (optional—you can make these mushrooms gluten-free as well)
- About 2 cups loosely packed shredded sharp white cheddar cheese
- Juice of ½ lemon
- A sprinkle of Old Bay Seasoning
- Finely chopped fresh chives and parsley, for serving

■ Preheat the oven to 425°F. Line a baking sheet with foil and top with parchment.

■ Mist the mushroom caps with cooking spray and season with salt and pepper. Parcook them for 8 to 10 minutes. Let them cool and drain cap-side up. Change the parchment paper to a clean sheet and season the inside of the caps with salt and pepper. (Leave the oven on.)

■ Heat a skillet over medium to medium-high heat. Melt the butter and add the celery, garlic, shallots, thyme, horseradish (if using), bay leaf, and salt and pepper to taste. Stir for 3 to 4 minutes. Add the sherry and let it mostly absorb, 1 to 2 minutes. Add the crab and heat through. Remove the bay leaf. Add the English muffin crumbs (if using). Cool the mixture a bit to handle, then stir in the cheddar.

■ Mound the stuffing into the mushrooms very generously. Bake the mushrooms to golden and set, 15 to 18 minutes. Top with lemon juice, Old Bay, and fresh herbs.

PINWHEEL STEAKS

SERVES 6

1½ pounds skirt steak or flank steak (for flank, horizontally halve the meat)

Salt and freshly ground black pepper

Crushed red pepper flakes (optional)

2 lemons, zest grated and reserved, lemons halved

1 cup shaved Parmigiano-Reggiano cheese

1 bunch flat-leaf parsley tops and/or celery tops

1 pound spinach, blanched (see Note), or 1 (16-ounce) package thawed frozen spinach, squeezed to remove excess liquid

¾ pound Gorgonzola cheese

2 to 3 cloves garlic, thinly sliced or shaved

EVOO, for drizzling

Nonaerosol olive oil spray or EVOO

▪ Pound the meat with mallet to a ⅛- to ¼-inch thickness. Cut the meat into 6 long strips, 4 to 5 inches wide and as uniform as possible.

▪ Season the meat with salt, black pepper, and pepper flakes (if using). Top with the lemon zest, shaved Parm, parsley, spinach, crumbles of Gorgonzola, and shaved garlic. Drizzle with EVOO, then roll up the meat as tight as possible. Tie each roll in three places with kitchen twine. Cut each roll into 3 pinwheels, slicing through the meat rolls and cutting between the tied strings.

▪ Preheat the oven to 350°F.

▪ Heat a large cast-iron or nonstick skillet over medium-high to high heat. Mist the pan with cooking spray or coat with EVOO. Add the rolls and brown on each side 2 to 3 minutes. Add lemons to pan, cut-side down, then transfer to oven 6 to 7 minutes more to cook to medium doneness.

▪ Remove strings and serve pinwheels doused with lemon juice.

Note: To blanch spinach, dip it in a pot of boiling salted water, then drain and cold-shock in a bowl of ice and water. Drain and squeeze dry.

Eggplant & Zucchini Parmigiana

PARMIGIANA di MELANZANE e ZUCCHINE
2 Medium, firm eggplants
2 Medium, firm zucchini – Salt
Non-aerosol cooking spray
1 teaspoon EACH:
 Granulated garlic
 granulated onion
 fennel pollen or
 ground fennel
 red pepper flake
 2 Tablespoons EVOO
2 Tablespoons butter
1 onion, finely chopped
4 cloves garlic, chopped
1 can, 15oz cherry tomatoes
or Italian diced tomatoe
1 jar 24oz passata, 3 cups
A handful of basil, torn
2 eggs, lightly beaten
1 ball fresh Mozzarella,
 thinly sliced
2 cups Parmigiano-Reggiano,
 freshly grated

John's Hibiscus Margarita

MAKES ONE COCKTAIL

- 2 ounces tequila blanco
- 2 ounces freshly squeezed lime juice
- 1 ounce hibiscus syrup from Wild Hibiscus Flowers in Syrup
- 1 hibiscus flower from syrup, for garnish

In a cocktail shaker, combine the tequila, lime juice, and hibiscus syrup. Add ice and shake vigorously. Strain into an ice-filled rocks glass. Garnish with the hibiscus flower.

The most comforting place to me in the world is the kitchen. This is why I cook. It's the room in my home that feels the safest and most nurturing and when I cook, I feel free. So when something bad or sad happens, I don't go to the kitchen to feel better. I'm already there.

CHICKEN AND ORZO SOUP WITH RANCH HERB SAUCE AND CRÈME FRAÎCHE

KEBABS WITH TZATZIKI AND GREEK RELISH

PORK PICCATA

Old Friends, New Friends

CHICKEN MILANESE WITH ESCAROLE SALAD

STUPID GOOD, SILLY EASY, STUFFED BREAD WITH SAUSAGE AND BROCCOLINI

SPRING PASTA PRIMAVERA WITH SAFFRON

CHICKEN PROVENÇAL

JOHN'S NEGRONI SPRITZER

Isaboo

Isaboo came into our lives on February 5, 2005: 02/05/2005. She left us on May 20, 2020: 05/20/2020. We all look for patterns when we suffer loss. Connections and reasons, a sign, the hint of a reason why.

On that day in late May, Isaboo had a lovely morning soaking up the near-summer sun on the back terrace. Under a light blanket and stretched out across one of her beds we'd brought outside, she lay beneath a canopy of grapevines that gave her shade and scented the air. Her shoulders were up, her head held high, she stared up at the vines and fruit, her nostrils fluttering, taking in the aroma of grapes and herbs and the flowers blooming in the backyard. Her daddy played his banjo, her favorite of his many instruments. She moved her upper body to the music as best she could. The cancer in her head had been kept at bay for as long as possible, managed with diet and pharmaceuticals—animal and human medicines. She'd survived a catastrophic back injury when she was thirteen, a fall of about twelve feet onto her spine that left her with three herniated discs. Her brilliant doctors gave us many months together beyond our initial projections at diagnosis. We hadn't thought we'd get to share the previous Christmas together, and now here it was spring.

Those last few days Isaboo became too weak to walk. John and I (mostly John) had been assisting her movement with a ten-point harness. She'd become thin and the skin on her pink underbelly was papery, scarred, and splitting from the friction of the harness. Her eyes were cloudy with bile from the cancer blocking her tear ducts. I washed her with cool water continually to clear her eyes and soothe her. She hadn't eaten in almost three days. I tried to hand-feed her lamb and rice, poached chicken, mashed carrots, even a bowl of warm bone broth. She had no appetite. She drank lots of water, always with ice. But she was expressing that she was tired, done, not herself. I believe she had been trying so hard, with every ounce of her will, to stay here for us.

And then, when our veterinarian, Dr. James Keller, with his wife kindly assisting, came to the backyard, John stopped playing and switched on some Bob Schneider, an Austin-based rock musician and our good friend. Isaboo knew his voice well and we listened to his music often; it was familiar to her.

Out on our terrace, under that bright golden bath

of sunlight, I curled up behind Isaboo, cradling her head and shoulders in my lap. I felt her breathing. The first shot, which would send her into a peaceful calm, was administered. I whispered in her ear, "We are better for knowing you. You have changed us and changed the world for so many other animals. You are loved and we know you love us. You are a fighter. You are tired. You can rest now. You can stop fighting now, and rest. Just rest. You can let go." John was too overwhelmed to watch the second shot. He stepped inside for a private moment. The second shot was administered. And before Dr. Keller told me she was gone, I already knew. I felt her pass right through me. I felt her in my soul, leaving this earth.

Our extremely gracious local (human) funeral home director made her a special coffin to fit her frame and a few of her favorite toys, her ball, and the embroidered pillow that bore her name and carried her scent. Imagine the compassion of a gentleman who comes to the passing of a dog during a pandemic wearing a suit. It was so kind and respectful. Our friend Steve, who built the home she had always known, asked to attend as well, and of course, Grandma and Auntie Ria were there, in their masks.

Because of this pandemic, we were with Isaboo more during the last months of her life than at any other time in our fifteen years together. Again, in loss we look for meaning. During the last months of her life, probably more than a year in terms of a dog's life and time on earth, we were never away from her side, indoors or out. In the garden or backyard, Isaboo held court on a chaise or on a bed of blankets.

We'd even make sure to take showers in shifts so that she was always with one of us. And every one of those days, including the day she died, her tail would wag. She knew how much and how deeply she was loved. She was very conscious and she never lost her faculties. She was Isaboo, same as she always was; her body just ran out of time.

The first thought I had immediately following her death was an overwhelming sense of gratitude. I have never felt such purity of emotion. I was filled with it, and it washed over me as it would again after watching my home burn down in front of me a few months later. When we suffer great loss, we can see more clearly all that we have to be grateful for.

In 2020 there were many hundreds of thousands of human lives lost to an insidious virus, airborne and indiscriminate. The number of souls, the loved ones affected by these deaths, is incalculable. The ocean of grief could be felt in all of our hearts and in the pit of our stomachs as we listened to the total number of sick and dying rise on the news each day. I remember sobbing when I first watched recordings of Italians singing to each other from their windows, into the dark of night, as their countrymen's deceased loved ones were loaded into trucks and carried away, far from them.

These losses of life have been and are made worse, crueler, because so many people had to spend their last days and hours alone. Death is a part of life. A good death is sharing the reflection of our lives in our final days with our loved ones around us, the comfort of their hands in ours. I feel so deeply grateful that I was there with Isaboo, but I'm sickened when I compare that to the lonely passing of these poor souls. I have never wished to change a day of my life or a negative circumstance in it, because each moment helps shape who and what we are today. This last year, with all my heart, I wished I could change the world and heal the holes in every heart. I wished I could give everyone the blessing of closure and the healing power of understanding the circle of life. I wished I could give the world that grace.

Isaboo is laid to rest in our small orchard high on a hill she loved. She would chase apples there, chew them to the core, and pop up to catch the next. She would roll in the tall grass and sniff the air and stare into the big blue sky. It's from that sky that she watches over all of us today.

When our home burned, we lost a lot of original art that meant so much to us. A portrait of Isaboo painted for me for my fiftieth birthday, by our dear friend Howard Stern, survived completely undamaged.

Chicken and Orzo Soup

WITH RANCH HERB SAUCE AND CRÈME FRAÎCHE

SERVES 4

RANCH HERB SAUCE

- ½ cup coarsely chopped fresh dill
- ½ cup coarsely chopped fresh flat-leaf parsley
- ½ cup coarsely chopped fresh chives
- ½ cup coarsely chopped fresh leafy carrot tops
- ¼ cup packed fresh tarragon or small basil leaves
- 2 cloves garlic, smashed
- ¼ cup fresh lemon juice, plus a few splashes for finishing
- ¼ cup EVOO
- Salt and freshly ground black pepper

SOUP

- 2 tablespoons butter or EVOO
- 2 carrots, cut into ¼-inch dice
- 2 large shallots or 1 onion, chopped
- Salt and freshly ground black pepper
- 1 cup orzo
- 2 (32-ounce) containers chicken stock or 3 (22-ounce) containers chicken bone broth
- 2½ to 3 cups pulled or bite-size pieces rotisserie chicken
- 2 cups fresh or thawed frozen green peas
- 3 to 4 cups baby lettuces or greens of choice, torn or coarsely chopped (optional)
- ½ to 1 cup crème fraîche, for serving

Talk about a spring fling! This recipe shows just how much you can jazz up a rotisserie chicken. I love to finish it with spring lettuces and lemon juice. The soup should be very thick but light in flavor—not overly brothy.

■ Make the ranch herb sauce: In a food processor, pulse the fresh herbs, garlic, and lemon juice until the herbs are finely chopped. With the machine running, stream in the EVOO until the sauce is smooth. Season with salt and pepper.

■ Make the soup: Heat a soup pot or medium Dutch oven over medium to medium-high heat. Add the butter. When the butter melts, add the carrots and shallots and season with salt and pepper. Cook, stirring often, until the vegetables soften, about 5 minutes. Add the orzo and cook, stirring often, until light golden, about 2 minutes. Stir in the bone broth and bring to a boil. Add the chicken and peas and cook until heated through, about 5 minutes.

■ Stir the herb sauce into the soup. Add the greens (if using) and stir until they wilt. Add a few squeezes of lemon juice to taste. Divide the soup among bowls and top each with a generous dollop of crème fraîche for stirring into soup.

Kebabs

WITH TZATZIKI AND GREEK RELISH

SERVES 4 TO 6

¼ cup Greek yogurt

Grated zest and juice of 1 lemon

¼ cup EVOO

4 cloves garlic, grated

2 teaspoons crushed red pepper flakes or freshly ground black pepper

2 teaspoons kosher salt

1 tablespoon packed finely chopped fresh oregano or 1 teaspoon dried

1 tablespoon packed finely chopped fresh thyme or 1 teaspoon dried

2 pounds boneless leg of lamb or boneless, skinless chicken breast, cut into 1½-inch pieces (large bite size)

1 small handful of fresh bay leaves (optional)

Nonaerosol cooking spray

Tzatziki Sauce (recipe follows)

Greek Relish (recipe follows)

▪ In a large bowl, combine the yogurt, lemon zest, lemon juice, EVOO, garlic, pepper flakes, salt, oregano, and thyme. Add the meat, toss to coat, and refrigerate for 30 minutes.

▪ Thread the meat onto metal skewers. If desired, add a fresh bay leaf every 3 to 4 pieces.

▪ Preheat a grill to medium-high for indirect heat. Mist the grill grates with oil.

▪ Cook the skewers 12 to 15 minutes, turning occasionally, starting over direct heat until browned, then moving to indirect heat. (The kebabs can also be broiled in the center of the oven under high, 12 to 15 minutes, turning occasionally.)

▪ Serve the kebabs with the tzatziki sauce and Greek relish.

(CONTINUED)

TZATZIKI SAUCE

MAKES ABOUT 1½ CUPS

½ seedless cucumber or
2 Persian (mini)
cucumbers, peeled and
grated

1½ teaspoons kosher salt

½ cup Greek yogurt

1 large or 2 medium cloves
garlic, grated

Juice of 1 lemon

2 tablespoons EVOO

Scant 1 teaspoon ground
cumin

½ cup mixed finely chopped
fresh dill and mint leaves

▪ Place the cucumber in a sieve,
sprinkle it with the salt, and let
drain 20 to 30 minutes, then press
out all of the excess liquid.

▪ In a small bowl, combine the
cucumber with the remaining
ingredients and refrigerate until
ready to serve.

Put in a fat handful of dill and mint. It makes the sauce!

GREEK RELISH

MAKES ABOUT 3 CUPS

½ seedless cucumber or
3 Persian (mini)
cucumbers, cut into
¼-inch dice

1 large heirloom or
beefsteak tomato or
2 vine tomatoes, seeded
and cut into ¼-inch dice

1 medium Vidalia or other
sweet onion, chopped

¾ to 1 cup pitted Kalamata
olives, chopped

1 handful of flat-leaf
parsley, chopped

Juice of 1 lemon

3 tablespoons EVOO

Salt and freshly ground
black pepper

▪ In a bowl, combine all the
ingredients and refrigerate until
ready to serve.

Pork Piccata

1½ pounds pork tenderloin

Salt and freshly ground black pepper or ground white pepper

1¼ cups AP flour

1 teaspoon granulated garlic

1 tablespoon grated lemon zest

1 tablespoon ground thyme or dried thyme

¼ cup EVOO

1 lemon, very thinly sliced

4 cloves garlic, thinly sliced

¼ cup drained capers

¼ cup fresh lemon juice

½ cup white wine

½ cup chicken stock

4 tablespoons (½ stick) butter

1 handful of fresh flat-leaf parsley, chopped, for garnish

■ Cut the tenderloin crosswise into eight equal pieces ¾ to 1 inch thick. Place the pork pieces between sheets of plastic wrap and pound into ¼- to ⅛-inch-thick medallions. Season the pork all over with salt and pepper.

■ On a large shallow plate, mix together the flour, granulated garlic, lemon zest, and thyme. Turn the pork in the flour to coat evenly. Transfer to another large plate as you coat the medallions.

■ Set up a frying station: Line a large rimmed baking sheet with foil. Set a wire rack inside the baking sheet.

■ In a large skillet, heat the EVOO (four turns of the pan) over medium-high heat. Working in batches, if needed, cook the pork, turning once, until browned on both sides, 4 to 5 minutes per batch. Transfer the pork to the baking sheet to drain. Reserve the skillet.

■ In the skillet the pork was cooked in, combine the sliced lemon, garlic, and capers and stir for a minute over medium-high heat. Whisk in the lemon juice, wine, and stock. Cook until reduced a bit, 3 to 5 minutes. Whisk in the butter to finish the sauce.

■ Transfer the pork to a platter or plates. Top with the sauce and garnish with the parsley.

Serve with sautéed spinach or roasted broccolini and crusty bread.

Chicken Milanese

WITH ESCAROLE SALAD

SERVES 4

4 boneless, skinless chicken breasts (8 ounces each)

Salt and freshly ground black pepper

1 cup AP flour

3 large eggs, beaten

1 cup dried breadcrumbs

½ cup panko breadcrumbs

1 cup finely shredded Parmigiano-Reggiano or pecorino cheese

1 tablespoon granulated garlic

1 tablespoon dried parsley

1 tablespoon grated lemon zest

1½ teaspoons dried oregano

1½ teaspoons dried rosemary

1½ teaspoons dried thyme

1 teaspoon crushed red pepper flakes

About 1½ cups olive oil or safflower oil, for shallow-frying

Escarole Salad (recipe follows)

■ Position a rack in the center of the oven and preheat the oven to 300°F.

■ Starting on the fat side of a chicken breast, cut horizontally across the breast but not all the way through. Open it up like a book. Pound the chicken to a ¼-inch thickness. Season with salt and black pepper.

■ Set up a breading station: Line up three shallow bowls on the counter. Spread the flour out in one, beat the eggs in the second, and mix together the breadcrumbs, panko, Parm, and seasonings in the third.

■ Set up a frying station: Line a large rimmed baking sheet with foil and arrange a wire rack inside the baking sheet. Put the baking sheet in the oven.

■ Pour the oil into a large skillet and heat the oil over medium-high heat.

■ Working with one cutlet at a time, coat both sides first in the flour and then the egg. Press into the breadcrumb mixture until completely coated. Add two pieces of breaded chicken to the oil and fry until deep golden, about 3 minutes per side. Transfer the chicken to the baking sheet in the oven to keep warm. Repeat with the remaining chicken and breading.

■ Divide the cutlets among four large plates. Top with escarole salad.

ESCAROLE SALAD

SERVES 4

Juice of 1 lemon

1 tablespoon white balsamic or white wine vinegar

1 teaspoon honey or sugar

2 teaspoons Dijon mustard

1 teaspoon fennel pollen or ground fennel

1 small bulb fennel, very thinly sliced by hand or on a mandoline

2 large ribs celery with leafy tops, very thinly sliced on an angle

1 large head escarole, coarsely chopped

1 small onion or ½ medium white onion, thinly sliced

1 cup shaved Parmigiano-Reggiano cheese (use a vegetable peeler)

Salt and freshly ground black pepper

■ In a small bowl, whisk together the lemon juice, vinegar, honey, mustard, and fennel pollen.

■ In a large bowl, toss together the chopped vegetables. Drizzle in the dressing, season with salt and pepper, sprinkle with Parm and toss again.

Bella Boo Blue

Triple B for short, Bella Boo Blue came into our lives and our backyard within weeks of Isaboo's passing. Joanne Yohannan, our friend who's SVP of operations at North Shore Animal League (a massive shelter in Long Island and a major recipient of our foundation's money), started texting us pictures of pit bulls looking for forever homes a few weeks before Izzy passed. A few weeks _after_ she died, we saw Bella's puppy face on John's phone, and that was it. I knew she was the one.

Bella is actually half pit bull and half Weimaraner. She'd been passed around quite a bit, and was fostered by another family after being rescued from a shelter that euthanizes. She is a singular beauty, with striking eyes. To be honest, she's also a little weird-looking—on certain parts of her body she seems to have bottle bristles spraying out. Like a hummingbird, she's every color. She has a blue-gray coat indoors, but when she hits the sun you see her mama. Her fur becomes iridescent, with orange pit bull highlights. I've always wanted a donkey; Eeyore was my favorite character in the world of Christopher Robin and Winnie-the-Pooh. But when we first met her, Bella looked more like a baby elephant—like Dumbo, with giant ears.

I fell in love with her at first sight, just as I had with Boo and Isaboo. Boo was originally named Boots. I adopted her when she was around two years old, so I simply shortened her name to Boo. Isabella is my favorite name, and I got her just after Boo had passed. So I combined Isabella with Boo and created the name Isaboo. Then I took Bella from Isabella, and I made that the front part of my third dog's name and Boo the middle. She had blue eyes and blueish fur when I got her, thus Bella Boo Blue. And every time I call her I'll think of my three girls.

I found Boo in answer to an open letter posted in the Pennysaver, a local circular of classified ads. I think my boyfriend at the time was looking for a motorcycle. What we saw was a plea from an already busy mom expecting, as I recall, twins. She had a young pit bull that had been cut to look like a boxer, cropped ears and tail (pit bull owners often did this to hide their dog's breed, or else

they would be denied homeowner's insurance). The letter was desperate, as most adult pit bulls lost their lives if they were brought to a shelter, and without an answer to her plea, that would likely be her dog's fate. The animal was young and required too much energy for a soon-to-be too busy new mom of two more children.

Boo had large brown eyes and was very human and expressive. She had a deviated septum that allowed her to talk like a human and grunt like a potbelly pig. She was very vocal and could run on in sentences, like Scooby. Her paws were scarred from trying to escape her backyard pen. Her scars reminded me of my hands, scarred from many years in the kitchen. She was awkward with a big, bold personality. She came home with us that day in my Ford Ranger. I spent the next few days breaking her of the rules she had been taught: not to jump up on people, to stay only on the linoleum floors of the house, and to be an obedient dog. I wanted her to become a full expression of herself. She loved to dance and sing along to the radio in the car. She slept late every day, loved butternut squash more than steak, and, most remarkably, this big-personality dog could fall into deep, daily meditations, like silent trances, while standing among the tender leaves of an overgrown ficus tree. Boo made it clear to me that I would live the rest of my life with a dog and that I would be a better human for it.

My grandpa Emmanuel had a black-nose pit bull. He also

had ten kids to look after! Pit bulls are actually perfect for a home like theirs, as they were originally bred to be nanny dogs, companions and protectors of infants and children. They are gentle and nurturing by nature, and want nothing more than to please the members of their pack or family. I've held many incredibly sweet pit bulls over the years who had suffered, been thrown into dog fights, wounded, abandoned, or tortured. But you wouldn't know it. Their capacity for love is extraordinary, matched by their strength, their resilience, and their ability to forgive.

Bella means <u>beautiful</u> in Italian, and our dog lives up to her name. She has a tiny butt, long legs and torso, and those Dumbo ears now look like a coiffed mane that draws you in to her blue, mysterious, and mesmerizing eyes. They've made even more striking by the darkness of the fur surrounding them, like Cleopatra in makeup, with David Bowie and Iman mixed in. She snuggles and nuzzles like no dog we've had and loves belly rubs so much that she can fall asleep on her back with her legs stretched wide open. It's a kooky pose for a sixty-five-pound (and counting) pup, but it shows how sweet and trusting she is.

Bella has odd eating habits. She loves roaming and grazing the herbs in our summer garden, including parsley and mint, and occasionally a little sage. She steals away large pieces of bark from the wood pile (too much fiber, for sure) and enjoys wedges of pumpkin, apple, and cheese, and noodles of all kinds. Oh, and she will steal a pita off my counter and sleep on it like it's a security blanket. I cook for her as I have for all my girls, but Bella is fussy and refuses to eat the same dish twice in twenty-four hours. She hides her treats and gnaw bones, burying them in the sofa or bed or of course in the backyard. Her favorite toy is Deadpool riding a unicorn (we've had to replace it half a dozen times).

Bella's paws are more like hooves, and while she may think and act like

a puppy, she has the strength of a bucking donkey. When she has an exciting dream, or she wants more room in the queen-size bed shared by her, John, and me, she bucks me with her hooves and haunches and I wake up covered in bruises. John looked at me one day while I was making a quick change for our show and he gasped in horror at my chest. I almost cried! It was just another Bella love mark, darkest just before they heal. She loves to gnaw on me as well. I think I might better have called her Bruce, the name Spielberg gave the shark in <u>Jaws</u>.

Training a puppy again after fifteen years required a learning curve. John would get so frustrated with her, he'd shout, "You're not making my life better!" I'd remind him that even though she looked full grown, she'd only been in this world a few months. I tend to be a little more patient with the accidents, and I was even impressed with a few of them. Bella knows we use our bathroom to go potty, and the shower is open in there, just a stone step up to get in. So she went in there to pee and poop. Logical! John, who was a germophobe even before the

pandemic, did not find it as charming as I did, and dumped half a bottle of bleach into the shower, ruining my new black bathmat.

Bella trained with Elizabeth Lajeunesse and loved going to her training center, Dog Logic, with her best friends Marin and Crumpet. My sister, Maria, drove, and off Bella went nearly every day that we were taping the show lest she get tangled in cables and cords, destroying lights and laptops). But she's a good pup with a big heart. Elizabeth had to work harder to train <u>us</u>—we are the old dogs in the scenario, and we're set in our ways. But eager to learn! Elizabeth was calm and collaborative, teaching us how to be better listeners and have more patience and persistence. Great lessons for any human, whether you belong to a dog or not.

Stupid Good, Silly Easy, Stuffed Bread

WITH SAUSAGE AND BROCCOLINI

SERVES 4

2 bunches broccolini, 1 inch of ends trimmed

3 tablespoons EVOO, plus more for drizzling

1 pound sweet Italian sausage with fennel, casings removed

2 cups ricotta

Salt and ground white or finely ground black pepper

⅛ teaspoon freshly grated nutmeg

1 small handful of fresh parsley, chopped

⅓ cup grated Parmigiano-Reggiano cheese

Grated zest of 1 small lemon

2 large shallots or 1 small onion, thinly sliced or chopped

4 cloves garlic, sliced

1 tablespoon Calabrian chile paste or 2 small red chiles, chopped

Juice of 1 small lemon

1 loaf Italian bread with sesame seeds on top

12 ounces shredded mozzarella cheese

Hot or sweet pickled cherry peppers

■ Set up a large bowl of ice and water. In a large pot of boiling salted water, blanch the broccolini for 3 minutes. Drain and cold-shock in the ice bath. Drain well and set aside.

■ Position a rack in the center of the oven and preheat the oven to 375°F.

■ In a skillet, heat 1 tablespoon of the EVOO (one turn of the pan) over medium-high heat. Add the sausage and brown and crumble. Transfer to a small platter lined with paper towels to drain.

■ In a bowl, season the ricotta with salt and pepper. Add the nutmeg, parsley, Parm, lemon zest, and a drizzle of EVOO.

■ Chop the broccolini into bite-size pieces.

■ In the same skillet, heat the remaining 2 tablespoons EVOO (two turns of the pan) over medium heat. Add the shallots, season with a little salt, and stir a couple of minutes to soften. Add

the garlic, chile paste, and broccolini and toss 2 to 3 minutes more. Add about ¼ cup water and the lemon juice, toss a minute more, and remove from the heat.

■ Halve the bread horizontally and scoop out excess interior softer bits from the top. Spread the bottom of the bread with the ricotta and top with sausage, broccolini mixture, mozzarella, and pickled peppers. Set the bread top over the filling and press to set the stuffed loaf. Wrap in foil with the seam on top of the loaf. Set the loaf on a sheet pan.

■ Bake the loaf for 20 minutes. Open the foil and increase the oven temperature to 425°F. Bake about 5 minutes more to brown.

■ Let stand 5 to 10 minutes, then remove from the foil and place on a large cutting board and cut into sections to serve.

Spring Pasta Primavera

WITH SAFFRON

SERVES 4

1½ cups vegetable or chicken stock

¼ teaspoon saffron threads (a fat pinch)

3 tablespoons EVOO

2 small zucchini (¾ pound), cut into ¼-inch dice (1½ to 2 cups)

¼ pound ramps (10 to 12), whites finely chopped and greens cut into 1-inch pieces, or 2 thin leeks (whites and light-green parts), halved lengthwise, well washed, and thinly sliced crosswise

½ pound asparagus, tough ends trimmed, thinly sliced on an angle

Salt and freshly ground black pepper

1 cup fresh or thawed frozen green peas

2 large cloves garlic, peeled

½ cup white wine (optional)

¾ cup half-and-half

Fat handful (several tablespoons) of chopped mixed fresh herbs: tarragon, torn basil or parsley, and chives, plus more for garnish

1 pound tagliatelle or other egg pasta

1 cup grated Parmigiano-Reggiano cheese

■ Bring a pot of water to a boil for the pasta.

■ In a small pot, combine the stock and saffron and simmer until reduced by half, allowing the saffron to bloom and the stock to concentrate its flavor.

■ Heat a large skillet over medium to medium-high heat. Add the EVOO (three turns of the pan), zucchini, ramp whites (or leeks), and asparagus and cook a few minutes to tender-crisp. Season with salt and pepper, stir in the peas, and grate in the garlic. If using white wine, add it and reduce until almost absorbed. Add the saffron stock and reduce a bit, then add the half-and-half and let simmer at a low bubble. Stir in the ramp greens and herbs.

■ Salt the boiling water and cook the pasta 1 minute less than the package directions for al dente. Before draining, ladle out about ½ cup of the starchy pasta cooking water, then drain the pasta. Add the pasta to vegetables and sauce, toss, then add the Parm and toss, adding a little starchy water if necessary.

■ Serve in shallow bowls. Garnish with more herbs.

If you can't find ramps, you can use any green onion. Leeks are perfect for this, no problem, and scallions are fine, too, or spring onions of any kind!

Chicken Provençal

MARINADE AND CHICKEN

4 large cloves garlic, chopped

½ cup packed chopped mixed fresh herbs: parsley, rosemary, and thyme

1 tablespoon grated lemon zest

1 tablespoon fennel seeds

2 teaspoons kosher salt

1 teaspoon freshly ground black pepper

1 cup crisp white wine

¼ cup EVOO

8 pieces boneless, skinless chicken, small breasts and thighs combined

TO PREPARE

4 tablespoons (½ stick) butter

2 shallots, cut into wedges

1 small onion, thinly sliced

1 small bulb fennel, thinly sliced

4 large cloves garlic, crushed with the side of a knife

1 cup loosely packed pitted Niçoise olives or green and black olives combined, coarsely chopped

2 tablespoons AP flour

1 cup chicken bone broth or stock

1 cup loosely packed or drained semi-dried tomatoes or plumped sun-dried tomatoes, coarsely chopped

Baguette

■ Marinate the chicken: In a bowl, toss together the garlic, herbs, lemon zest, fennel seeds, salt, pepper, wine, and EVOO. Add the chicken, cover, and refrigerate for at least 1 hour and up to 1 day.

■ Preheat the oven to 400°F.

■ To prepare, heat a large heavy pot over medium heat and add 2 tablespoons of the butter. Remove the chicken from the marinade (shaking off the excess marinade but reserving it). Add the chicken to the pan and brown, then remove from the pan.

■ Add the remaining 2 tablespoons butter, the shallots, onion, fennel, and garlic and sauté to soften, 5 to 6 minutes. Add the olives, sprinkle in the flour and stir. Add half the reserved marinade (discard the rest). Stir and let bubble for 2 to 3 minutes. Add the broth and let thicken a bit.

■ Add the tomatoes and slide the chicken back into the pan and nest into the sauce. Transfer to oven and roast for 20 minutes or until juices run clear.

■ Serve with crusty bread.

COCKTAIL BY JOHN

John's Negroni Spritzer

MAKES ONE COCKTAIL

1½ ounces gin
1½ ounces Campari
¾ ounce red vermouth
2 dashes Angostura bitters
½ orange
Club soda
Lemon twist, for garnish

Add the gin, Campari, vermouth, and bitters to a rocks glass. Fill the glass with ice, squeeze the orange over it, and drop the orange into the glass. Top with club soda. Stir gently and garnish with a lemon twist.

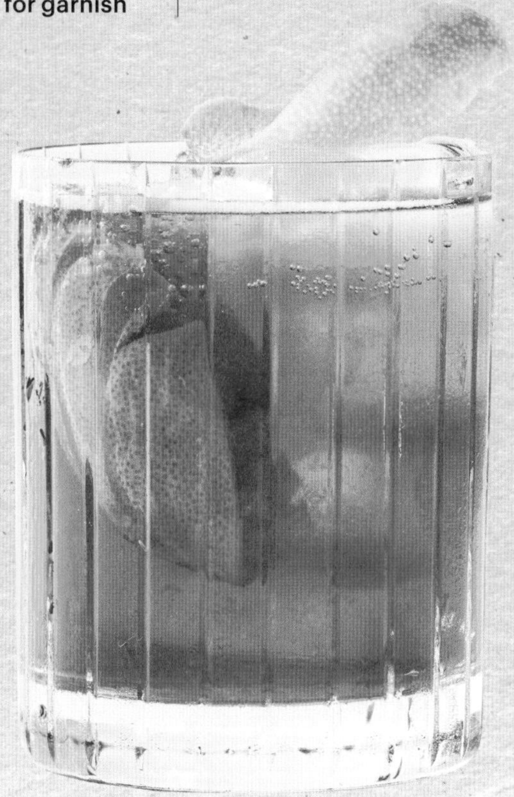

Pretty early on during lockdown, we realized we needed some version of a social life, a way to bond, entertain, share our feelings, and spend time with our friends from New York and beyond. So the Rach and John Cook-Along was born. The fun began with the invitees choosing a specific cuisine or technique to focus on. The recipes weren't necessarily in season. They were just what my friends felt like cooking when it was time to cook.

CRAB FRA DIAVOLO AND SPAGHETTI

PAPPARDELLE WITH LAMB RAGU

PORCINI AND GREENS RISOTTO

JAEGER SPAETZLE AND MUSHROOM CREAM SAUCE WITH
SPICED RED CABBAGE

SALMON EN CROÛTE

Cook-Alongs

SPAGHETTI AND ROASTED IMPOSSIBALLS

PUMPKIN RISOTTO WITH SAGE, BROWN BUTTER, AND NUTS

MOROCCAN CHICKEN TAGINE

BEEF STEW WITH DIJON MUSTARD AND SHERRY MUSHROOMS

JOHN'S MOROCCAN MAR-TEA-NI

See You Next Tuesday Cooking Club

It seems that in this past year, the farther the world has drawn us away from each other, the closer we've become to the people we love. For so many of us, the thinner the thread is pulled, the more careful we are with it.

On November 1, 2020, my mind was on the election and I was full of worry about what would happen to our country and my second home, New York City, in the days after the polls closed. We hadn't set foot in our Manhattan apartment in eight months and counting, by far the longest John and I had been away in our almost twenty years together. I missed so much about the city (see page 202 for more on that), but one major gaping hole in our lives was our friends. We hadn't seen them, or broken bread with them as we loved to do, since we arrived upstate back in March. We missed them, and we missed the long dinners we'd host or attend, eating and drinking and talking until well past our bedtime. For months it had been me and John, my sister and mom popping by, and nobody else.

What made us feel sane and social again despite all of that were Cook-Alongs. Pretty early on during lockdown, we realized we needed some version of a social life, a way to bond, entertain, share our feelings, and spend time with our friends from New  York and beyond. So the Rach and John Cook-Along was born. They're a lot of advance work, but they're worth it. We started doing Cook-Alongs to comfort ourselves, because we couldn't go to New York—and then, when we lost our home, as a way not to focus on that all the time. It was a much-needed mechanism to keep us from letting ourselves go down the rabbit hole of loss. Spending time with people gets your head out of your own world and into others' worlds. And so you join the world again—even if it's only possible through a thing I never knew existed: Zoom.

Cook-Alongs are great because they require focus, fun, food, and there's always a drink, recipe courtesy of John. In a way they're better than an actual dinner party because there's real group interaction—when we have people over, I'm usually in the kitchen

cooking and cleaning as I go, and missing a lot of the conversation happening in the dining room. The Cook-Along fun begins with the group choosing a specific cuisine or technique to focus on. Next, I write a recipe in my notebook for us all to cook together virtually, and John comes up with a perfect cocktail to go with it. I call my partner in procurement, Michelle Boxer, who helps me send our "guests" the ingredients—but I don't share a formal recipe with them. Instead, on the appointed night, I text a series of photos of the mise en place, all the prep work step by step. Then, closer to game time, John sends the specifics for the cocktail.

We did our first Cook-Along in June, with our friends the Antonoffs. Jack Antonoff, the uber talented musician and producer, was our closer at the last SXSW party we threw, performing as Bleachers. He is a force of inspiration and energy on and off stage, and makes amazing granola, I might add. Cooking along with us was Jack's brilliant sister Rachel, a fashion designer. She's a go-to for me: I'm a loyal customer, and her jumpsuits (I call them my onesies) are so chic and comfortable, I could live in them. Also, the lovely Carlotta "Carl" Kohl, a beautiful and super-artistic photographer/producer (and Jack's girlfriend), would be cooking with us as well. Truth be told, the girls are all in on the food. Jack works on the cocktails. Occasionally Jack and Rachel's parents, Shira and Ricky, would join in, too.

We happened to start our Cook-Alongs on a Tuesday night, and thus Tuesdays quickly became my favorite night of the week, as we had a fun activity to look forward to that felt different from what we recorded for our shows. And so, we legit became the "See You Next Tuesday Cooking Club" (fill in the inappropriate acronym here). Whether you get the joke or not, OUR food is amazing! We now do Cook-Alongs with other friends, but this club, with Jack and Co., is our longest running one, focusing on plant-based dishes and occasionally seafood.

Our second longest running Cook-Along gang was a handful of John's bandmates: Shawn Pelton, _Saturday Night Live_ drummer and legendary session musician; his wife, Elaine Caswell, preeminent vocalist who plays a hell of a fiddle; Neal Coomer, who will sing the pants off anyone within hearing range; and his husband, Daniel Konicek, resident artist and fabulous dancer. Each time we cook together this gang writes and records a theme song based on the dish, and they send me the lyrics, framed and enhanced by Daniel's artwork (see page 135). It's a quid pro quo, in a good way.

Another pair we've cooked along regularly with is Harlan Coben, _New York Times_ bestselling novelist, and his wife, Anne Armstrong-Coben, a pediatrician and senior associate dean of admissions at Columbia Medicine. They love seafood and pasta, so we'd cook risottos and mussels and pasta fra diavolo. (I wish I could remember which one got the review, "This is the best fucking pasta I've ever had!" from one of their sons.) Anne's biggest stress during lockdown was that she loves her job, offering counsel and support to young people, but she hasn't been able to hug them or even go near them. And she's a hugger! Me, too. It's kind of crushing to have to hold that back in yourself. Harlan and Anne were the last guests we had in our apartment in New York City before relocating permanently upstate last year. I remember hugging them then. It was hard. Not emotionally—physically! They're much taller than we are. As close as we can become on Zoom or FaceTime, physical contact can't be replicated by a computer. Standing six feet away doesn't cut it either. But this next best thing held us over. Anne gets a gold star for her prep work. She's never running late, but always early. I think she and Harlan make their drinks early, too!

Austin is my home away from home, and one of its native sons, musician Bob Schneider, is a great friend of ours. We cooked with him and his family on the regular, and during one call, I think it was shrimp tacos and salsas, Bob said that what he'd learned from the process and

preparation was a deep appreciation for my recipes and what goes into them. His sincerity filled my heart and made me blush. (For many cooks and service people, compliments bring out our awkwardness.) Bob was the first artist we asked to perform at our first Feedback party fourteen years ago, our big old rock concert that runs every year during South by

Southwest in Austin. Bob and John's band, The Cringe, are the only two acts that have played all fourteen years, and a few times they shared the stage together. Bob is a gifted artist in many media and disciplines (he has painted us several perfect copies of Picassos) and he kinda looks like John's much taller brother.

We also cooked along with our friends Mike and Britt Pritchard. We'd met them years ago at the Hotel St. Cecilia in Austin. We were there for South by Southwest, specifically for our event, Feedback, and we were having a drink and sharing a plate nearby. The St. Cecilia, named for the patron saint of musicians, is a popular spot for bands, actors, and artists who come to Austin for performances, premieres, or festivals. On this trip, the Pritchards were celebrating their anniversary. The weekend ended up becoming the anniversary of our friendship, as well. In a move I'd never seen him make, John introduced himself to the pair and politely told Mike what a big fan he was—Mike is best known to music lovers as Mike Dirnt of the band Green Day. We ended up sharing a table and the next few days together. We've been very close since, and would try and visit each year in Italy or at the holidays. To other people, he's a rock star. To us, he's a friend with the fastest wit and an endless string of puns to brighten any conversation and keep you on your toes. His wife, Britt, is beautiful inside and out, and what a force of nature! She kicked cancer (kicked it in the ass and then some) and is a mom of two. She loves design and is an inspiration to all.

Years ago, we started a movable feast tradition along with our friends Patti Galluzzi, Michael Stipe, and Thomas Dozol. We would pop into one another's homes, one after another, and nosh on nibbles at one, main at the next, dessert at the last. Patti has the most sincere and joyful laugh, she's a wonderful baker, active in many social and charitable initiatives, and is a busy, thoughtful mom and friend and a former bigwig at MTV. Michael, front man for R.E.M, has one of the rarest and most moving voices in music. He's brilliant but unassuming, and conversations with him are fun-filled and illuminating. Thomas, his

partner, is an artist and a thinker as well, and has a calm about him that makes me envious. When the feast group assembled again to cook along virtually, Michael did the work, as Thomas was self-quarantining after traveling from abroad. The meal was beautiful, hearty, and healthy, a porcini risotto with spinach and semi-dried tomatoes, finished off by a dessert that Patti had made and shipped to all of us. Michael loved it so much, he made the meal again for his mom. He was home with her during quarantine. Later, he sent pictures of himself making it again on his own and serving it to her, and it just overwhelmed me with a wave of emotion. (It doesn't hurt that his mom happens to look a lot like my mom.) I just burst into tears at the beauty of it. It was the same when the Antonoffs' parents, Shira and Ricky, joined us and they made food together. Before the pandemic was over, Jack would be onstage with Taylor Swift winning a Grammy for Album of the Year, and here he was in a T-shirt with his family, all working together to cook and eat. I really love that.

   We cooked with Brooke Johnson, my former boss, mentor, and advisor who has become a lifelong trusted friend and travel mate, and her wife, Marianna Rosett. We cooked with Paul Franklin—winemaker and retired TV executive who worked at CBS and helped secure the future of the show I still work on to this day—and his wife, Jan. We cooked with the Klausners, friends of John's from law school who now love me more because I feed them.

One big surprise came when we scheduled a Cook-Along with our friends Zanna Roberts Rassi and Mazdack Rassi, the co-founders of Milk Makeup (my daily go-to), among their myriad other interesting and successful endeavors. They wanted to make spaghetti and meatballs with plant-based Impossible meat, rather than beef or beef and pork—Impossiballs, I called them. The Rassis have beautiful twin daughters, Juno and Rumi, and Zanna was psyched to get hands-on and roll meatballs with her girls. But when we logged in for the Cook-Along, we had a surprise cook in the kitchen, a friend who had joined

their pandemic pod, Justin Theroux (with his pit bull, instant respect and love)! We had never met, so what fun to get the ball rolling by rolling some balls. Ha! What a beautiful table this pod set. Justin did an amazing job, but, Zanna, next time I'm going to make sure you get your hands dirty!

John and I hosted two vinyl parties from here that went on for hours, as part of Gary Dell'Abate's vinyl club. (You may know Gary from <u>The Howard Stern Show,</u> but we know him as a vinylphile, like

John and me.) It was a couple dozen people, and everyone had to pick a record based on a theme that Gary chose. For the parties we hosted upstate, John planned them and ordered every record that everyone

chose. In some cases, he spent days hunting down an album. When he couldn't find it, people were kind enough to send/lend their personal copy of the record. Because we couldn't pour it ourselves, we sent along wine and snacks for all. For the first party I got help with snacks from Love Mary, my friend Mary Giuliani's

frozen app boxes; for the second I went even easier, with a Goldbelly gift card, allowing everyone to order snacks at will.

During each party, each participant had to introduce their song and explain what it meant to them. People from all over the country joined— and even outside of it. (Fred Armisen was in London and still made it to both parties.) We all have different lives and professions, but music brings us together. (We just happen to think it sounds better on vinyl— but don't tell our friend Howard Stern that. He thinks vinyl sucks.) We talk about one another's song picks, and it brings back flashes of memory from our whole lives. And these vinylphiles have crazy facts! You'll never hear those songs the same way again. It's cool and cathartic; it marries music and food, and marries us all to each other. It helped us all a lot during this really dark time.

Zoom itself, which, like everyone else, I had zero awareness of before March of 2020, has been an education. You have to relearn many things you were taught as a child: Only speak when spoken to, let people finish their thoughts, be patient with commentary. For the Italian in me, this is a challenge. In person, our family talks over one another, each louder than the person already speaking. That's how you win the floor! And we all can hear everything through the cacophony. I think Zoom has improved (if only marginally) my skills of patience and listening, in spite of the occasional, inevitable, and excruciating (for me) lag in connection.

When and if the world "goes back" to what it was pre-pandemic, I hope the Cook-Alongs live on. When you cook _for_ someone, everyone's food is the same. When we cook along _with_ each other, we each bring our own hands and palate to the dishes. Each plate will be different, with its own personality, although it's made from the same recipe. It becomes a collective, communal experience of shared excitement but also individual influences, more than just eating a tasty dinner. It's basically sanctioned "playing with your food."

Crab fra Diavolo and Spaghetti

1 pound crabmeat (I use king leg meat, but lump or claw meat is great as well), picked through for any bits of shell or tendon

Juice of 1½ lemons

2 teaspoons Old Bay Seasoning

2 tablespoons EVOO

2 tablespoons butter

2 large shallots, finely chopped

1 small rib celery, finely chopped

4 cloves garlic, chopped

1 large bay leaf

1 tablespoon Calabrian chile paste or 1½ teaspoons crushed red pepper flakes

1 teaspoon fennel pollen or chopped fennel seeds

½ cup dry sherry, dry vermouth, or white wine

2 cups passata or 1 (14-ounce) can tomato puree

1 (14-ounce) can crushed tomatoes or Italian cherry tomatoes

12 to 16 ounces egg spaghetti or linguine

½ cup chopped mixed fresh herbs: chives, dill, and parsley

¼ cup drained hot pickled chile peppers, chopped (optional)

■ Bring a pot of water to a boil for the pasta.

■ Toss the crabmeat with the lemon juice and Old Bay.

■ In a large skillet, heat the EVOO (two turns of the pan) over medium heat. Add the butter and melt to bubble. Add the shallots, celery, garlic, bay leaf, chile paste, and fennel pollen. Stir 2 to 3 minutes, then add the sherry, passata, and canned tomatoes. (If using cherry tomatoes, crush before adding.)

■ Salt the boiling water and cook the pasta 1 minute less than the package directions for al dente.

■ Add the crab to the sauce. Before draining the pasta, ladle out ½ cup of the starchy pasta cooking water, then drain the pasta and toss with sauce and crab, adding a little starchy water if necessary to keep it loose. Adjust the seasoning and top with the herbs and pickled chiles (if using).

I cooked this with my friends bestselling author Harlan Coben and his wife, Anne Armstrong-Coben. This meal can also be made with seared scallops, shrimp, scrubbed mussels, or a mixture for a fancy holiday course or just to spice up a Wednesday. Add them when you would add the crab.

FRA DIAVOLO

Pleased to meet you
Won't you guess my name?
I'm hot as hell
Gonna drive you insane

Chorus:
FRA DIAVOLO
FRA DIAVOLO
FRA DIAVOLO
FRA DIAVOLO

Verse 1:
Naples Calabrese?
My roots are kinda hazy
Long Island's joy & pride?

Hangin' with Sinatra
Slathered on the pasta
Always there, table-side

Pleased to meet you
Won't you guess my name
I'm hot as hell
Gonna drive you insane

LA LEGGENDA DI
FRA DIAVOLO

HEY, FRA...
YOUR PLACE
OR MINE?

Pappardelle with Lamb Ragu

3 tablespoons EVOO

1 pound lamb tenderloin, very thinly sliced against the grain, at an angle

Salt and freshly ground black pepper

2 ribs celery, finely chopped

1 small onion, finely chopped

1 large shallot, finely chopped

4 cloves garlic, chopped or grated

1 large fresh bay leaf

1 tablespoon fresh rosemary, finely chopped

1 tablespoon finely chopped fresh sage

Scant 1 teaspoon crushed red pepper flakes (a healthy pinch)

2 tablespoons sun-dried tomato paste

½ cup red vermouth

1 cup beef or chicken bone broth or stock

1 (28-ounce) can Italian crushed tomatoes

1 pound pappardelle

2 tablespoons butter, cut into pieces, or 2 tablespoons EVOO

1 cup grated pecorino or Parmigiano-Reggiano cheese, plus more for serving

■ Bring a large pot of water to a boil for the pasta.

■ In a Dutch oven or heavy-bottomed pan, heat 2 tablespoons of the EVOO (two turns of the pan) over medium to medium-high heat. Working in two batches, add the lamb, season, and brown. Transfer to a platter.

■ Add the remaining 1 tablespoon EVOO (one turn of the pan) and the celery, onion, shallot, garlic, bay leaf, rosemary, sage, pepper flakes, and salt to taste and stir to soften a few minutes. Stir in the tomato paste, then return the browned lamb to the pan. Add the vermouth and let it absorb and cook off. Add the stock and crushed tomatoes, reduce the heat to low, and cook, stirring occasionally, for 20 minutes.

■ Salt the boiling water and cook the pasta 1 minute less than the package directions for al dente. Before draining, ladle out about 1 cup of the starchy cooking water. Drain the pasta, return to the hot pot, add the butter, pecorino, lamb ragu, and cooking water as needed, until sauce and pasta meld and sauce is glossy. Toss 1 minute more.

■ Serve in shallow bowls, taking care to distribute the lamb. Top with more cheese.

Porcini and Greens Risotto

SERVES 4

- 6 cups vegetable stock, homemade (recipe follows) or store-bought
- 1 cup dried sliced porcini mushrooms
- 1½ pounds spinach or chard, tough ends trimmed, stems separated from leaves
- 3 tablespoons EVOO
- 1 onion or 3 large shallots, finely chopped
- 4 cloves garlic, finely chopped
- 1 small handful of fresh rosemary, finely chopped
- 1 small handful of fresh thyme, finely chopped
- Salt and freshly ground black pepper
- 1½ cups Arborio, Carnaroli, or other short-grain rice
- 1 cup white wine (crisp, not oaky or too sweet)
- 1 cup loosely packed semi-dried tomatoes, roughly chopped
- ⅛ teaspoon freshly grated nutmeg
- 3 tablespoons butter, cut into pieces
- 1 cup grated pecorino cheese, plus more for serving
- 1 cup walnuts, roughly chopped and lightly toasted in the oven or small skillet

In a saucepot, heat the stock and porcini over medium heat to reconstitute mushrooms, about 20 minutes. Remove the porcini and chop. Reserve stock.

Finely chop the stems and chop the leaves of the spinach or chard and keep them separate.

In a risotto pot (wide, round-bottomed pan) or deep skillet, heat the EVOO (three turns of the pan) over medium to medium-high heat. Add the onion, garlic, stems, rosemary, thyme, and salt and pepper to taste. Soften a couple of minutes, then add the rice and stir a minute more. Add the wine and let it absorb. Add a few ladles of reserved stock and stir vigorously.

Continue to add stock every few minutes and continue to stir. (Do not use last few spoons of stock, as grit may collect at the bottom.)

Risotto will take about 18 minutes from first addition of wine and liquids.

Stir in the semi-dried tomatoes. During the last 5 minutes, add the chopped greens in bunches, letting each bunch wilt before adding the next. Add the nutmeg and porcini and melt in the butter and pecorino. Add the walnuts in the last minute.

Serve the risotto in shallow bowls and pass extra cheese.

(CONTINUED)

VEGETABLE STOCK

MAKES 1½ QUARTS

1 bulb garlic, halved
  horizontally

2 carrots, coarsely cut

2 ribs celery with tops,
  coarsely cut

1 onion, halved

1 bulb fennel, quartered

1 leek, quartered

Kosher salt

1 teaspoon black
  peppercorns

1 large bay leaf

Bundle of thyme, sage, and
  parsley stems

A few slices of lemon

EVOO

■ Preheat the oven to 400°F.

■ In a pot, combine the garlic, carrots, celery, onion, fennel, leek, salt, peppercorns, bay leaf, herb bundle, and lemon slices. Coat with oil, roast 12 to 15 minutes to soften. Add about 3 quarts water, move pot to stovetop over medium heat, and simmer 60 minutes. Let cool, then strain.

Jaeger Spaetzle and Mushroom Cream Sauce

WITH SPICED RED CABBAGE

SERVES 4

MUSHROOM CREAM SAUCE

4 tablespoons (½ stick) butter

1½ pounds cremini or white mushrooms, rubbed clean with a damp cloth, then sliced

2 large shallots or 1 small onion, chopped

2 large cloves garlic, chopped

1 tablespoon fresh thyme, finely chopped

1 teaspoon paprika

Salt and freshly ground black pepper

1 tablespoon tomato paste

2 tablespoons brandy

½ cup white wine

½ cup vegetable stock

½ cup heavy cream

SPAETZLE

4 eggs

⅔ cup whole milk

2 cups AP flour

2 teaspoons salt

¼ teaspoon freshly grated nutmeg

½ teaspoon ground white pepper

4 tablespoons (½ stick) butter

FOR SERVING

Chopped mixed fresh herbs: parsley and dill

Spiced Red Cabbage (recipe follows)

■ Bring a large pot of water (5 to 6 quarts) to a boil for the spaetzle.

■ Make the mushroom cream sauce: In a large deep skillet or wide saucepot, melt the butter over medium to medium-high heat. When it foams, add the mushrooms and brown. Add the shallots, garlic, thyme, paprika, and salt and pepper to taste and soften for 3 minutes. Stir in the tomato paste, then stir in the brandy. Add the wine and stir a minute more. Add the vegetable stock and bring to a boil, then reduce the heat to low and add the cream.

■ Make the spaetzle: In a bowl, whisk up the eggs and milk. In a separate bowl, whisk together the flour, salt, nutmeg, and white pepper. Add the flour mixture to the egg mixture and stir to combine. It should have the consistency of a very thick pancake batter. Add a little water if you need to thin it.

■ Place the butter in a wide skillet and heat over medium-low until barely melted and warm. Salt the boiling water, place a spaetzle maker over the pot, and add one-third to one-half of the batter. Drop the batter into the boiling salted water, moving the maker handle fairly quickly back and forth to cut the dumplings and drop them. When they float, about 2 minutes, remove them to the skillet of melted butter. Repeat to make all the spaetzle. (Note: If you, like most of America, do not have a spaetzle maker, you can use a pasta colander. Put the dough into the colander, hold it over your boiling water, and press the dough through with a rubber spatula.)

■ Top the spaetzle with the mushroom sauce and chopped herbs and serve with the spiced red cabbage.

(CONTINUED)

For the Antonoffs, by special request. A beautiful vegetarian dinner.

SPICED RED CABBAGE

SERVES 4

1 tablespoon EVOO

2 tablespoons butter

1 small head red cabbage, thinly sliced

1 red onion, quartered and thinly sliced

1 sweet-tart apple, such as Honeycrisp, peeled and finely chopped

1 large fresh bay leaf

1 tablespoon Peppery Cumin and Caraway Spice Blend (page 49)

½ teaspoon ground allspice

⅛ teaspoon freshly grated nutmeg

3 tablespoons apple cider vinegar

2 tablespoons light brown pourable sugar or regular brown sugar

1 cup chicken stock

Salt and freshly ground black pepper

■ In a Dutch oven, heat the EVOO (one turn of the pan) over medium to medium-high heat. Melt the butter into the oil, then stir in the cabbage, onion, apple, bay leaf, spices, vinegar, brown sugar, and stock. Season with salt and pepper. Partially cover the pot and cook, stirring occasionally, until the cabbage is just tender, 35 to 45 minutes. (If the pot gets dry or the cabbage starts to brown during cooking, reduce the heat.) Cover to keep warm. If needed, reheat over medium-low before serving.

Burning Down the House

"Your roof is on fire!" John and I heard the man in our backyard cry out. He had a cigar in one hand, a beer in the other, and had just run over to our home from a nearby common-use trail perched at a bird's-eye view, on a ridge of the mountain behind our property. He had been out ATV-ing with a friend when he spotted the flames.

Earlier that day, August 9, John had left the house to play golf with friends who had driven hours to see him. It was his first time in months seeing anyone socially. I was up earlier than usual to make boxed lunches for the three guys, so each could eat in his cart safely, socially distanced from one another. This was an exciting day for both of us because it marked the start of our summer vacation, after months of straight work: taping the talk show from home, recording a twenty-episode run of <u>30 Minute Meals</u> for Food Network, writing for the magazine, and all of our other many responsibilities. We were planning to spend the next few weeks relaxing with our puppy Bella Boo, spending some time on our boat out on Lake George, and reading the stacks of books we'd each been piling up. John was going to finish an album and I was finally going to have time to paint and study Italian.

If John had a good day on the golf course, he'd be in a happy mood and I could make anything for dinner. If he didn't play well, he'd want pasta, so that was the safest bet. John had cleaned the fireplace in our living room and stocked the wood. It was a gorgeous day with a nice breeze, and it was going to be a cool evening, perfect for pasta and a crackling fire.

Cut to the Good Samaritan in our backyard, who'd already called the fire department. John and I were eating dinner, and we ran outside and looked up to see small balls of flame and debris shooting from the top of the chimney. The roof was on fire. I left my phone on the counter, dinner on the table, and ran upstairs to grab what I could of our personal things—letters, notebooks, photos, medicines, and necessities. By the time I ran into our bedroom I could hear the fire in the walls. I had been through live fire simulations with Leary Fire Fighter Foundation (I'm a huge supporter and I'm on the board), so I knew to get out. I turned and was met by the mask of a firefighter. "Go! Go now!" John was heading up the stairs and I sent him back down, as we'd have to leave it all. "The fire's in the walls," I told him. "Get the dog. We have to leave."

Bella was just a few months old and was trembling in my lap when we pulled away from our driveway in flip-flops, the clothes on our backs, and little else. Our poor pup, who had already been through so much, found herself in another scary scene, surrounded by big men in terrifying outfits, flashing lights, smoke, and the overpowering scent of fire everywhere.

We drove to our guesthouse across the street and watched as our home, which I'd drawn the first plan of myself on a notebook page, burned and burned and burned. Fifteen years of memories and a lifetime of scrapbooks, photos, my notebooks, John's music charts, all the things we had gathered to build our home and lives together—would it all be lost?

There are no hydrants in the woods where we live. So many firefighters came to our rescue, but we live on a mountainous dirt road, difficult to navigate, and water trucks would take time. The fire raged. John and I didn't fully process it, or feel the full extent of our loss, right away. As we stood on a stoop watching our home burn like a giant bonfire in the black night, we just kept talking each other through next steps, and notifying everyone in our lives who needed to know. We were frozen in time and stoic in demeanor, just functioning through the work of evaluating what to do next.

The fire chief told the local news station that the kitchen was saved, but ultimately it was not. The walls still stood the next day, but the damage of fire and chemicals and water was too great. The day after, the ruins caught up and burned again, but the fire was quickly put out. I'd hoped that at

least my pizza oven would survive the damage. I'd worked thirty-five years to pay for it, and it still stood after the double-whammy of fires. Then, a few days later, collapsing debris fell on the oven and cracked it. It would be lost as well.

The fire was deemed an accident, the result of some debris shooting out of the top of the chimney (which we'd had cleaned twice that year) and onto the roof, which caught fire and never went out. When the fire investigators, insurance teams, and remediators were done with their work, the excavation teams came in to remove what was left. We would get back some items, even art and books, thanks to the specialists whose job it is to rebuild stuff, and in turn rebuild the humans to whom that stuff mattered.

We were grateful to be safe, and looked forward with hope to the day we could bring anything we'd saved back into our lives and our rebuilt house. Still, the shock of seeing a big empty hole where your home stood for fifteen years is not easy to put into words. Even knowing how fortunate we were to have a secure place to land, to look out and over the cement basement, all that remained of my true happy place, gave me an overwhelming feeling of being erased, of part of me dying even as I remained here, among the living.

The full brunt of the loss washed over John and me in waves, and thankfully our waves crested on different days. For me, one hit at

3 A.M. a couple of days later, when I shot upright in bed and realized I had lost most of my mom's letters and cards—her essence, captured in her own words and handwriting. Mom has advanced macular degeneration and it's become a struggle for her to write, as she's blind in the center of her field of vision. Next I thought of her high school ring, which she gave to me as a young woman. Gone. And from when I was a kid to the present day, my notebooks have always been my most prized possessions, full of thoughts and recipes and doodles, my life on paper. How many if not all were lost or damaged? I cried for hours and wandered in circles,

remembering a moment when I was little and my mom asked me why every single creature I drew carried a purse. "That's not a purse," I said, offended. That was where the fish or dog or person I was drawing kept <u>their</u> notebooks and pencils.

For John, the tsunami hit on his birthday a few weeks later. "Happy" birthday? The idea of it broke him. I had some paving stones put into our small yard so we could bring down a heavy ceramic table from our former terrace that had survived the fire. My sister made a display of gifts piled in a little wagon by the garage. I ordered a collapsible banquet table to be delivered, and linens and flowers to go on it, so we could seat six people—some family and friends—safely, socially distanced, outside. And I cooked and cooked and cooked a feast for many more than six, so there would be leftovers for all. Maria made multiple mini desserts so everyone could safely serve themselves and enjoy. John came back from hitting golf balls by himself, took one look at all we'd done, and lost it. "I gotta get out of here!" he said, and broke down. He was overwhelmed by the idea of gathering and of celebrating when so much had been lost. It was incongruous. Everyone understood. I packed up the food and rolled the gifts into the garage and tried to let John let it all out. He finally opened his presents right around midnight, after calling everyone to apologize for his behavior. But his outburst was long overdue. He had lost everything, and he needed to grieve.

Then there was the cussing phase we both experienced. Every time we would reach for a favorite pair of sweats or socks or face cream—"Oh, f*ck! That's gone, too." The few items that survived the fire all reeked of smoke. And every time we went up to our garden for a tomato or vegetables, we had to look at the rubble and yellow caution tape. "Yup, that happened. . . ." Insert stream of expletives here.

Losing our home crushed John and me. It also helped me understand loss in a new way. It made us resourceful, committed to each other and our lives, and it has become a study in gratitude. Every day since our house fire, we've remembered all the things that made up the fabric of our lives and how much we miss them. When you lose things, all you have are memories of them. But you appreciate everything in a more complete and meaningful way. In this way, our losses have enriched us.

This experience was another circle of loss and gratitude and hope. It was another life shift for us, another new beginning, like the loss of Isaboo, and the arrival of Bella, and the pandemic itself—coming home and moving forward. We all paddled through the year of pressure and loss, trying to keep our heads at the waterline. We'd take a deep breath and reach out and stroke forward. As exhausted as we are from it, I believe our best days are on the horizon, an island oasis waiting for us all.

This one's for my friend Carlotta! I serve it with a simple sautéed vegetable medley: blanched green beans sliced on an angle, bias-cut celery, baby carrots, and leeks or shallots. Sauté all in butter, then add broth to gently braise the vegetables.

Salmon en Croûte

SERVES 4

SPINACH FILLING

1 pound spinach or 1 (16-ounce) package frozen spinach, thawed

Salt

2 tablespoons EVOO

2 shallots, finely chopped

2 large cloves garlic, finely chopped

Ground white pepper

Freshly grated nutmeg

Juice of ½ lemon

A splash of white wine

½ cup crème fraîche or 4 ounces cream cheese

¼ cup freshly grated Parmigiano-Reggiano cheese

¼ cup dried breadcrumbs, toasted

SALMON AND PASTRY

1 tablespoon butter, at room temperature

2 tablespoons Dijon mustard

1 tablespoon chopped fresh thyme

2 tablespoons chopped fresh dill

2 sheets puff pastry, thawed in fridge for 2 hours before rolling

4 skinless salmon fillets (about 6 ounces each)

Salt and freshly ground black pepper

Egg wash: 1 egg beaten with 2 teaspoons water

■ Make the spinach filling: For fresh spinach, wash and stem the spinach. Set up a bowl of ice and water and bring a pot of water to a boil. Salt the boiling water, cook the spinach for 1 to 2 minutes, and drain. Cold-shock in the ice bath and drain well. Wring out excess liquid in a clean towel and chop. For the thawed frozen spinach, wring out the excess liquid in a clean towel and finely chop. Loosen it up with your fingertips.

■ In a skillet, heat the EVOO (two turns of the pan) over medium heat. Add the shallots and garlic and season with salt and white pepper. Add the spinach, nutmeg, lemon juice, and wine. Let it absorb while mixing in the crème fraîche. Stir in the Parm and breadcrumbs and remove from the heat to cool.

■ Prepare the salmon and pastry: Preheat the oven to 425°F. Line two baking sheets with parchment paper.

■ In a small dish, combine the butter, mustard, thyme, and dill. Roll out the puff pastry just a bit to smooth the seams from the packaging and cut each sheet in half across to form 2 rectangles. Place 2 rectangles on each lined baking sheet. Season the salmon with salt and pepper and rub each fillet with the mustard mixture. Set a salmon fillet in the center of each pastry rectangle, mustard-side down. Dividing evenly, shape a layer of the spinach mixture on each fillet, gently setting it in place with your hands. Brush the edges of the puff pastry with egg wash (to help seal the package). Starting at a long side, fold the pastry up over the salmon. Trim the ends a bit and tuck in the sides to form a packet. Flip the whole package over and score the top in a crosshatch pattern with a paring knife to vent. Brush the packets with egg wash.

■ Transfer to the oven and bake until the pastry is deep golden brown, 25 to 30 minutes.

Feed It Forward

My house burned to the ground on August 9. I was scheduled to conduct the last day of a virtual kids' cooking camp with a live demo on Zoom on August 14. Friends and colleagues asked if I would prefer that another chef or cook stand in for me, as we were trying to rebuild our lives in the guesthouse and, in my case, learn how to work in a new kitchen with no pantry to speak of. Regardless, the idea of not showing up for kids I made a commitment to was inconceivable to me. This fired me up and riled me up. I'm stronger than a five. I do not let people down. Game on! Let's roll some Impossible meatballs, people!

In the long days and months of lockdown, families were struggling with chores, working from home, juggling meals, and entertaining kids who were unable in many places around the country and the world to go to camp or even just hang out with their friends in the park. They were disappointed, sad, and bored. My holding company's chief digital officer, Jo Gryfe, and Andrew "Kappy" Kaplan—our VP of culinary operations and director of Yum-O! and the Rachael Ray Foundation—came up with the cooking camp concept. Lee Brian Schrager, my dear friend and the genius behind the gastronomic-philanthropic events SoBe and NYC Wine and Food Festivals (which include our Burger Bash events), put together a team to help us make it happen. While it was offered for free for kids who wanted to attend, corporate sponsorships and optional grassroots donations helped us to raise more than 400,000 dollars for Boys & Girls Clubs of America and our culinary scholarship fund at Florida International University's Chaplin School of Hospitality & Tourism Management. So many friends and huge talents including Bobby Flay, Andrew Zimmern, Carla Hall, and Anne Burrell joined in the fun and taught classes, with up to 10,000 "campers" Zooming in from all over the world for each one.

I think kids are smarter than adults in many ways, and especially in the kitchen. I remember when I was little, how it made me feel to be in there with my mom or my grandpa and be given a direction like "Rachael, stir the sauce well and wash and dry the greens, please." I wasn't given a lesson in how to do these things, but I figured it out based on what I'd absorbed from the time I'd spent in the kitchen, practically

since infancy. As I grew older, I was taught to respect the heat of a stove, how to hold a knife, how to control the temperature of a pan. But first I remember feeling the confidence of being trusted to do tasks in the kitchen that benefited the family and helped provide our next meal. In the kitchen, kids as young as four can pick up valuable basic skill sets, and they can also discover self-esteem and another pathway to creativity.

Kids are great in class and in groups because they are so frank, and they see right through anything other than sincerity and total honesty. Once I confirmed that I would teach and cook in front of 10,000 Zooming families, my first appearance after losing our home, the largest concern of my colleagues was the topic of the fire. They

suggested that I not mention it. As far as I was concerned, this would be the same as lying to these kids and families, as our loss had been all over the news. So I opened with it. I told them I was adjusting to a new kitchen, "Because, as you may have heard, my house burned down. But I'm safe!" I told the kids and their families. "When scary things happen, it's important to listen to the grown-up helpers—parents, teachers, first responders, and firefighters—and follow directions. We had been scared," I admitted, "but we were safe and fine because we listened and did as we were told." I continued: "Life will bring us sad days and losses, but they make us stronger. No matter what happened to us yesterday, any day that we have shelter and food and a place to cook it and someone to share it with, we're among the luckiest people in the world today." Then we made spaghetti and meatballs together.

That hour and a half on Zoom was one of my most soul-saving moments after the fire—and all summer, actually. Cooking with thousands of kids from across the U.S. and around the world, and seeing the pictures families posted of everyone hanging in the kitchen cooking together, made my broken heart whole again. In the week since the fire, I'd slept maybe ninety minutes at a time, max. That night was the first time I slept through the night. I fell into bed, exhausted and happy and grateful, with my pillow, my pup, and a goodnight kiss from my husband. No nightmares or bad dreams. That giant communal Cook-Along full of beautiful, earnest young people reminded me just how wonderful the world really was, still is. It comforted me. That feeling was even better than eating a delicious bowl of spaghetti.

Halibut in Tomatillo Sauce 🐟

@rachaelray · 2020-7-13

The dish that made it all happen ✨ Full video on IGTV! #fyp #learnontiktok #howto #skillbuilding #letscook #learnfromme #tiktoktips #foryoupage

Roll out pizza dough

in adobo or you can use powdered Chipotle. Chipotle is a smoked chili pepper.

Spaghetti and Roasted Impossiballs

SERVES 4

TOMATO-BASIL SAUCE

2 tablespoons EVOO

2 tablespoons butter

4 cloves garlic, thinly sliced, crushed through a press, or grated

Salt

2 (28-ounce) cans San Marzano tomatoes

1 (24-ounce) jar tomato passata or 3 cups canned tomato puree

1 small handful of basil leaves, torn

Sprinkle of sugar (optional)

PASTA AND MEATBALLS

1 (1-pound) box spaghetti or linguine

Salt

2 tablespoons butter and/or EVOO

1 cup loosely packed grated Parmigiano-Reggiano and/or Pecorino Romano cheese

Roasted Impossiballs (recipe follows)

1 small handful of basil leaves, torn

▪ Make the tomato-basil sauce: In a large saucepot, combine the EVOO (two turns of the pan) and butter and set over medium to medium-low heat. Stir in the garlic, season with salt, and cook until very fragrant, 1 to 2 minutes, making sure not to burn the garlic. Stir in the tomatoes and passata and bring to a light bubble, then reduce the heat a bit, add the basil and the sugar (if you like a sweeter sauce) and cook for 20 to 30 minutes.

▪ Cook the pasta: Bring a large pot of water to a boil for the pasta. Salt the water and cook the pasta 1 minute less than the package directions for al dente. Before draining, ladle out about a cup of the starchy pasta cooking water, then drain the pasta and return it to the pot.

▪ Add the butter to the pasta along with the cheese and some pasta water. Add about half of the tomato-basil sauce and stir vigorously with tongs to emulsify the sauce with the pasta.

▪ Add the meatballs to the sauce remaining in the pot and stir to coat. Serve the pasta family-style or divide among shallow bowls. Top with the meatballs, more sauce, and remaining basil and pass more cheese at the table. There will be extra sauce.

ROASTED IMPOSSIBALLS

MAKES ABOUT 24 MEATBALLS

2 (12-ounce) packages plant-based ground meat

½ to 1 cup breadcrumbs

3 to 5 tablespoons whole milk (use the larger amount if using more breadcrumbs)

1 egg, lightly beaten

1 cup loosely packed grated Parmigiano-Reggiano and/or Pecorino Romano cheese

1 big handful of flat-leaf parsley, finely chopped

1 teaspoon dried oregano

1 teaspoon crushed red pepper flakes (optional)

1 teaspoon fennel seeds or fennel pollen (⅓ palmful)

Kosher salt

Nonaerosol cooking spray

■ Preheat the oven to 425°F. Line a baking sheet with foil and then parchment paper.

■ Place the plant-based meat in a large bowl.

■ Place the breadcrumbs in a small bowl and moisten with the milk.

■ Add the moistened breadcrumbs, egg, cheese, parsley, oregano, pepper flakes (if using), and fennel seeds to the plant-based meat. Season with salt. Mix together, plump into a round in the bowl, and score the round into 4 quarters. Working with one quarter at a time, break up and roll into 6 meatballs (a total of 24). Arrange the balls on the lined baking sheet and lightly mist with cooking spray.

■ Place in the oven and roast until lightly browned, about 15 minutes. Remove and let rest.

I'm a meatball freak. I must have one hundred recipes for them, but now my husband only wants this one. I've locked myself in the jail cell of Impossiballs.

Pumpkin Risotto

WITH SAGE, BROWN BUTTER, AND NUTS

SERVES 4

ROASTED PUMPKIN

1 small sugar or cheese pumpkin (about 2 pounds; 1½ pounds trimmed)

Nonaerosol cooking spray

Salt and freshly ground black pepper

Freshly grated nutmeg

Olive oil for drizzling

Ground pink peppercorns

RISOTTO

6 cups chicken or vegetable stock

3 tablespoons EVOO

1 small to medium onion, finely chopped

2 cloves garlic, grated or chopped

Salt and freshly ground black pepper

1½ cups Arborio or Carnaroli rice

1 cup white wine

5 to 6 tablespoons butter

18 to 20 fresh sage leaves

1 cup grated Parmigiano-Reggiano cheese

Pumpkin seeds, hazelnuts, or walnuts, toasted, for garnish

■ Position a rack in the center of the oven and preheat the oven to 425°F. Line a sheet pan with parchment paper.

■ Make the pumpkin puree: Halve the pumpkin vertically through the middle. Scoop out all of the seeds and save about ½ cup for garnish.

■ With half of the pumpkin, keep the skin on, mist with cooking spray, and season with salt, pepper, and nutmeg.

■ With the other half of the pumpkin, cut off the top and bottom and with a sharp knife, strip off the skin like you would a melon. Cut into slices and then into bite-size pieces. Toss the pieces in a bowl with a drizzle of olive oil, salt, black pepper, pink pepper, and nutmeg.

■ Place the halved pumpkin cut-side down at one end of the lined sheet pan and spread the cut-up pumpkin over the other end.

■ Transfer to the oven and roast until the pieces are browned at the edges and the top of the roasted half is browned and starting to collapse, 25 to 30 minutes. Remove from the oven and let cool until able to handle. If toasting the pumpkin seeds in the oven, leave the oven on and reduce the oven temperature to 350°F.

■ Meanwhile, to toast the seeds, rinse them and dry very well. Spread the seeds on a baking sheet, mist with cooking spray, and season with salt, pepper, and nutmeg. Transfer to the oven and bake until golden brown. Make sure you babysit and shake the pan every now and then as they

(CONTINUED)

When we made this for a Cook-Along, we added shaved truffle on top for friends who'd voted for a mushroom risotto but got this instead. Shortcuts: Use pre-cut pumpkin or butternut squash for the roasted pumpkin pieces and store-bought pumpkin puree (not pie filling!).

cook. You want them as dry and crisp as possible. To toast in a skillet, follow the seasoning directions above, then toast over medium heat in a dry skillet, shaking the pan to make sure they don't burn. Turn the heat off and let sit. Turn the heat back on and give them a second toast.

■ When the pumpkin has cooled, scoop the flesh out of the roasted half into a food processor and puree.

■ Make the risotto: In a small pot, heat the stock over low heat.

■ In a risotto pot (wide, round-bottomed pan) or deep skillet, heat the EVOO (three turns of the pan) over medium heat. Add the onion and garlic, season with salt and pepper, and cook until tender, 2 to 3 minutes. Add the rice and stir for 1 to 2 minutes to toast. Add the wine and stir, stir, stir using a round spoon to get into the round corners. After the wine is

fully absorbed, begin adding warm stock, a few ladles at a time. Stir, stir, stir to develop the starch. As the stock is absorbed, add more stock, a few ladles at a time. (From the time you add your first liquids, it will take 18 minutes to cook.)

■ When the rice is about 5 minutes away from being done, place a small skillet over medium heat and add the butter. When the butter foams, add the sage leaves and cook until they're crisp and the butter is brown. Transfer to a paper towel to drain.

■ Add the pureed roast pumpkin and browned butter to the risotto pot. Stir in the Parm and half of the sage leaves.

■ Serve the risotto in warm shallow bowls and top with nuts, the remaining crispy sage, pumpkin seeds, and chopped roast pumpkin.

Moroccan Chicken Tagine

SERVES 4

TAGINE

1 preserved lemon

3 tablespoons EVOO

8 pieces of bone-in chicken legs and thighs, skin removed

Salt and freshly ground black pepper

3 tablespoons butter

1 large or 2 medium onions, chopped

4 cloves garlic, crushed with the flat side of a knife

1 small piece fresh turmeric, peeled and finely chopped

2-inch piece fresh ginger, peeled and finely chopped

3 tablespoons ras el hanout, Moroccan spice blend, or Tagine Spice (recipe follows)

1 cup chicken bone broth or stock

1 cup Moroccan or medium Mediterranean olives (green or black), pitted or whole

COUSCOUS

3 cups chicken stock or mixed stock and water

2 tablespoons butter

Salt

2 cloves garlic, chopped

1½ cups couscous

1 cup finely chopped mixed fresh herbs: mint, parsley, and cilantro

■ Make the tagine: Pull the flesh off the preserved lemon rind (discard the seeds), finely chop the flesh, and set aside for the couscous. Finely chop the rind.

■ In a tagine or a large Dutch oven, heat the EVOO (three turns of the pan) over barely medium heat (if you go too hot you will damage the tagine). Season the chicken pieces with salt and pepper. Brown the chicken pieces on both sides and remove. Add the butter and melt. Add the onion, garlic, turmeric, ginger, preserved lemon rind, chopped pickled pepper (if using; see Note), and spice blend. Sweat the onion to soften for about 5 minutes. Add the chicken and stock, cover, and simmer, stirring occasionally, until cooked through, 45 to 50 minutes. Stir in olives to serve.

■ Make the couscous: In a saucepan, heat the stock, butter, garlic, reserved chopped lemon flesh, and salt to taste and bring to a boil. Stir in the couscous, remove from the heat, cover, and let stand for 5 minutes. Add herbs and fluff with a fork.

■ Serve chicken and olives with couscous.

(CONTINUED)

When I host Zoom Cook-Alongs with friends, they pick the recipe they want to learn and I ship them any ingredients they'll need that they may not have in their pantry. For this one, which I did with John's band members, I had to send everyone tagines, those cone-shaped pots, so they could make this insanely delicious dish properly!

TAGINE SPICE

MAKES ABOUT ⅓ CUP

You can use ras el hanout or other store-bought Moroccan blends, but I like to make my own house blend. I usually start with whole seeds and peppercorns that I toast before grinding, but this version uses all ground spices for a small shortcut. You can quadruple the amounts here and store in a jar for 6 months.

1½ teaspoons ground coriander

1½ teaspoons ground cumin

1½ teaspoons ground turmeric

1½ teaspoons sweet paprika or pimentón (smoked paprika)

1 teaspoon ground white pepper

1 teaspoon freshly ground black pepper

1 teaspoon ground ginger

1 teaspoon garlic powder

¼ teaspoon ground cinnamon or smoked cinnamon

¼ teaspoon cayenne pepper

⅛ teaspoon ground allspice

⅛ teaspoon ground cloves

■ In a small bowl, mix together all the ingredients.

Beef Stew

WITH DIJON MUSTARD AND SHERRY MUSHROOMS

SERVES 4 TO 6

BEEF STEW

1 cup AP flour

1 tablespoon ground sage

Salt, finely ground black pepper, and ground white pepper

2½ pounds beef chuck, cut into large bite-size cubes

4 to 6 tablespoons (½ to ¾ stick) butter

1 large onion, chopped

6 large shallots, halved and sliced

1 large fresh bay leaf

½ cup Cognac or other brandy

½ cup white wine

½ cup Dijon mustard

2 cups beef bone broth or stock

1 tablespoon Worcestershire sauce

3 to 4 cups bite-size bias-cut root vegetables: carrots, parsnips, and parsley root (all peeled)

1½ pounds baby potatoes

¼ cup grainy Dijon mustard

SHERRY MUSHROOMS

4 tablespoons (½ stick) butter

1 pound white mushrooms, cleaned and quartered

Salt and freshly ground black pepper

2 tablespoons fresh thyme

4 cloves garlic, chopped

½ cup dry sherry

Juice of ½ small lemon

■ Make the beef stew: In a shallow bowl, season the flour with the sage, salt, black pepper, and white pepper. Heat a Dutch oven over medium to medium-high heat. Dredge the meat in the seasoned flour. Add 4 tablespoons butter to the pan and, working in batches, cook the meat until browned. Add the onion and shallots to the pan (with more butter if necessary) and season with salt and black pepper. Add the bay leaf, partially cover, and cook until softened, 7 to 8 minutes. Add the Cognac and let it absorb. Add the wine, regular Dijon, bone broth, and Worcestershire. Slide the beef into the sauce, reduce the heat to very low, cover, and simmer for 1½ hours.

When we do a Cook-Along with John's band, they all propose ideas but they <u>never</u> pick what Elaine—who sings and plays the violin—wants! This one's for you, Lainey!

■ Add the root vegetables and potatoes and cook until tender, 30 to 40 minutes more. Stir in the grainy Dijon to finish the stew's sauce. Discard the bay leaf.

■ Meanwhile, make the sherry mushrooms. In a skillet, melt the butter over medium-high heat. Add the mushrooms and brown. Season with salt and pepper, add the thyme and garlic, and toss for 2 minutes. Stir in the sherry and lemon juice.

■ Serve the stew topped with mushrooms, with crusty bread on the side.

EAT THIS NOW

CARBONARA

CAR-BON-ARRRA (RR!)
CAR-BON-ARRRA (RR!)

C - A - R - B - O - N - A - R - A
C - A - R - B - O - N - A - R - A

So fucking good it's here to stay
Don't care if I get fat & round
Jus' makes me happy when I here the sound of

CAR-BON-ARRRA (RR!)
CAR-BON-ARRRA (RR!)

Couple of eggs, some rigatone
Guanciale or *fried lardon*
Pepper, parm, *EVOO*
TLC & we're *good to go*

CAR-BON-ARRRA (RR!)
CAR-BON-ARRRA (RR!)

C - A - R - B - O - N - A - R - A
C - A - R - B - O - N - A - R - A

Big Commander *stir it up*
Gotta sip on sump'n when I *eat my sup*
Raise a glass we *toast to you*
& welcome sweet Belle Boo Blue

CAR-BON-ARRRA (RR!)
CAR-BON-ARRRA (RR!)

COCKTAIL BY JOHN

John's Moroccan Mar-Tea-Ni

MAKES ONE COCKTAIL

1½ ounces vodka
¾ ounce Lillet Blanc
½ ounce freshly squeezed lemon juice
¼ ounce simple syrup
2 ounces chilled mint tea
2 dashes orange bitters
Fresh mint leaf, for garnish

In a cocktail shaker, combine the vodka, Lillet, lemon juice, simple syrup, mint tea, and bitters. Add ice and shake vigorously. Strain into a chilled martini glass. Garnish with a mint leaf.

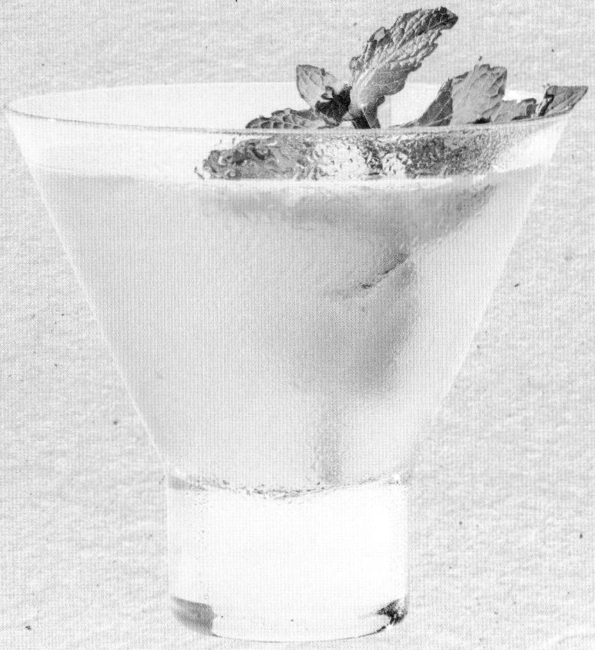

Because of my work schedule, I typically see very little of fall up here in my Adirondack Mountains home. This year, I saw the seasons change from spring to summer, summer to fall, fall to winter. I relished in the foliage and crisp, cold nights and the first turning of the leaves. A true moment of grace.

SPICY PESTO PASTA WITH SWEET CORN AND ZUCCHINI

DEVILED CORN CHOWDER

FRESH TOMATO SOUP

GRILLED CHEESE WITH BLACKBERRY AND BALSAMIC

QUICK GREEN CHILI WITH QUESADILLA TOP

PETITE FILET SANDWICHES WITH HORSERADISH-
DIJON SAUCE AND FALL SALAD

PASTA ALLA GRICIA WITH ROASTED HEN OF THE WOODS AND SHALLOTS

Harvest

BRAISED PORK SHOULDER DINNER: BRAISED PORK SHOULDER,
GARLICKY MASHED POTATOES AND PARSNIPS, GREEN BEANS
AND SHALLOTS, AND HARD CIDER CRAN-APPLE SAUCE

EGGPLANT AND ZUCCHINI PARMIGIANA

MOULES MARINIÈRES WITH GARLIC BREAD

SMOKED PROSCIUTTO-WRAPPED CHICKEN THIGHS AND
ESCAROLE AND APPLE SALAD

FRENCH-STYLE CHICKEN CASSEROLE À LA NORMANDE

ROASTED TOMATO AND BREAD SOUP (PAPPA AL POMODORO ARROSTO)

JOHN'S BOBBING FOR APPLES

The Season of Me?

In the months after we were sent home from school—literally and figuratively—people I interviewed on the show, along with friends and family, all had visions of who they'd become given all this time to develop themselves. In follow-ups I learned that most of us didn't get to most of those projects. Whether it was our goal weight, finishing that pile of books on the nightstand, or learning to knit, even when we were holed up at home almost all the time, life still happened and we were distracted and overwhelmed by what was happening all around us. And all that free time vanished before our eyes.

I grew up surrounded by people who lived every moment of every day to the fullest. No matter how many hours my grandfather and mother put into their day jobs, when they came home, they were joyful, cooking and telling stories, laughing, crying, being vibrant. They never thought, I have to work so hard and then I'll collapse at the end of the day. It was, I have to work so hard and then I get to go home and enjoy my family. Grandpa toiled as a stonemason, carrying rocks, real back-breaking stuff. Then he'd come home at night and tend his garden and cook for his children and serenade them in the moonlight. It was a hard life—my mother was one of ten kids. But their quality of life was about the time they could share and their passion for life itself, not the love of money. They didn't settle. They always made time to share time. That's how I try to be: work hard and play hard no matter the hour or day.

As a kid I pretty much wanted to be my mom. I wanted to wear the clothes she did, and go to important jobs, and work as hard as she did, and be as strong as she was. I still want to work hard, and measure myself not by how I look or what I earn, but by what I achieve and share and give people. That's what makes me happy. That you can put your shoulder into your work and make something—a recipe, a TV show, a book, a magazine—is exciting to me. That's also what I love about food. In a fairly short amount of time I can take a random pile of things and use hard work and alchemy and magic and unicorns, and then sprinkle stardust over everything, and it changes into something delicious. Music, art, design—they all take serious effort, but they bring magic to life and make the impossible real.

At the outset of lockdown, I thought, OK. I can't work like I did, with some things I was working on put on hold. And we can't take the trips we had planned. So I'll make the most of this. I'll read books and conquer the drums and become the world's best watercolor painter. John and I will finish taping the last episodes of the daily show from home for a few weeks, and then I'll have The Summer of Me. I thought all this time would magically appear in my calendar. Why did a workaholic like me think I would manage an eleven- to twelve-week vacation? Goofy. So, yeah, spoiler alert: That did _not_ happen. Summer of Me? Didn't happen.

I will always put more on my plate than can reasonably fit, and therefore push myself harder than anyone else pushes me. Those first episodes recording from home took a while to make, as we were trying to figure out how to do it, just John and me. It was a relief to switch over to make 30 Minute Meals from our guesthouse, because the Food Network production team had a genius plan to record using robotic cameras. We decided next to do a free summer camp for kids, benefitting the Boys & Girls Clubs of America. My free time was about keeping up with the magazine, shows, and oh yeah, writing this book. As usual, I filled up my dance card, and I never got around to painting watercolors or improving my skills on the drum kit. It was the same for so many people. Just because they weren't heading to office buildings, it didn't mean they weren't busy from dawn to dusk and

beyond. So many of us found ways to create _more_ work for ourselves. I did. During what was to be the Summer of Me, I was constantly working for other people.

I said to John one day, "I'm jealous of you. You get to play golf and do things. I'm always stuck here. I just wish I had more _life_ in my life." Then Mary Curran, my friend and the former hairdresser of our show, told me she'd been taking Italian lessons. Her teacher began to offer them remotely for private tutoring during the pandemic. She said, "I love him! He's hard but he's so cool. He gives tons of homework!" I said, "Can you ask him if he'll take on a new student?" It's the one thing I've done during this whole year for myself. It's so important for me to always find a way to learn, a way to better myself. Even the week my house burned, with everything I cared about in it, I made it to Italian class. In fact, throughout August and into fall, it was the thing I looked forward to. It was my "me time."

My professor, my commendatore, is a spiritual cheerleader and firm believer that adult brains can absorb a new language. His name is

Lorenzo Miraglia. We try to meet on Zoom every week or so. There have been some stumbling blocks: I always have to change the time or the day, and sometimes I fall behind on homework. But Lorenzo is endlessly patient. He reminds me in texts in Italian to take a moment every two hours, for five minutes, to think, breathe, turn off the stress and turn on the switch of learning and possibility, and practice writing one sentence in Italian. And he sends jokes. But they're in Italian so I have to translate them, too.

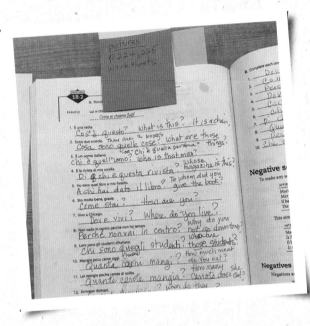

Then there's the homework. I keep a diary in Italian every single day. I try to translate recipes. It's hard at 5:30 in the morning to write instructions for Risotto with Walnuts, Spinach, and Semi-Dried Tomatoes in Italian. My diary in Italian is in the equivalent of kindergarten sentences. "Today we went on our boat. Its name is _Delicious_. I think I looked like a dog with its head out the car window." Lorenzo giggles enough to make me believe he appreciates how I think and what I write, regardless of how simplistic. He's probably being kind.

So two big things I learned in lockdown were 1) I can't escape my own nature. And 2) I had to take a first step and dedicate some time to me. Those Italian lessons were and remain a godsend. Maybe this year I'll become fluent in Italian, the fittest woman on earth, or the drummer I dream about being. I have picked up a paintbrush. I'm working on it. They're not for sale just yet. I'm taking one bite at a time.

Forgive me if you speak perfect Italian! My lessons have advanced beyond trying to translate my own recipes, but this was my first for class.

Pasta con Pesto di Cavolo Nero

500 g cavolo nero, 1 mazzo grande
Sale
150 g di noci
75–100 g formaggio pecorino
Succo di 1 limone
6–7 cucciaio d'olio extravergine d'oliva (EVOO)
2 spicchio d'aglio
Noce moscata, grattugiata, circa ⅛ cucciaino, piacere
Pepperoncino, circa ½ cucciaino, piacere
500 g fusilli lunghi o linguine o chitarra

1. Lavare e pulire il cavolo nero. Rimuovere i gambi arricciando le dita attorno alle foglie e tirare i gambi o le costole con la mano opposta, rimuovendole. Cuocere in una pentola con acqua bollente salata per circa 12–15 minuti, fino a quando il cavolo nero non sia ben cotto. Lasciare scolare e raffreddare.

2. Tritare grossolanamente il cavolo nero e aggiungerlo al robot da cucina con le noci, il pecorino, succo di limone, EVOO, il aglio, la noce moscato e il pepperoncino. Frullare tutto ad ottenere un compost abbastanza omogeneo.

3. Cuocere la pasta in acqua bollente sallata 1 minuto in meno rispetto alle indicazioni, riservare circa 1 tazza di acqua bollente e scolare la pasta. Unire acqua, pesto e pasta e sevire il piatto caldo.

DOSI PER 4 PERSONE (PER SECONDI PIATTI) O 6–8 PERSONE (PER PRIMI PIATTI)

Spicy Pesto Pasta

WITH SWEET CORN AND ZUCCHINI

PESTO

Salt

2 cups packed fresh basil leaves

½ cup packed fresh mint leaves

½ cup pistachios or pine nuts, lightly toasted

2 large cloves garlic, grated or pasted

1 jalapeño, seeded and coarsely chopped

1 teaspoon crushed red pepper flakes

Juice of 1 small lime or lemon or a splash of white wine vinegar

¾ cup grated Pecorino Romano cheese

¾ cup grated Parmigiano-Reggiano cheese

About ⅓ cup EVOO

PASTA

1 tablespoon EVOO

2 tablespoons butter

1 firm medium zucchini—halved lengthwise, seeded, and cut crosswise into ¼- to ½-inch pieces

2 ears corn, husked, kernels cut from cobs

1 leek (white and light-green parts), halved lengthwise, well washed, and thinly sliced

Salt and freshly ground black pepper

1 pound spaghetti or tagliatelle

■ Make the pesto: Set up a bowl of ice and water. Bring a large pot of salted water to a boil. Add the basil to the boiling water and cook for 15 seconds. Using a spider or a slotted spoon, transfer the basil to the ice bath, then transfer to a kitchen towel to drain. (Keep the pot of water hot for the pasta.)

■ In a food processor, pulse the basil, mint, toasted nuts, garlic, jalapeño, pepper flakes, and lime juice until a thick paste forms. Add the Romano and Parm and pulse a few times. With the machine running, slowly stream in the EVOO. Mix until the pesto is almost smooth.

■ For the pasta: Bring the large pot of water back to a boil.

■ In a large skillet, heat the EVOO (one turn of the pan) over medium heat. Melt the butter into the oil. Add the zucchini, corn, and leek and season with salt and pepper. Cook until the leek softens, 5 to 6 minutes.

■ Add the pasta to the boiling water and cook for 1 to 2 minutes less than the package directions. Before draining, scoop out about ¾ cup of the starchy cooking water. Drain the pasta and add to the skillet along with the pesto. Toss, adding pasta water as needed to coat the pasta in the pesto.

Deviled Corn Chowder

SERVES 4

3 tablespoons butter

1 leek (white and light-green parts), halved lengthwise, well washed, and sliced crosswise into ½-inch-wide half-moons

2 shallots or 1 small red onion, chopped

4 cloves garlic, sliced

1 pound (1 large or 2 medium) russet potatoes, peeled and cut into ½-inch pieces

2 jalapeños, 2 red Fresno peppers (for less heat), or 1 of each, chopped

1 tablespoon smoked paprika (sweet or hot)

1 tablespoon chile powder (ancho for mild or Gebhardt for medium heat)

1 tablespoon mustard powder

2 large bay leaves

Salt and freshly ground black pepper

3 tablespoons AP flour

1 quart chicken stock or vegetable stock

3 cups fresh scraped corn or 3 cups frozen fire-roasted corn kernels

1 tablespoon hot sauce, preferably Frank's RedHot

1 tablespoon Worcestershire sauce

1 cup half-and-half

1 cup shredded sharp cheddar cheese (optional)

TOPPINGS

Chopped fresh cilantro or flat-leaf parsley

Pickled jalapeño rings

Oyster crackers or saltines

Crumbled Ritz crackers

For a meatier option that will cool down the spice, add some crabmeat and diced avocado.

■ In a large pot, melt the butter over medium-high heat. Add the leek, shallots, garlic, potatoes, jalapeños, smoked paprika, chile powder, mustard powder, and bay leaves. Season with salt and black pepper. Cover the pot, leaving the lid ajar, and cook, stirring occasionally, until the vegetables soften, about 5 minutes.

■ Sprinkle the flour over the vegetables and stir for a minute to coat. Whisk in the stock and bring to a boil. Stir in the corn, hot sauce, and Worcestershire. Cover and simmer until the chowder thickens, about 10 minutes. Reduce the heat to medium-low and add the half-and-half and cheddar (if using). Stir until the cheese melts. Discard the bay leaves.

■ Serve the chowder in shallow bowls with your choice of toppings.

Fresh Tomato Soup

5 to 6 large tomatoes (3 to 3½ pounds)

2 tablespoons EVOO, plus more for drizzling

2 tablespoons butter

2 medium or 1 large Vidalia onion, chopped

Salt and freshly ground black pepper

1 large leafy sprig basil, plus torn leaves for topping

2 cups vegetable stock or chicken bone broth or stock

If you've never made homemade tomato soup, you're missing out! It's a great way to use up the end-of-summer glut, so here's a classic version.

▪ Set up a large bowl of ice and water. Place a sieve or colander in the sink. Bring at least 4 inches of water to boil in a large pot.

▪ Using a paring knife, remove the core from the top of each tomato and score the bottom of the skin of the tomato with an "X." When water boils, gently place the tomatoes in the water and let them roll around 1 full minute. Transfer the tomatoes to the ice bath using a spider or tongs. Scoop out of the ice bath and set in the sieve to drain and cool. Working over the sieve, peel the tomatoes, letting them drain a bit as you work. Slice and chop the tomatoes and place in a bowl.

▪ In a soup pot, heat 2 tablespoons EVOO (two turns of the pan) over low heat. Add the butter and when it melts into the oil, add the Vidalia onions and season with salt and pepper. Let the onions sweat 10 to 15 minutes—do not let the onions brown. Add 1 cup water, increase the heat to medium-high, and let the water absorb and cook the onions to absolute mush.

▪ Add the tomatoes, basil, and stock and cook at a medium boil for 20 minutes to break down the tomatoes. Remove the basil stem and puree the soup using an immersion blender (or transfer to a food processor or high-powered blender and puree, then return to the pot). Simmer gently over the lowest heat until ready to serve. Top with a few small leaves of torn basil, a drizzle of EVOO, and black pepper to taste.

Grilled Cheese

WITH BLACKBERRY, BALSAMIC, AND BASIL

MAKES 3 SANDWICHES

1 to 1½ cups blackberries

2 tablespoons aged balsamic vinegar or balsamic drizzle (see Note)

½ cup basil leaves (a handful), stacked, rolled, and very thinly sliced

2 tablespoons EVOO

2 tablespoons butter

6 slices (½ to ¾ inch thick) sesame Italian bread

8 ounces Fontina cheese, sliced

▪ Place the berries in a bowl, add the balsamic and basil, and mash with a fork to combine and macerate the berries.

▪ Preheat a griddle or large skillet over medium-low heat.

▪ In a small bowl, combine the EVOO and butter and microwave 45 seconds. Brush one side of the sliced bread lightly.

▪ Flip 3 of the slices buttered-side down and build cheese sandwiches with Fontina and blackberries, then more cheese. Top with the remaining 3 slices buttered-side up. Grill the sandwiches until deeply golden and the cheese has melted, then cut in half.

Note: To make about ¼ cup balsamic drizzle, mix ½ cup balsamic vinegar with 2 tablespoons light brown sugar in a saucepan over medium heat and reduce until thick and syrupy.

Quick Green Chili

WITH QUESADILLA TOP

SERVES 4

CHILI

1 (15-ounce) can or 1 (16-ounce) pouch roasted tomatillos

2 tablespoons olive or canola oil

1 pound ground pork or ground chicken

Salt and freshly ground black pepper

1 tablespoon ground coriander

1 tablespoon ground cumin

1 tablespoon dried oregano

1 onion, chopped

4 cloves garlic, chopped or sliced

2 cups thawed frozen New Mexican frozen Hatch green chiles (mild, medium, or hot) or 4 (4-ounce) cans green chiles

1 (14-ounce) can spicy vegetarian refried beans

2 cups chicken stock

1 tablespoon lime juice

Jalapeño hot sauce

TOPPING

6 taco-size flour tortillas

2 cups shredded Monterey Jack or pepper Jack cheese

Pickled jalapeños

Chopped fresh cilantro and/or scallions

■ Make the chili: In a food processor, puree the tomatillos.

■ In a Dutch oven or deep skillet, heat the oil (two turns of the pan) over medium-high heat. Add the ground meat and season with salt and pepper. Cook, breaking up with a wooden spoon, until lightly browned, about 8 minutes.

■ Stir in the coriander, cumin, and oregano. Add the onion and garlic and reduce the heat to medium. Cook, stirring, until the onion softens, about 6 minutes. Stir in the tomatillo puree, Hatch chiles, refried beans, and chicken stock. Bring to a vigorous simmer over medium-high heat. Reduce the heat to medium and simmer, stirring often, until the flavors meld, about 15 minutes. Stir in the lime juice and hot sauce to taste.

■ Meanwhile, make the quesadilla top: Heat the tortillas over the open flame of a gas stove or in a hot cast-iron or stainless-steel skillet until charred in spots, about 2 minutes over a flame or 1 to 2 minutes in a skillet. Transfer the tortillas to a work surface, then cut in half and then into wide strips or triangles.

■ Position an oven rack in the center of the oven and preheat the broiler.

■ Divide the chili among four broilerproof bowls. Top with the tortilla pieces, letting them hang off the edge of the bowl all the way around. Sprinkle the Jack cheese on top of the tortillas. Broil until the cheese is bubbling and the top is browned in spots, about 4 minutes.

■ Serve the bowls on plates (the bowls will be hot). Top with the pickled jalapeños and cilantro and/or scallions.

Petite Filet Sandwiches

WITH HORSERADISH-DIJON SAUCE AND FALL SALAD

PETITE FILET SANDWICHES

MAKES 4 SANDWICHES

4 petite filets (1½ to 2 pounds total) or beef tenderloin medallions

Kosher salt and coarsely ground black pepper

Nonaerosol olive oil cooking spray

1 cup sour cream or crème fraîche

¼ cup finely chopped fresh chives

2 rounded tablespoons Dijon mustard

2 rounded tablespoons prepared horseradish

1 tablespoon Worcestershire sauce

1 clove garlic, grated or pasted

4 sandwich rolls, warmed, or a warm baguette

TOPPING

Finely chopped white onions or very thinly sliced shallots

Thinly sliced cornichons (sliced lengthwise)

Upland cress

■ Preheat the oven to 375°F. Bring the steaks to room temperature.

■ Meanwhile, heat a large cast-iron skillet over medium-high heat.

■ Pat the steaks dry and season liberally on both sides with salt and pepper. Mist the pan with the cooking spray, add the meat, and cook until browned, 2 to 3 minutes per side.

■ Transfer the steaks to a large rimmed baking sheet and bake until an instant-read thermometer registers 130° to 135°F when inserted horizontally into the steaks, about 5 minutes. Transfer the steaks to a cutting board to rest while you make the sauce. (The temperature should reach 145°F as the meat rests.)

■ In a small bowl, stir the sour cream, chives, mustard, horseradish, Worcestershire, and garlic. Season with salt and pepper.

■ Thinly slice the meat. Slice rolls or a baguette and spread the cut sides generously with the horseradish sauce. Sprinkle the onion on the roll bottoms, then arrange the cornichons on top. Top with the upland cress, the sliced beef, and the roll tops.

(CONTINUED)

Before you yell at me, petite filet is less expensive than filet mignon, and this sandwich, with all the fixings, is a delicious way to eat a steak.

FALL SALAD

SERVES 4

8 cups chopped mixed romaine lettuce and escarole

½ cup walnuts, toasted and chopped

1 cup sharp cheddar cheese crumbles

½ cup chopped mixed fresh herbs: flat-leaf parsley and dill or tarragon

Fall Salad Dressing to taste (recipe follows)

■ In a large bowl, toss all the ingredients together.

FALL SALAD DRESSING

MAKES ABOUT 1 CUP

2 tablespoons pure maple syrup

1 tablespoon soy sauce or tamari

3 tablespoons apple cider vinegar

1-inch piece fresh ginger, peeled and grated, or 1 teaspoon ground ginger

2 cloves garlic, grated, or 1 teaspoon granulated garlic

2 tablespoons grainy mustard

½ cup EVOO

Salt and freshly ground black pepper

■ In a small bowl, whisk the maple syrup, soy sauce, vinegar, ginger, garlic, mustard, and EVOO until smooth. Season with salt and pepper. Transfer the dressing to a bottle or a jar with a lid.

Store this dressing in a squeeze bottle in the fridge. It will keep for a week to 10 days. Use it on salads and sandwiches.

Pasta alla Gricia

WITH ROASTED HEN OF THE WOODS AND SHALLOTS

SERVES 4

12 ounces hen of the woods (maitake) mushrooms, pulled into thin strips

2 large shallots, halved lengthwise and very thinly sliced crosswise

Nonaerosol olive oil cooking spray

Salt and freshly ground black pepper

2 tablespoons chopped fresh thyme

½ pound meaty guanciale or pancetta or smoked pancetta

1 tablespoon EVOO

1 pound spaghetti

1 cup grated Pecorino Romano cheese

Grated zest of 1 lemon

▪ Position a rack in the upper third of the oven and preheat the oven to 475°F. Line a large baking sheet with foil and top the foil with parchment.

▪ Arrange the mushrooms and shallots on the baking sheet in a single layer. Mist evenly and liberally with the cooking spray and season generously with salt and pepper. Sprinkle with the thyme.

▪ Transfer to the oven and roast until the mushrooms are crispy and fragrant, about 20 minutes, stirring halfway through cooking.

▪ Place the guanciale in the freezer for 10 minutes. Once it's firm, slice it into thin ½-inch-long pieces.

▪ Meanwhile, bring a large pot of water to a boil for the pasta.

▪ Heat a large skillet over medium-low heat. Add the EVOO (one turn of the pan) and add the guanciale. Cook until the fat renders, about 15 minutes. Season with pepper and remove from the heat.

▪ Salt the boiling water, add the pasta, and cook for a minute or two less than the package directions for al dente. Before draining, ladle out 1½ cups of the starchy cooking water, then drain the pasta.

▪ Add the pasta, half the Romano, and ¾ cup of the pasta water to the skillet. Toss the pasta for 1 minute to coat, adding more pasta water if needed to thin the sauce.

▪ Transfer the pasta to a large bowl and top with the remaining Romano, a pile of crispy mushrooms and shallots, and a little lemon zest.

Braised Pork Shoulder Dinner

BRAISED PORK SHOULDER

SERVES 6 TO 8

1 boneless pork shoulder (3 to 4 pounds), trimmed and cut into 3- to 4-inch pieces

Salt

2 tablespoons olive or vegetable oil

2 onions, chopped

About ¼ cup mixed chopped fresh herbs: sage and thyme leaves

1 large fresh bay leaf

1 tablespoon juniper berries (optional)

Freshly ground black pepper

¼ cup apple cider vinegar

¼ cup Worcestershire sauce

2 (12-ounce) bottles hard cider

¾ cup crème fraîche or heavy cream

½ cup finely chopped fresh chives

■ Preheat the oven to 300°F. Bring the pork to room temperature.

■ Pat the pork dry with paper towels. Season liberally all over with salt. In a large Dutch oven, heat the oil (two turns of the pan) over medium-high heat. Add the pork and cook until browned on all sides. Transfer the pork to a platter or baking sheet.

■ Add the onions, herbs, bay leaf, and juniper berries (if using) to the Dutch oven. Season with salt and pepper and cook, stirring often, until the onions start to soften, about 3 minutes. Add the vinegar and cook, stirring often, until it evaporates, about 1 minute. Stir in the Worcestershire and cider.

■ Return the pork to the pot. Cover and braise until the meat is fork-tender, about 2½ hours. Transfer the pork to a plate and tent with foil to keep warm.

■ Put the Dutch oven back on the stovetop and bring the juices to a simmer over medium heat. Simmer until the juices are reduced by half, 8 to 10 minutes. Whisk in the crème fraîche, return the pork to the sauce, and reduce the heat to low. Simmer until the sauce thickens, about 10 minutes more. Remove the bay leaf. Top with chopped chives.

(CONTINUED)

GARLICKY MASHED POTATOES AND PARSNIPS

SERVES 6 TO 8

- 3 large parsnips (about 1 pound), peeled and cut into 1-inch cubes
- 3 pounds russet or Yukon Gold potatoes, peeled and cut into cubes a little larger than the parsnip cubes
- 4 large cloves garlic, smashed and peeled
- Salt
- 1 cup whole milk, half-and-half, or heavy cream
- 2 tablespoons butter
- White pepper or finely ground black pepper
- ¼ teaspoon freshly grated nutmeg
- Chopped chives or parsley, for serving

■ In a large pot, combine the parsnips, potatoes, and garlic with cold water to cover by a couple of inches. Bring to a boil over high heat, season generously with salt, and cook until tender, 20 to 25 minutes.

■ Meanwhile, in a small pan, heat the milk and butter over low heat until the milk is warm and the butter melts.

■ Drain the vegetables. For a smooth mash, pass the vegetables through a food mill. For a more rustic mash, transfer the vegetables to a large bowl and smash with a potato masher. Stir in the milk mixture. Season with pepper and the nutmeg. Transfer to a serving bowl and top with the chives or parsley.

GREEN BEANS AND SHALLOTS

SERVES 6 TO 8

- Salt
- 2 pounds green beans, trimmed
- 4 tablespoons (½ stick) butter, cut into small pieces
- 8 small or 3 to 4 large shallots, chopped
- 1 cup chicken stock

■ Set up a bowl of ice and water. In a large deep skillet, bring a few inches of water to a boil.

■ Salt the water, add the green beans, and cook until crisp-tender, 3 to 4 minutes. Using a slotted spoon, transfer the green beans to the ice bath to cool. Drain the green beans.

■ Pour the water out of the skillet. Add the butter to the skillet. Heat over medium-low heat until the butter melts. Add the shallots and cook, stirring occasionally, until very tender and lightly caramelized, about 15 minutes.

■ Add the stock and green beans. Remove from the heat and cover until ready to serve. If needed, reheat the green beans over medium-low heat until heated through, about 5 minutes.

HARD CIDER CRAN-APPLE SAUCE

SERVES 6 TO 8

- 2 large sweet-tart apples, such as Honeycrisp, Braeburn, or Northern Spy—peeled, cored, and cut into 1-inch pieces (about 1½ cups)
- 1 (12-ounce) bag whole cranberries
- 1 cup hard apple cider, apple juice, or water
- ¼ cup packed light or dark brown sugar
- ¼ cup granulated sugar
- ½ teaspoon kosher salt
- 1 tablespoon lemon juice

■ In a medium saucepan, combine all of the ingredients and bring to a boil over medium-high heat. Reduce the heat to medium and cook, stirring often, until the sauce thickens and the apples are very tender, about 25 minutes.

Eggplant and Zucchini Parmigiana

2 firm medium eggplants

2 firm medium zucchini

Salt

1 teaspoon granulated garlic

1 teaspoon granulated onion

1 teaspoon fennel pollen or ground fennel seed

Crushed red pepper flakes, for sprinkling

Nonaerosol cooking spray

2 tablespoons EVOO

1 tablespoon butter

1 onion, finely chopped

Pinch of sugar

4 cloves garlic, chopped

1 teaspoon chopped fresh oregano

1 (14- to 15-ounce) can cherry tomatoes or Italian diced tomatoes

1 (24-ounce) jar passata

¼ cup chopped fresh basil, plus a handful of fresh basil leaves, torn

2 large eggs, lightly beaten

1 (8-ounce) ball fresh mozzarella, thinly sliced

2 cups freshly grated Parmigiano-Reggiano cheese

Trim the tops off the eggplants and zucchini. Using a vegetable peeler, peel half of the skin off the eggplants in long strips, leaving a strip of skin between peeled sections. (The eggplants will look striped.) Slice the eggplants and zucchini lengthwise into ¼-inch-thick planks or steaks. Salt the eggplants and zucchini and arrange in a single layer on kitchen towels. Let sit for 30 minutes. Using a paper towel, press on the vegetables firmly to remove the excess moisture.

Preheat the oven to 450°F. Line three large sheet pans with parchment paper.

Arrange the vegetable planks on the sheet pans in a single layer. Sprinkle with the granulated garlic, granulated onion, fennel pollen, and a little bit of pepper flakes. Mist the vegetables with the cooking spray and roast until lightly browned all over, 10 to 12 minutes. Let the vegetables rest until they are cool enough to handle. Move one of the oven racks to the center position.

In a large Dutch oven or deep saucepan, heat the EVOO (two turns of pan) over medium heat. Melt the butter into the oil, then add the onion. Season with salt and sugar and cook, stirring often, until the onion softens, about 5 minutes. Add the garlic and oregano and a pinch of pepper flakes. Stir in the canned tomatoes, passata, and ¼ cup basil. Bring the sauce to a bubble, then reduce the heat to a simmer and let the sauce cook while the zucchini and eggplants cool.

Pour one-quarter of the sauce into a 9 × 13-inch baking dish. Whisking constantly, slowly pour the eggs into the remaining sauce. Arrange one layer of eggplant on top of the sauce. Top with a layer of zucchini. Top with another one-quarter of the sauce, one-third of the cheeses, and some torn basil. Repeat two more times, ending with a layer of cheese.

Bake until the sauce is bubbling and the cheese is golden brown, 30 to 40 minutes. Let stand for 10 minutes before serving.

Moules Marinières

WITH GARLIC BREAD

SERVES 4

GARLIC BREAD

1 baguette, split lengthwise, then halved crosswise

3 tablespoons butter

3 tablespoons EVOO

2 cloves garlic, chopped or pasted

A handful of fresh flat-leaf parsley, finely chopped

MUSSELS

4 pounds mussels

2 tablespoons olive oil

6 tablespoons (¾ stick) butter

2 large shallots, finely chopped

4 cloves garlic, finely chopped or thinly sliced

Grated zest and juice of 1 lemon

Salt

1 teaspoon crushed red pepper flakes

1½ cups white wine

½ bunch fresh flat-leaf parsley, leaves only, finely chopped

■ Make the garlic bread: Preheat the oven to 350°F.

■ Arrange the baguette pieces, cut-side down, on an oven rack and toast until crisp, about 7 minutes.

■ In a small pan, melt the butter and EVOO. Add the garlic, swirl 1 minute, and remove from the heat. Brush the baguette halves liberally with the garlic butter and sprinkle with the parsley. Slice into 3-inch pieces and set aside.

■ Prepare the mussels: In a large pot or bowl, soak the mussels for 15 minutes in very cold water. Drain.

■ Heat a large pot or Dutch oven over medium to medium-high heat. Add the olive oil (two turns of the pan) and 2 tablespoons of the butter. When the butter melts, add the shallots, garlic, and lemon zest. Season with salt and the pepper flakes. Stir until the

shallots soften, 3 to 4 minutes. Add the wine and bring to a boil. Add the mussels, cover the pot, and cook until the mussels open, 6 to 8 minutes, stirring once halfway through cooking. Discard any mussels that don't open. Stir in the remaining 4 tablespoons butter, the parsley, and lemon juice.

■ Arrange half of the garlic bread around the inside edge of the pot. Serve the mussels from the pot, setting out small bowls for guests. Place an empty bowl on the table for discarding the shells. Serve with the remaining bread.

"Fisherman's mussels" are one of the easiest and most impressive dishes you can make. Just gobble them up with some delicious bread to soak up the sauce and that's dinner!

Smoked Prosciutto-Wrapped Chicken Thighs

AND ESCAROLE AND APPLE SALAD

SERVES 4

SMOKED PROSCIUTTO-WRAPPED CHICKEN THIGHS

SERVES 4

- 8 boneless, skinless chicken thighs
- Salt and freshly ground black pepper
- 2 tablespoons EVOO, plus more for drizzling
- 1 teaspoon ground sage
- 2 cloves garlic, finely chopped
- 16 thin slices speck (smoked prosciutto)
- ⅓ cup dry vermouth or crisp, dry white wine
- ½ cup chicken stock
- Juice of ½ lemon
- 2 tablespoons butter

■ Heat a large cast-iron or nonstick skillet over medium-high heat.

■ Season the chicken with salt and pepper, drizzle with EVOO, then sprinkle with the sage and garlic. Wrap each chicken thigh with 2 slices of speck, layering to cover the chicken.

■ Add 2 tablespoons EVOO (two turns of the pan) to the skillet. Add the chicken and cook until cooked through, about 4 minutes on each side. Add the vermouth and stock. Cook until slightly reduced, about 2 minutes. Stir in the lemon juice and butter to create the sauce.

■ Divide the chicken among four plates. Top with the sauce.

This is a rich, protein-packed, satisfying meal. Big, chunky croutons in the salad are all the starch you need, trust me.
   Serve the chicken thighs with the escarole salad alongside.

ESCAROLE AND APPLE SALAD

SERVES 4

CROUTONS

2 Italian sesame rolls or a few thick slices of stale bread

2 tablespoons EVOO

2 tablespoons butter

Salt and freshly ground black pepper

SALAD

About 8 cups (total) roughly torn or coarsely chopped escarole and romaine hearts

1 firm sweet-tart apple, such as Honeycrisp, quartered and thinly sliced

Juice of ½ lemon

1 cup (total) celery tops and fresh flat-leaf parsley leaves

½ small bulb fennel, very thinly sliced

1 small onion, very thinly sliced

Blue Cheese-Basil Vinaigrette to taste (recipe follows)

■ Make the croutons: Preheat the oven to 400°F. Line a small baking sheet with foil.

■ Tear the bread into bite-size pieces. In a medium skillet, heat the EVOO (two turns of the pan) over medium heat. Add the butter and when it melts, add the bread and toss to coat. Season with salt and pepper and arrange the bread in a single layer on the baking sheet. Bake until golden, 10 to 15 minutes.

■ Make the salad: In a large bowl, toss the greens and half the croutons. In a small bowl, toss the apple with the lemon juice. Add the apple, celery tops and parsley, fennel, and onion to the bowl. Toss with some of the dressing.

BLUE CHEESE-BASIL VINAIGRETTE

MAKES ABOUT 1¾ CUPS

1 cup EVOO

¾ cup crumbled blue cheese

10 to 12 small fresh basil leaves

⅓ cup white wine vinegar

1 tablespoon fresh thyme

2 cloves garlic, smashed and peeled

1½ teaspoons crushed red pepper flakes

1 teaspoon salt

1 teaspoon freshly ground black pepper

1 teaspoon sugar

■ In a food processor, blend the dressing ingredients until smooth. Transfer to a squirt bottle or a jar with a lid.

The dressing will keep for about 10 days in the refrigerator.

French-Style Chicken Casserole à la Normande

2 tablespoons olive oil

8 pieces bone-in, skin-on chicken—2 thighs, 2 drumsticks, and 2 breasts cut in half

Salt and freshly ground black pepper

6 slices slab or thick meaty bacon or smoked pancetta, cut into lardons or small dice

3 large shallots, chopped

2 ribs celery with leafy tops, chopped

1 bay leaf

2 tablespoons fresh thyme, chopped, plus more for garnish

2 large cloves garlic, chopped or crushed

3 tablespoons Cognac (or other brandy) or, Calvados

2 tablespoons AP flour

1 (12-ounce) bottle or can hard cider or ½ cup cloudy cider plus 1 cup white wine

½ cup chicken bone broth or stock

3 tablespoons butter

2 Opal apples or other crisp apples, sliced into 8 wedges each

¼ teaspoon freshly grated nutmeg

½ cup heavy cream or crème fraîche

Crusty baguette, warmed in the oven, for serving

■ Position a rack in the slot just below the center and preheat the oven to 375°F.

■ In a large Dutch oven or other ovenproof pot with a lid, heat the oil (two turns of the pan) over medium to medium-high heat. Working in two batches, brown the chicken to crisp the skin. Season with salt and pepper and remove to a platter.

■ Drain off all but 2 tablespoons of chicken fat from the pot, then add the bacon and render until lightly crisp. Remove to a platter.

■ Add the shallots, celery, bay leaf, thyme, and salt and pepper. Cook a couple of minutes to soften. Stir in the garlic. Stir in the Cognac and let it absorb. Sprinkle in the flour and stir to combine. Whisk in the cider and cook to reduce by half. Add the bone broth and cook for 1 minute to thicken. Return the chicken and bacon to the pan.

■ Cover, transfer to the oven, and cook for 20 minutes. Uncover and cook for 20 minutes more.

■ Meanwhile, in a skillet, melt the butter over medium heat. Add the apples and sauté until tender-crisp, 5 to 6 minutes. Season with salt and the nutmeg.

■ When the chicken is done, return the Dutch oven to the stovetop and set over low heat to simmer, then stir in the cream. Stir in the sautéed apple and garnish with some thyme. Serve with crusty baguette.

This is a classic from northern France that my mom made for us when I was a girl and that now I make for her. Opal apples don't turn brown, so they are wonderful for cooking and serving in salads and savory dishes alike.

Roasted Tomato and Bread Soup

(PAPPA AL POMODORO ARROSTO)

SERVES 4

About 6 tablespoons EVOO, plus more for serving

2 tablespoons butter

6 cloves garlic, smashed

½ to ¾ pound stale bread, cut into small cubes

½ cup grated Parmigiano-Reggiano cheese, plus more for serving

1 red onion, halved and thinly sliced

1 tablespoon fresh oregano or 1 teaspoon dried

Salt and red pepper flakes (spicy) or ground black pepper (milder)

8 or 9 large vine or hothouse tomatoes, cored and halved

2 to 3 cups chicken or vegetable stock

A few small fresh basil leaves, for serving

▪ Position a rack in the center of the oven and preheat the oven to 375°F. Line two sheet pans, one medium and one large, with parchment paper.

▪ In a skillet, heat 2 tablespoons of the EVOO (two turns of the pan) and the butter over medium heat. When the butter foams, add 2 cloves of the garlic and the bread and toss to coat. Add the Parm and toss. Transfer to the smaller baking sheet and roast until deeply golden. Remove from the oven, set aside, and increase the oven temperature to 425°F.

▪ Arrange the onion and remaining garlic on the larger sheet pan and toss with 3 or 4 tablespoons EVOO, the oregano, salt, and red or black pepper. Top with the halved tomatoes and sprinkle with more EVOO. Transfer to the oven and roast until soft and the skins are loose and browned, about 40 minutes.

▪ When cool enough to handle, peel the tomatoes and transfer to a pot. Add the toasted bread and the stock. Puree with an immersion blender and keep warm over low heat. Add a few small leaves of basil, adjust the seasoning, and serve. Pass extra EVOO, pepper flakes, and Parm at the table.

COCKTAIL BY JOHN

John's Bobbing for Apples

MAKES ONE COCKTAIL

1 ounce vodka
½ ounce Calvados or applejack
½ ounce freshly squeezed lemon juice
½ ounce cinnamon simple syrup (see Note)
3 to 4 ounces sparkling hard cider
Dehydrated apple slice, for garnish

In a cocktail shaker, combine the vodka, Calvados, lemon juice, and cinnamon simple syrup. Add ice and shake vigorously. Strain into an ice-filled Collins glass. Top with cider and garnish with an apple slice and a straw.

Note: To make cinnamon simple syrup: Heat and stir equal parts sugar and water, along with 2 or 3 cinnamon sticks, until the sugar melts. Let cool and store in the refrigerator.

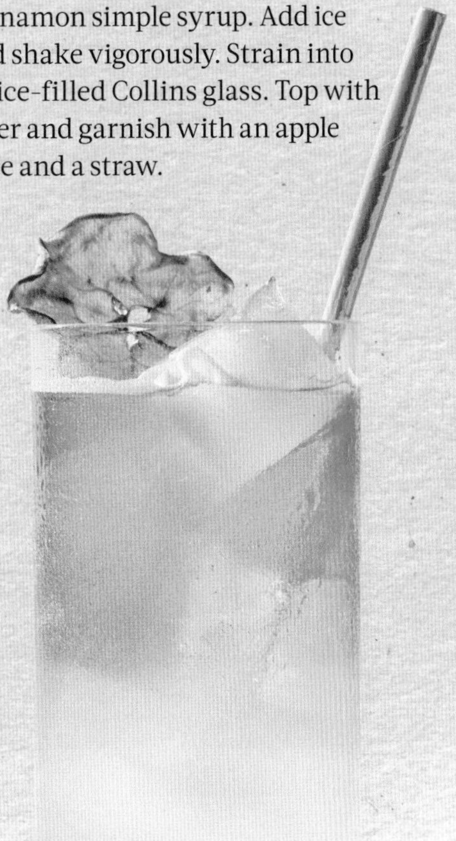

October

I miss New York City, my second home. I miss everything about it. I know I need to be upstate right now. I need to care for my mom. We need to oversee the rebuilding of our home. But we are going back to New York as soon as we can. And in the meantime, I can cook my way through some of my NYC cravings.

5-SPICE CHICKEN WITH BLACK AND GREEN BEANS

SESAME-MUSHROOM RAMEN

JAPANESE CURRY WITH CHICKEN AND EGGPLANT

MOROCCAN NACHOS

THAI SPICED STUFFED OMELETS WITH CUCUMBER SALAD

Yearning

SWEET 'N' SPICY PASTA ALLA NORMA

THAI CHICKEN WITH BASIL AND PEPPERS

DEVILED SLASHED CHICKEN WITH CHEESY TWICE-BAKED
BUTTERNUT SQUASH

SPICY CUMIN LAMB, BEEF, OR PORK WITH WIDE NOODLES AND
CRUSHED CUCUMBER SALAD

PAD THAI WITH CHICKEN OR SHRIMP

JOHN'S LEGENDS OF THE FALL

Things I Miss About New York City

Where can I begin about a city that is so iconic to the world? How can I express my love for my second home, the place where I spent most weekdays before all of this began? I'm just 250 miles north of the city, but it might as well be the moon. Sometimes I close my eyes and visit it, and when I do, I have four New Yorks in my heart and mind.

My first New York is the magical one of my childhood. My mom saved all year long to take her children to New York City at least once a year—usually more, but always at Christmas. My first memory of New York was like being in a real-life snow globe. Every holiday season we would slide down as if our minivan or Ford four-door were a sleigh, driving on icy I-87 straight into this enchanted land of light and sound and wonder. We'd see a Broadway show, like <u>Fiddler on the Roof</u> (which I saw with both Chaim Topol and Zero Mostel as Tevye!) and we'd go to either <u>The Nutcracker</u> at the Met or the <u>Christmas Spectacular with The Rockettes</u> at Radio City Music Hall. We would take a carriage ride through Central Park and eat dinner at Mamma Leone's, where Pasquale was always our waiter. He wore a badge of honor on his service coat with the number of his years of service. The dining room was a little village; the lounge was a grotto painted to look like the island of Capri. Strolling troubadours filled the air with arias and songs like "O Sole Mio," my grandfather's favorite. I would put black olives on my fingers and make my mamma giggle as I ate them off. She would order Chauvenet Red Cap sparkling wine, and Pasquale would pour us kids little pony glasses of it. He'd hoist me on his shoulder and let me sing along as we tromped around the dining room. We'd eat spaghetti and meatballs or lasagna and then meat or fish and vegetables, and for dessert spumoni and crispy fried dough with powdered sugar snow. The next day we'd see the tree in Rockefeller Plaza with its choir of golden angels trumpeting before it. We'd go to FAO Schwartz and run free among the store's five stories, playing with every toy imaginable and driving little cars literally into each other. We might have a haircut on the top floor and a tea party before or after, and at the end of our play and our day we could choose any one toy we wanted most of all as our Christmas gift, with high hopes that Santa might bring more on Christmas morning.

My next New York is cinematic. An endless Woody Allen dreamscape with a sprawling soundtrack of Broadway classics and jazz standards scoring an endless loop of shots of bridges and skyline, streetlamp-dotted streets, neighborhoods, and parks. Every scene is populated with interesting people (and dogs), and they all have a certain way about them. No matter their language, they all have something to say, and they say it in such a way that the ordinary becomes a tale that you'll tell over and over. No two people look alike or dress alike, and just watching them pass by is fascinating, as each individual sparks a backstory in your mind. When I was a young woman, New York was a character to me. I was the short girl always in the background of events and at the edge of the party. This New York pushed me to say what I felt. It gave me a voice.

New York number three is my dark but comforting city. The Nine Inch Nails NY. I am a huge fan of the band; Trent Reznor is brilliant. I love his work because at once it scares me and excites me. New York at night is an edge you walk between what could be and what will be. What choices will you make? Where will this night take you? What will happen next and will you still be in control of it? I was mugged twice in New York, which I don't wish on anyone, but I still, decades later, would happily stride and ride into the unknown of nights in the city. I thrive at night and have since I was a child. I feel my best self under the

shade and the cover of darkness. I can laugh too loud, dance too hard, and make my stand. At night in New York, you see strange, unusual, and sometimes scary things. You talk to strangers. You can get lost and then found again. I feel free and dangerous, as I beat my inner drum louder and pulse through the cold or the heat or the wet of the streets until I'm exhausted, until I somehow find my way back home. I am a New Yorker.

My last New York is my love story. When I fell in love with John, literally the night we met, I knew I wanted to spend part of every day with him for as many days as I lived. We talked until dawn that first night and we have spoken, screamed, or whispered to each other every day since. I wasn't living in New York City when we met—after that second mugging I moved back upstate. I would stay in town for a few weeks at a time to make shows for Food Network—and I met John on one of these stints. When I wasn't in town, he and I would leave lengthy messages for each other during the day until we could speak at night. I asked him to share the small moments of each day—the little things I was missing, that only happen in the city. He left one message that I've saved to this day, more than twenty years later, from lunch al fresco at Cipriani Downtown. The weather demanded eating outside, but after he and his friends sat down, a construction crew came back from their break and it was a cacophony of Transformer-like machinery. John and his friends asked for extra napkins and stuffed them in their ears, and went on with their meal, sipping Negronis and wine, eating pasta, salads, and veggie risotto in the warmth of the sun. His messages with stories like this made me fall hopelessly in love, and we are still here, but sadly have not been there—New York—in far too long.

I miss the city. I miss everything about it. I know I need to be upstate right now. My mom is eighty-six and at high risk, so I need to care for her (from a safe social distance). We need to oversee the rebuilding of our home. We need to be safe and stay safe ourselves. But we are going back to the city, all four of my New Yorks, in the year to come. Until then, here's what I miss most. . . .

✱ **My neighborhood.** I bought my apartment because of its proximity to The Strand bookstore and the Union Square green market. I love books. Real books. I love to cook with real food passed to me by the hands of the people who grow it. It's taken a toll on my back over the last fifteen years as I come home from either place like a pack mule, weighed down so heavily with produce or the latest nonfiction releases that I have to take a block in small, hard sprints, then take a break.

✱ **The Studio.** I miss seeing my work family. We celebrate each day in small ways. There's a game of daily trivia on the chalkboard with my friend Chad—he plays for beers, I play for money for Yum-o, and we all play together for fun. On every birthday we have Prosecco and songs and ridiculous meals. Our studio family has seen marriages, births, sicknesses, and even deaths. We have a growing family of adopted animals and many extended visits among our three shows and three audiences and double-digit numbers of guests a day. I miss our family. Every day is a circus, a cavalcade of clowning, filled with joy, even through our occasional tears.

✳ **Takeout and delivery.** NYC is a beautiful microcosm of the planet, its people, and its food. And in New York you can get takeout from almost any cuisine on earth delivered in an hour or less. Truth be told, most workdays, even after I've cooked three meals on the show, I still want to go home and cook our dinner. But it gives me a sense of security knowing I can give myself a night off, anytime. (Also, I miss having a corner deli that delivers toilet paper, water, Aleve, and such.)

✳ **Fluff and fold.** I iron my sheets. No kidding. Even in COVID times with no guests allowed, I stand there ironing our sheets. Take care of your good shoes, your winter coats, and your linens–this is how I was raised. A washer and dryer can be evil twins in your life. They beep and bump and grind and break and leak. And they remind you around the clock that the laundry is never done. But in the city: the glory of fluff and fold. I miss it. I miss having the laundry picked up, one door buzzer, in the morning and having it come back in mint condition, except for maybe a lost sock or two, before dinner is on the table. Fluff and fold service spoils you for the rest of your life. It's just such a treat to have all your sheets and towels come back like you just bought them at a Bloomingdale's white sale. And while I may lose a sock in the city, how did I lose a pillowcase in my own laundry room yesterday? How did that happen?!

✳ **Live music.** I miss the ability to walk to Webster Hall and see Green Day or to pile a few too many into a cab and go hear John play a gig with The Cringe. I miss epic shows at MSG and Barclays. I miss obscure tiny stages at unknown pop-up venues. I miss live music and its ability to make you feel ageless. I miss the abandon of it, the feeling of the music literally vibrating through you. I've watched *2001* with a live symphony and seen Bruce Springsteen front row on Broadway. The last show we saw, poetically, was by my hero David Byrne: *American Utopia*. His song "This Must Be the Place"–which inspired this book's title–featured in it, and that was the place to be.

* **Dinner parties.** Yes, we Zoom as often as we can with friends. It's fun and soul-saving in months spent apart, but it can't replace the magic of sitting at a table and breaking bread together. I miss reading eyes and expressions and the sound of live laughter and small comments and asides that can't happen on Zooms. I miss the breaking of a wine stem and the pot left in the oven, the music we would play tailored to the night and the guests. I miss the "One more round?" Or "Is there espresso?" I miss the unexpected that can happen when we get together, in person.

* **The pace of the city.** I love walking outside in the woodsy Adirondacks. But I miss the sidewalks of a big city. Light, quick steps, all of your senses alert. A city feels alive. It's a living, breathing entity that you're always trying to keep in time with.

* **People-watching.** Well, enough said. Imagine. And whatever you imagine, some cool, unique, fascinating New Yorker just did it!

* **Parades.** Halloween, St. Paddy's, Pride. Even though we complained about the traffic and noise sometimes, we take it back now, and deep down we love the pomp and circumstance, the funk and grandeur, and the sense of community.

* **Street fairs.** Actually, I don't miss them at all.

* **Restaurants.** The pandemic of 2020 hit our frontline workers the hardest because, as their title connotes, they put themselves into the fire to save our lives or comfort us as best they could when the battle

was lost. They sacrificed sleep, contact with their own loved ones, and in too many cases their lives for the hope of saving more of us, strangers to them. My heart aches for all of them. And right behind them I think of everyone in my own extended family, the restaurant, food, and hospitality world. I miss all of our haunts in all of the boroughs of New York City, large and small. I don't know how many of the countless places we hold dear in memories will still be standing when we get back. I've supported many initiatives to help keep them going, but I know without sweeping government intervention, many will close. So I dream of them at night; they appear in my mind like scenes from old, favorite movies.

✴ **Dogs.** I miss seeing the daily critter parade in the city. We're preparing Bella as best we can to one day join canine pals in the city. I actually got lost in thought the other day about what the weather might be like on her first New York outing and what she'd be wearing—which collar or hoodie or fleece or vest. She loves an accessory more than I do; our big, sixty-five-pound (and counting) girl jumps with joy at the wave of a fleece or the taco costume she chose on a field trip to Petco.

✴ **Parks.** Some of my most loved pictures of Isaboo were taken in Washington Square Park, her favorite squirrel zoo. She could sit on a blanket there for hours, or linger on a bench in the sun, and have a stare-down with a single squirrel. I can't wait to walk Bella through the arch and into her neighborhood park, or past our Christmas tree that the arch frames each December. I daydream about taking her on Wednesdays and Saturdays to Union Square to help me hunt for seasonal veggies and blue eggs and flowers that will make us both sneeze. The woods are wonderful, but city parks are special, too. They're spectacles and gathering places that can keep you aware of the state of the world and its energy, both its beauty and its cruelty. You'll see the best of us and the least fortunate of us, but it's a place to find who else is out there, and to walk through it all and reflect.

✴ **Noise.** I miss the sound of my block, wedged between two major parks and two large firehouses. I miss stopping and saying a silent prayer, lending my heart and hope to each alarm or siren, wishing all safe home and well. I miss the sounds of struggles and celebrations, the marches, the voices of protest or joy. I miss the symphony of millions of people living within a few square miles.

✳ **Museums and public art.** At our end of Manhattan we love to visit the Whitney Museum of American Art, currently the only museum membership cards in our wallets. The neighborhood itself has become living art with the High Line Park and now The Vessel, a towering piece of architecture behind Hudson Yards resembling a giant beehive that we love to climb. New York has public art everywhere, contributing to the layered personality and style of the city itself.

✳ **Cocktail bars.** Lounging with friends before dinner is often in a location separate from dinner in NYC. John is an avid mixologist and loves the performance art of watching the great bartenders in action. He puts on quite a show here at home, but our kitchen counter doesn't have the same ambience of places like Bar Pisellino, with its silver trays and drinks in proper glasses and salty treats to go with them–right across the way from a restaurant by the same owners, Via Carota. Until we meet again, at least we have a tasty drink before dinner to look forward to.

✳ **Movies.** I remember when I was a kid, we used to get dressed up to see movies at Radio City. The Rockettes would dance before the film and at intermission mom would treat us all to a chocolate bar. We saw *Mame, Caravan,* and *Lawrence of Arabia* there. The Ziegfeld was our other holiday theater haunt. In the last couple of years, John and I have become exclusive with the Alamo Draft House in Brooklyn, because it's an experience. They run preshow programming specific to the movie–like newsreels and music videos of Elton John before they run *Rocket Man* or a piece on the top ten stunts Tom Cruise has done himself before *MI5.* The popcorn is popped fresh and topped with real butter and you can add cheese or truffle. The food is great and the cocktails top shelf. It's like hanging at a really cool friend's house for the afternoon or evening. We have a great TV at home, and a comfy enough sofa, but we have to run our own concession stand. It's a drag.

✳ **The views**. When I fell for John, his tiny apartment didn't really have a bedroom, but instead, a sleeping loft reached by ladder. He did however, have a little roof space that had a garden where he grew

tomatoes and basil. I was smitten. Look at him, a little farmer growing basil in the city! It's one of the reasons I fell for him. Now we have a large roof space with vegetables and herbs and flowers that we've been nurturing for the better part of two decades. We also have a double-wide deck with an outdoor mattress where we go and read books and look up at the Empire State Building. I miss our little treehouse in the city. I feel like in a way we've lost both our homes this year because we haven't seen that one in so long–seven months and change as I write this, and it looks like it will be longer.

✳ **Diners.** They're barber shops with food: You go to confess and console and decompress. A diner is the best place to solve a problem, with food and with friends. Diners are home, and in New York, everyone has theirs. I miss ordering from ours every once in a while. In the city, it feels like the height of luxury to call for a bacon, egg, and cheese for John and a tomato, egg, and cheese for me. That fresh crusty Kaiser roll–always on a roll!–is mind-blowing. And when the delivery guy arrives and that buzzer sounds, it's like Christmas. I miss going to the diner and just sitting, Seinfeld-style, and getting my kvetch on, getting something out of my system while taking in familiar food. For a second you always wonder, How do they have a nine-page menu? How is all that food fresh? How can you train a tiny staff to make it all? Then you think, I don't care! I'm going to get whatever I want. And you pick something from the improbably long specials list and enjoy this moment–a beautiful, perfect thing.

✳ **Having more hours in the day.** Time is different in a city. Our days upstate start at 4 or 4:30 A.M. and we are exhausted by 7 P.M. In New York we would get up at 6 or 6:30 and rarely eat dinner before 9. There are somehow more hours in a city day. That pulse is hard to keep your finger on when you're 250 miles away from the vein. When I work past 8 or serve supper late, I feel like I'm dancing out of time. We definitely feel older up here.

✳ **The smell.** This may be a hard sell, but I miss the scent of New York. The city's perfume is a unique mix of exhaust, construction dust, weed, cigarettes, and food carts with pretzels, roasted nuts, dosa, hot dogs, or shawarma.

✳ **Even some of the rats.** On days when I'd have to be at the gym by 5—early enough that some folks were still on their way in from the prior evening's festivities—the trash would be piled high a couple times a week, ripe for the picking. You may have seen a viral video of the famous pizza-loving subway rat? Well, he has cousins. I have to admit I have a strange affection for the ballsy moves some of them make to get their breakfast. Like George in the *Seinfeld* episode with the Frogger challenge, I'd hop off and on the sidewalk and cross the street to bob and weave and give way to those bold New York City rats.

✳ **Shopping.** Yes, in my lifetime I am awestruck by the ability, from Etsy to Amazon, The Strand to Goldbelly, to shop for literally anything online. But I make a Chanukah/Christmas/Holiday gift list that's thirty pages long, which I love to shop for in person. I head to my favorite haunts—niche, interestingly curated small businesses where you can make discoveries of the things that make the person receiving the gift gasp a little. I love that quick inhale that accompanies the look of true surprise and delight. For so many, it was hard to give at all last year because it became about just keeping up with food and a roof. But it's exactly that circumstance that made me wish I could give one special treat to literally every person on earth. We all needed and deserved those little gasps of wonder last year.

5-Spice Chicken

WITH BLACK AND GREEN BEANS

SERVES 4

RICE

1½ cups chicken broth

1 cup white rice

CHICKEN AND MARINADE

1 pound boneless, skinless chicken breasts or thighs, thinly sliced (if using breasts, halve them horizontally, then thinly slice crosswise into strips)

1 tablespoon soy sauce

1 tablespoon Shaoxing wine, dry sherry, or white wine

1 tablespoon Chinese 5-spice powder

STIR-FRY

3 to 4 tablespoons fermented black beans (available online and at Asian markets)

¼ cup Shaoxing wine, dry sherry, or white wine

4 tablespoons peanut oil or other neutral oil

12 ounces green beans, sliced on an angle in 1-inch pieces

2 shallots or 1 small onion, thinly sliced

4 cloves garlic, chopped

1½-inch piece peeled fresh ginger, finely chopped or cut into thin matchsticks

2 tablespoons black bean sauce or hoisin sauce

2 tablespoons soy sauce

Splash of Chinese black vinegar or rice vinegar

½ to 1 teaspoon chile-garlic paste (optional)

1 tablespoon toasted sesame oil

1 bunch scallions, thinly sliced on an angle

■ Make the rice: In a small pot, bring the broth to a boil over medium-high heat. Stir in the rice, reduce the heat to low, cover, and simmer for 15 minutes. Remove from the heat and let stand for 5 minutes more. Fluff the rice with a fork.

■ Marinate the chicken: In a resealable plastic bag, place the chicken and the marinade ingredients and stir to combine. Marinate at room temperature for 15 minutes.

■ Prepare the stir-fry: In a small bowl, cover the fermented beans with the wine.

■ In a large nonstick skillet, heat 2 tablespoons of the oil (two turns of the pan) over medium-high heat. Add the green beans and shallots and stir-fry for 5 minutes. Stir in half of the garlic and half of the ginger and stir-fry until fragrant, a minute or two. Transfer the green beans to a platter.

■ Return the pan to the stovetop and heat the remaining 2 tablespoons oil (two turns of the pan) over medium-high heat. Add the chicken, the black bean sauce, soy sauce, black vinegar, chile-garlic paste (if using), and the remaining ginger and garlic. Return the green beans to the skillet and toss to coat. Add the fermented bean mixture and toss again. Add the sesame oil and scallions and toss to combine. Stir-fry until the chicken is cooked through, about 5 minutes.

■ Divide the rice among shallow bowls. Top with the chicken.

Sesame-Mushroom Ramen

SERVES 4

4 large eggs

1 quart vegetable stock

¾ to 1 pound hen of the woods (maitake) mushrooms, pulled into bite-size pieces

Nonaerosol olive or canola oil cooking spray

Salt and coarsely ground black pepper

2 shallots, halved and thinly sliced

2 tablespoons safflower oil or olive oil

4 cloves garlic, thinly sliced

2-inch piece fresh ginger, peeled and cut into very thin matchsticks or grated

2 leeks (white and light-green parts), quartered lengthwise, well washed, and thinly sliced

1 tablespoon chile-garlic paste (optional)

¼ cup Shaoxing wine or dry sherry

1 quart chicken broth (or vegetable broth for vegetarian)

1 small bunch (8 ounces) rainbow or Swiss chard, stems separated from leaves, stems chopped

½ cup or a generous handful of dried porcini or mixed dried mushrooms

¼ cup black garlic shoyu, soy sauce, or liquid aminos

¼ cup well-stirred tahini

¼ cup white miso

1 (9-ounce) package ramen noodles

2 carrots or 6 multicolor baby carrots, very thinly sliced

9 to 12 ounces smoked chicken, very thinly sliced (optional)

4 small stacks of shiso leaves, thinly sliced, or ½ cup chopped fresh cilantro

¼ cup toasted sesame seeds

½ cup finely chopped fresh chives

Toasted sesame oil, for drizzling

Position a rack in the upper third of the oven and preheat the oven to 450°F. Line a large sheet pan with parchment paper.

Set up a medium bowl of ice and water. Place the eggs in a medium pot, add cold water to cover, and bring to a boil over high heat. Remove from the heat, cover, and let stand for 2½ minutes (you want the eggs to be jammy in the center). Drain the water out of the pan and then shake the pan to crack the shells. Transfer the eggs to the ice bath. Let cool, then peel the eggs. Set the eggs aside while you make the ramen.

In a medium pot, heat 2 cups of the vegetable stock with the dried mushrooms. Let simmer until softened, about 5 minutes.

Arrange the fresh mushrooms on the baking sheet. Mist with cooking spray and season with salt and pepper. Roast for 10 minutes. Using tongs, toss the mushrooms and then add the shallots to the baking sheet. Continue roasting until the mushrooms are crisp on the edges, 10 to 15 minutes more.

Meanwhile, in a soup pot, heat the oil (two turns of the pan) over medium-high heat. Add the garlic, ginger, leeks, and chile-garlic paste (if using). Stir for 2 minutes. Stir in the Shaoxing wine and cook, stirring often, until the wine is absorbed, 3 to 4 minutes. Add the remaining 2 cups vegetable stock, the chicken broth, and the chard. Bring to a boil over high heat, stirring occasionally.

■ Bring a large pot of water to a boil for the ramen. Using a slotted spoon, transfer the reconstituted porcinis to a work surface and chop them up. Add them to the soup pot. Pour the mushroom soaking liquid into the soup pot, leaving the last few tablespoons in the pan to avoid any grit that may have settled in the pan.

■ In a medium bowl, whisk together the shoyu, tahini, and miso. Whisk in about 1 cup of the stock from the soup pot, then pour the mixture back into the pot.

■ Drop the ramen into the boiling water and cook for 5 minutes, then drain.

■ Divide the ramen among four bowls. Top each with carrots, chicken (if using), and shiso. Add the broth to the bowls, then top with the roasted mushrooms. Sprinkle each portion with sesame seeds and chives. Drizzle with a little toasted sesame oil. Halve the eggs and divide among the bowls.

Japanese Curry

WITH CHICKEN AND EGGPLANT

2 firm Japanese eggplants or 1 small firm eggplant, halved and thinly sliced on an angle

Salt

1½ cups chicken bone broth or stock

3 tablespoons white miso

2 tablespoons Chinese light soy sauce

2 tablespoons Chinese dark soy sauce

1½-inch piece fresh ginger, peeled and cut into matchsticks

3 boneless, skinless chicken breasts, halved horizontally, then thinly sliced

1 tablespoon cornstarch dissolved in 3 tablespoons water

1 teaspoon sugar

About 5 tablespoons high-temperature cooking oil, such as peanut or safflower

¾ pound green beans, trimmed

1 red or white onion, sliced

4 cloves garlic, sliced

¼ cup curry powder, curry paste, or homemade spice blend (see Note)

Cooked rice or ramen noodles, for serving

1 bunch scallions, thinly sliced on an angle

▪ On a kitchen towel or paper towels, arrange the eggplant slices in a single layer. Salt generously on both sides, then let rest for 15 minutes. Using a paper towel, pat the eggplant dry.

▪ In a small saucepan, bring the broth, miso, light soy sauce, dark soy sauce, and ginger to a simmer over medium heat. Let the sauce simmer while you cook the chicken and eggplant.

▪ In a medium bowl, toss the chicken with the cornstarch mixture and the sugar. Season with salt.

▪ In a large nonstick skillet or cast-iron skillet, heat 2 tablespoons of the oil (two turns of the pan) over high heat. Working in batches, if needed, cook the chicken until browned all over, adding more oil as needed, 5 to 6 minutes per batch. Transfer the chicken to a plate.

▪ Add 2 tablespoons oil (two turns of the pan), the eggplant, green beans, and onion to the skillet. Cook, stirring constantly, until the green beans are crisp-tender, 4 to 5 minutes. Return the chicken to the pan and add the garlic, curry spice blend, and the soy/miso sauce. Simmer for 5 minutes to meld the flavors.

▪ Serve the curry over rice or ramen. Top with the scallions.

Note: In place of the curry powder, make this quick homemade blend: 1 tablespoon each ground turmeric, ground cumin, ground coriander, and mustard powder.

Note: If you don't have ras el hanout, make this quick blend: ½ teaspoon ground cumin, ½ teaspoon ground coriander, and ¼ teaspoon ground cinnamon.

Moroccan Nachos

SERVES 4 TO 6

SPICY HUMMUS

2 (14-ounce) cans chickpeas, drained and rinsed

3 tablespoons tahini paste

3 tablespoons white miso (or double the tahini)

2 cloves garlic, peeled and smashed

1 tablespoon sumac

2 teaspoons Aleppo pepper powder, hot paprika, or chili powder

1½ teaspoons ras el hanout (Moroccan spice blend) or a homemade spice blend (see Note)

Grated zest and juice of 1 lemon

2 tablespoons EVOO

Salt

MEAT TOPPING

3 tablespoons EVOO

1 pound ground chicken, lamb, or beef

1 small yellow or red onion, finely chopped

4 cloves garlic, finely chopped or grated

Salt and freshly ground black pepper

1 tablespoon ground cumin (scant palmful)

1 tablespoon ground coriander (scant palmful)

1½ teaspoons ground turmeric (½ palmful)

1 teaspoon Aleppo pepper powder, chili powder, or hot paprika (⅓ palmful)

1 teaspoon smoked paprika (pimentón)

Grated zest and juice of 1 lemon

1 cup Moroccan green olives

1 cup loosely packed mixed fresh cilantro and flat-leaf parsley, chopped, to finish and garnish

NACHOS

2 (8-ounce) bags pita chips, sea salt or multi-grain

2½ to 3 cups shredded mozzarella cheese

Labneh or Greek yogurt, for dolloping

Hot pickled Italian cherry peppers or jalapeño peppers, to taste

2 plum or vine tomatoes, seeded and chopped

1 white onion, finely chopped, or scallions, thinly sliced on bias

■ Make the hummus: In a food processor, combine about two-thirds of the chickpeas, the tahini, miso (if using), garlic, sumac, Aleppo pepper, ras el hanout, lemon zest and juice, and EVOO. Process until smooth, adding water as needed to thin a bit. Adjust the salt. Transfer to a bowl. Mash the remaining chickpeas and stir them into the hummus.

■ Position a rack in the center of the oven and preheat the oven to 450°F. Line a large baking sheet with parchment.

■ Make the meat topping: In a large deep skillet, heat the EVOO (three turns of the pan) over medium-high heat. Add the meat and brown. Add the onion, garlic, and salt and black pepper to taste and cook until the onions are soft, 3 to 4 minutes. Add the spices and stir a few minutes. Add about ¾ cup water and let it absorb. Add the lemon zest and juice, olives, and half the cilantro and parsley.

■ Assemble the nachos: Arrange the chips on the lined baking sheet and top with the hummus, meat, and mozzarella. Bake until browned and bubbling.

■ Serve topped with dollops of labneh or Greek yogurt, the hot peppers, tomatoes, onion, and the remaining cilantro and parsley.

Thai Spiced Stuffed Omelets

WITH CUCUMBER SALAD

Sausage or Mushroom
Filling (recipes follow)

8 large eggs

1-inch piece fresh ginger,
grated or minced

1-inch piece fresh turmeric,
trimmed and grated, or
½ teaspoon ground
turmeric

2 cloves garlic, grated or
minced

1 small Thai bird's eye chile,
minced (optional)

1 teaspoon fish sauce

1 teaspoon ground white
pepper

2 tablespoons peanut oil

Thai Cucumber Salad
(recipe follows), for
serving

■ For each omelet, prepare your filling first.

■ In a bowl, whisk together the eggs, ginger, turmeric, garlic, chile (if using), fish sauce, and white pepper.

■ In a 12-inch nonstick skillet, heat 1 tablespoon of the oil (one turn of the pan) over medium-high heat, swirling the pan to coat. Pour in half the egg mixture and swirl the pan again to settle the eggs and let them form a skin. Use a silicone spatula to pull back the edges of the omelet and swirl the pan to settle the eggs again. Cover the pan with a lid for well done or let stand off the heat for a minute to keep the eggs soft on top for a softer stuffed omelet.

■ Let cool for a minute or two in the pan, add your filling to the middle of the omelet, and fold in the edges toward the middle. Use a plate to help you flip the stuffed omelet over so that the seam is on the bottom. Repeat to make the second omelet.

■ Serve the omelets with the cucumber salad.

(CONTINUED)

I like to make these for brunch the morning after a possibly too-fun night. There's a sausage option and a mushroom one for our vegetarian friends. Both are fun to look at and even more fun to eat.

SAUSAGE FILLING

MAKES ENOUGH FOR 1 STUFFED OMELET

1 tablespoon peanut oil

¼ pound spicy bulk breakfast sausage

3 to 4 ounces green beans (a handful), finely chopped

1 shallot, chopped

2 cloves garlic, chopped

1-inch piece fresh ginger, minced or grated

1 small plum tomato or ½ vine tomato, chopped

2 teaspoons fish sauce

1 teaspoon soy sauce

2 teaspoons superfine sugar

2 Thai bird's eye chiles, minced (optional)

■ In a small-medium skillet, heat the peanut oil over medium-high heat. Add the sausage and brown and crumble. Add the green beans, shallot, garlic, ginger, and tomato and stir-fry 2 minutes. Add the fish sauce, soy sauce, sugar, and chiles (if using) and toss to combine. Remove from the heat.

MUSHROOM FILLING

MAKES ENOUGH FOR 1 STUFFED OMELET

1 tablespoon peanut oil

½ pound mushrooms, a mixture or all of same type (shiitakes, hen of the woods, and/or cremini), wiped clean, stemmed, and finely chopped

¼ cup grated carrot

¼ cup fresh green peas

2 shallots, finely chopped

2 cloves garlic, finely chopped

2 teaspoons fish sauce

1 teaspoon soy sauce

2 teaspoons superfine sugar

2 Thai bird's eye chiles, minced (optional)

■ In a small-medium nonstick skillet, heat the oil over medium-high heat. Add the mushrooms and brown for 3 to 4 minutes. Add the carrot, peas, and shallots and cook 3 to 4 minutes more. Add the garlic, fish sauce, soy sauce, sugar, and chiles (if using) and toss to combine. Remove from the heat.

THAI CUCUMBER SALAD

SERVES 4

Juice of 2 limes

3 tablespoons peanut oil or other neutral oil

1 tablespoon fish sauce

1 tablespoon superfine sugar

3 Thai bird's eye chiles, minced

1 clove garlic, grated or minced

1 cup packed Thai mint or mint and cilantro leaves, a generous handful of each, chopped

2 English cucumbers, halved, seeded, and thinly sliced

½ red onion, halved and thinly sliced

½ cup chopped salted roasted peanuts

■ In a bowl, whisk together the lime juice, oil, fish sauce, sugar, chiles, garlic, and chopped herbs. Add the cucumbers, onion, and peanuts and toss to coat. Serve or chill until ready to serve.

Sweet 'n' Spicy Pasta alla Norma

SERVES 4

1 large, firm eggplant

Salt

7 tablespoons EVOO

4 cloves garlic, thinly sliced

1 tablespoon Calabrian chile paste

½ cup red vermouth

2 cups jarred or 1 (14-ounce) can lightly drained semi-dried tomatoes

1 (24-ounce) jar passata or 1 (28-ounce) can Italian crushed tomatoes

A handful of basil leaves, torn

1 pound casarecce, strozzapreti, or other short pasta

Grated ricotta salata or pecorino

Finely chopped fresh flat-leaf parsley and/or mint

Using a vegetable peeler, peel half of the skin off the eggplant in long strips, leaving a strip of skin between peeled sections. (The eggplant will look striped.) Trim the top and bottom off the eggplant. Slice the eggplant lengthwise into ¼- to ½-inch-thick planks, then cut the planks into 2-inch-wide strips. Salt the eggplant and arrange in a single layer between two kitchen towels. Fold the towel up and weight with a heavy skillet to press the moisture out of the eggplant. Let sit for 15 to 20 minutes.

Bring a large pot of water to a boil for the pasta.

In a deep skillet, heat 2 tablespoons EVOO (two turns of the pan) over medium heat. Add the garlic and swirl for a minute. Stir in the chile paste, then stir in the vermouth and semi-dried tomatoes. Return to a simmer over medium heat and let cook until the alcohol cooks off, about 2 minutes. Using a wooden spoon, break up the tomatoes, then stir in the passata and basil. Bring the mixture to a bubble over medium-high heat, then reduce the heat to medium-low and let the sauce simmer, stirring occasionally, while you cook the eggplant.

In a large nonstick skillet, heat the remaining 5 tablespoons EVOO (five turns of the pan) over medium to medium-high heat. Add the eggplant and cook until it is browned on both sides, 6 to 8 minutes per side.

While the eggplant cooks, salt the boiling water, add the pasta, and cook for 1 minute less than the package directions for al dente. Before draining, scoop out ½ to ¾ cup of the starchy cooking water, then drain the pasta.

Add the pasta and eggplant to the sauce, adding the pasta cooking water as needed to keep the pasta moist and emulsify the sauce. Season with salt. Top the pasta with the cheese and parsley and/or mint.

Thai Chicken

WITH BASIL AND PEPPERS

SERVES 4

SAUCE

1½ tablespoons each dark and light soy sauce (or 3 tablespoons tamari or soy sauce of choice)

1 tablespoon oyster sauce

1 tablespoon fish sauce

3 tablespoons light brown sugar or granulated sugar

½ cup chicken bone broth or stock

CHICKEN AND VEGETABLES

3 tablespoons high-temp cooking oil, such as peanut or safflower

1¼ to 1½ pounds boneless, skinless chicken breasts (halved horizontally)

2 large red peppers, sliced (about 3 cups)

4 to 5 Thai bird's eye chiles or 1 jalapeño, finely chopped

4 large shallots, thinly sliced lengthwise

4 large cloves garlic, chopped

1½-inch piece fresh ginger, peeled and chopped

1 cup Thai basil leaves or a handful of basil tops, torn

½ cup Thai mint or regular mint leaves, coarsely chopped

Cooked jasmine rice, for serving

■ Make the sauce: In a medium bowl, whisk together the soy sauce, oyster sauce, fish sauce, sugar, and bone broth.

■ Cook the chicken and vegetables: In a large nonstick skillet, heat 2 tablespoons of the oil (two turns of the pan) over medium-high to high heat. Add the chicken in a single layer and brown, then remove and set aside. Add the remaining 1 tablespoon oil (one turn of the pan), all the peppers, and shallots and toss 2 to 3 minutes. Add the garlic and ginger and toss again. Return the chicken to the pan, add the sauce, and cook a minute or two to thicken. Wilt the basil and mint into the dish and remove from the heat.

■ Place the rice in shallow bowls and top with chicken and peppers and serve.

Deviled Slashed Chicken

WITH CHEESY TWICE-BAKED BUTTERNUT SQUASH

SERVES 4

SQUASH

2 medium butternut squash

Nonaerosol cooking spray

½ teaspoon smoked paprika (pimentón)

Freshly grated nutmeg

Salt and freshly ground black pepper

CHICKEN

½ cup prepared mustard, brown or yellow ballpark-style

2 tablespoons cayenne pepper sauce, preferably Frank's RedHot

2 tablespoons Worcestershire sauce

2 cloves garlic, chopped

2 bone-in, skin-on chicken breasts

2 whole chicken legs

Salt and freshly ground black pepper

2 teaspoons granulated onion

FOR FINISHING

½ cup sour cream

3 tablespoons finely chopped chives

2 cups shredded sharp or mild orange cheddar cheese

Chopped celery tops, parsley, and scallions

Celery sticks

Carrot sticks

■ Roast the butternut squash: Preheat the oven to 425°F. Line a baking sheet with parchment paper.

■ Halve the squash lengthwise and remove the seeds. Mist with oil and season with the smoked paprika, a sprinkling of nutmeg, and salt and pepper to taste.

■ Set the squash on the baking sheet cut-side down and roast until tender, 30 to 35 minutes. Set aside to cool. Leave the oven on and increase the oven temperature to 450°F.

■ Roast the chicken: Line another baking sheet with parchment paper.

■ In a bowl, combine the mustard, hot sauce, Worcestershire, and garlic. Make slashes in the meat 1 inch apart on the thighs and drumsticks and across the breasts. Season the chicken with salt, pepper, and granulated onion. Rub the paste into and evenly over the chicken.

■ Arrange the chicken on the lined baking sheet and roast until a meat thermometer reads 170° to 175°F, 25 to 30 minutes. Remove chicken from the oven and let rest.

■ Finish the squash: While chicken rests, scoop out the flesh from the cooled squash into a bowl, keeping the shell and a thin layer of flesh intact. Add the sour cream, 2 tablespoons of the chives, and 1½ cups of the cheddar. Mash and mix together to combine.

■ Preheat the broiler. Stuff the flesh back into the squash shells and top with remaining ½ cup cheddar. Run under the broiler to brown. Garnish with the remaining 1 tablespoon chives.

■ To serve, set a squash half on each plate. Top the chicken with chopped celery tops, parsley, and scallions and divide among plates. Serve with celery and carrot sticks.

Spicy Cumin Lamb, Beef, or Pork

WITH WIDE NOODLES AND CRUSHED CUCUMBER SALAD

SERVES 4

MEAT AND MARINADE

1 tablespoon cornstarch

2 tablespoons Shaoxing wine or sherry

1 tablespoon neutral oil

1 teaspoon salt

1 to 1¼ pounds lamb, beef, or pork tenderloin, halved lengthwise for beef or pork, well trimmed of silver skin or tendons, very thinly sliced

SAUCE

¼ to ⅓ cup chile oil, store-bought or homemade (recipe follows), to taste

¼ cup Shaoxing wine or sherry

1½ tablespoons Chinese light soy sauce

1½ tablespoons Chinese dark soy sauce

½ cup chicken bone broth or stock or vegetable stock

NOODLES AND VEGETABLES

2 tablespoons cumin seeds (2 scant palmfuls)

1 tablespoon Sichuan peppercorns

1 tablespoon coriander seeds

2 tablespoons neutral oil

Salt and freshly ground black pepper

½ head small cabbage, shredded

2 ribs celery with leafy tops, very thinly sliced on an angle

1 red or white onion, quartered and thinly sliced

2 to 4 green or red chile peppers, seeded and thinly sliced or finely chopped

7 to 8 cloves garlic, sliced or chopped

2-inch piece fresh ginger, peeled and finely chopped

1 pound wide-cut wheat or semolina pasta, such as pappardelle, or wide Chinese noodles (also known as planed noodles or pulled noodles)

FOR SERVING

2 scallions, sliced on an angle

½ bunch cilantro, chopped

Crushed Cucumber Salad (recipe follows)

I like to make my own chile oil for this, but store-bought is fine.

■ Marinate the meat: In a medium bowl, combine the cornstarch, wine, oil, and salt. Add the meat, toss to coat, and refrigerate for at least 1 hour or up to a few hours.

■ Make the sauce: In a bowl, whisk together the chile oil, wine, both soy sauces, and the chicken broth. Set aside.

■ Prepare the noodles and vegetables: Bring a large pot of water to a boil for the noodles.

■ In a dry skillet, toast the cumin seeds, Sichuan peppercorns, and coriander seeds over medium heat until fragrant. Grind in a spice mill. Set the spice blend aside.

■ In a large skillet, heat the oil (two turns of the pan) over medium to medium-high heat. Add the marinated meat, season with salt and pepper, and brown a couple of minutes.

■ Add the cabbage, celery, onion, and spice blend to the skillet and let wilt. Add the chiles, garlic, and ginger and toss 3 to 4 minutes more. Add the sauce and bring to a bubble, then reduce the heat to low.

(CONTINUED)

■ Add the pasta or noodles to the boiling water. For the pasta, cook for 1 minute less than the package directions. For the Chinese noodles, follow the package directions. Drain and toss with the sauce.

■ Serve the noodles right from the pan, garnished with scallions and cilantro. Serve the cucumber salad on the side.

CHILE OIL

MAKES ABOUT ½ CUP

2 tablespoons crushed red pepper flakes

2 tablespoons chile-garlic paste or sauce

1 teaspoon Chinese 5-spice powder

1 small bay leaf

1-inch piece fresh ginger, sliced

½ cup neutral oil

2 teaspoons ground Sichuan peppercorns

2 tablespoons sesame seeds

■ In a small jar, combine all the ingredients. Let sit for 1 hour to several weeks. Strain before using.

This is easy to keep in the pantry for weeks and is a great way to use up chile products if you keep a lot on hand.

CRUSHED CUCUMBER SALAD

SERVE 4

1 English cucumber, sliced on an angle into ¼-inch-thick slices

2 tablespoons Chinese black vinegar or rice vinegar

1 tablespoon Chinese light soy sauce or other soy sauce of choice

1 tablespoon toasted sesame oil

1 tablespoon chile oil, store-bought or homemade (recipe above)

2 teaspoons superfine sugar

3 cloves garlic, chopped or grated

Salt

½ red or white onion, halved through the root end, then thinly sliced crosswise

4 scallions, chopped or thinly sliced

3 tablespoons sesame seeds

■ Place the cucumbers in a zip-top bag and crush a bit with a mallet so the cucumbers will absorb the dressing. In a medium bowl, whisk together the vinegar, soy sauce, sesame oil, chile oil, sugar, garlic, and salt to taste. Add the cucumbers and onion and toss to coat. Garnish with scallions and sesame seeds and serve.

Pad Thai

WITH CHICKEN OR SHRIMP

SERVES 4 TO 6

SAUCE

- 1 tablespoon tamarind paste
- 2 tablespoons fish sauce
- 1 tablespoon rice vinegar
- 1½ tablespoons dark soy sauce
- 1½ tablespoons Chinese light soy sauce
- 3 tablespoons light brown sugar

NOODLES AND PROTEIN

- 4 tablespoons high-temperature cooking oil
- 1¼ pounds boneless, skinless chicken breasts, thinly sliced, or 1 pound peeled and deveined shrimp, tails removed
- 2 (8-ounce) packages rice noodles
- 1 large egg
- 2 medium or 6 baby carrots, cut into thin matchsticks
- 2 large shallots, halved and thinly sliced
- 2 Thai chiles, thinly sliced
- 1½-inch piece fresh ginger, peeled and cut into matchsticks
- 4 large cloves garlic, thinly sliced
- 1 cup Thai basil or basil leaves, torn or shredded
- ½ cup Thai mint leaves, chopped
- 1 bunch scallions, very thinly sliced on an angle
- 2 cups mung bean sprouts
- ¾ cup dry-roasted peanuts, chopped
- Lime wedges, for squeezing

■ Make the sauce: In a small bowl, whisk together the tamarind paste, fish sauce, vinegar, both soy sauces, and brown sugar. Set aside.

■ Prepare the noodles and protein: Bring a large pot of water to a boil for the noodles.

■ In a large skillet, heat 2 tablespoons of the oil (two turns of the pan) over high heat. Add the chicken or shrimp and brown, about 5 minutes for chicken and 3 to 4 minutes for shrimp. Transfer to a platter.

■ Drop the noodles into the boiling water, give it a stir, and cook for 5 minutes. Before draining, scoop out 1 cup of the cooking water. Drain the noodles.

■ In a small nonstick skillet, heat 1 tablespoon of the oil over medium-high heat. Beat the egg with a fork and add to the pan, swirling to cover the pan to make a thin omelet. Brown the bottom, then roll and slide out of the pan to cool. Slice into long strips.

■ In the large skillet, add the remaining 1 tablespoon oil (one turn of the pan). Add the carrots and shallots and toss for 2 minutes. Add the chiles, ginger, and garlic and toss. Return the chicken or shrimp to the pan along with the reserved sauce and most of the basil and mint (save some for garnish) and toss. Add most of the scallions and toss 1 to 2 minutes more. Add the noodles, toss lightly 1 to 2 minutes, adding some of the reserved cooking water to loosen the sauce if needed. Add the egg ribbons and bean sprouts and toss gently to combine.

■ Garnish with the peanuts and the remaining herbs and scallions. Serve with lime wedges for squeezing.

PASTA con le SARDE

- ¼ c golden raisins · ¼ c EVOO · 2 t lemon zest
- ½ t saffron threads · 1 small bulb fennel, finely chopped
- 1 small onion, finely chopped · 4 cloves garlic, sliced
- 1 T Calabrian chili paste or red pepper flakes
- 1 pound fresh sardine filets, coarsely chopped
- Salt · 1 pound bucatini · juice of ½ lemon
- parsley, celery leaves, mint & fennel fronds
- 1 cup Panko, deeply toasted

Soak raisins in boiling water to soften them.
Heat a large pot of water to a boil. Heat EVOO
in large skillet, 4 turns of the pan, add saffron
and lemon zest to oil, stir, add fennel and onion
and season with salt, sauté to soften,
add chili paste or flakes then sardines.
Cook sardines until opaque and
firm then add lemon juice & reduce
heat. Season the boiling water with salt.
Add bucatini and cook pasta
a minute or so less than package
directions for al dente. Remove about
⅔ - ¾ cup of water just before draining
the pasta. Chop 1 cup of parsley, celery
leaves, mint & fennel fronds, combined. Toss
pasta with sardines, adding water as needed to
emulsify. Add herbs, pine nuts and top with toasted Panko.
— Serves 4 —

John's Legends of the Fall

MAKES ONE COCKTAIL

2 ounces vodka

1 ounce cranberry juice

½ ounce orange juice

½ ounce simple syrup

3 ounces sparkling hard cider

Flamed orange peel (see Note)

1 sprig fresh rosemary

In a cocktail shaker, combine the vodka, cranberry juice, orange juice, and simple syrup. Add ice and shake vigorously. Strain into an ice-filled Collins glass. Top with hard cider and garnish with a flamed orange peel, a rosemary sprig, and a straw.

Note: To flame an orange peel: Hold a quarter-size piece of orange peel above the drink zest-side down. Light a match, hold it between the peel and the drink, and squeeze the peel to express the oils. The orange oils should flare up. Drop the peel into the drink.

By Thanksgiving Day I'd already prepared and performed at least a dozen variations on a turkey dinner for my show. And then, on November 26, the <u>actual</u> Thanksgiving Day, I made (again) roast turkey, stuffing, mashed potatoes and parsnips, cranberry, green beans and shallots, twice-baked stuffed butternut squash, cider gravy. . . . By the time I was done cooking, I wanted to eat anything <u>but</u> turkey.

MARVELOUS MUSHROOM SOUP WITH MARSALA

PAPPARDELLE BOSCAIOLA

PUMPKIN-STUFFED PASTA OR GNOCCHI WITH BROWN BUTTER
AND SAGE SAUCE AND WALNUTS

TURKEY SCHNITZEL WITH CRANBERRY SAUCE, BRUSSELS SPROUTS
WITH APPLES, AND STUFFING BALLS

Giving Thanks

TURKEY BREAST ROULADE AND SIMPLE GRAVY

TRAY BAKE TURKEY BREAST AND ROAST VEG WITH
WORCESTERSHIRE-CIDER GRAVY AND CRACKED CRANBERRY SAUCE

GIVING THANKS LASAGNA

PILGRIM SANDWICH

JOHN'S FRENCH 50

Giving Thanks

Question: What do you think of when you first get out of bed on Thanksgiving Day? When you walk downstairs early that morning to get the bird in the oven, are you thinking, Yay, let's enjoy each other and the bounty we're blessed with! Or is it more like, What needs to go in which oven? Is the turkey defrosted? What side dish goes in next? Where can I store things? Where can I hide the dirty pots? Do I have enough serving dishes? Where did I put the gravy boat? What topic is Aunt Whoever going to bring up that sets everyone aflame? When can I start drinking and still be able to perform all of these tasks? Why did I have to make this so complicated?!?! And if you're not hosting, are you panicked about whether you're bringing enough or the right thing?

This is what happens to pretty much every home cook I know. Our minds awake to worries and to-do lists as we try to make this meal feel formal and impressive. We're not thinking about how lucky we are. We're not consumed with gratitude but with stress. Thanksgiving has become a day we fear. We overplan and overthink. This day should be about being grateful for time together, but it's become a thing to joke about on <u>SNL</u>. We lament to our friends about our relatives, or the casserole that's not right, the turkey that's ever so slightly dry, the pie crust that's not "perfect." We will eventually get to the moment when someone says grace or gives a toast, and everyone goes around the table and shares what they're grateful for. But for the most part, Thanksgiving can be a real source of stress and aggravation.

One big reason I have a job is that I help people fix things that go wrong on Thanksgiving by solving their cooking challenges and getting them through their "food trauma." Our strongest numbers all year are for the November shows and

magazine, which are all about trouble-shooting this one meal on this one day. I love helping people and I <u>totally get</u> what's behind it all, but it shouldn't be this hard.

Spending the holiday this year with only a few immediate family members forced us all to rethink a whole lot of our traditions. And maybe that's a good thing. Maybe it's made us more mindful of what Thanksgiving should be, and what food should be: Simple. Less, not more. Plenty, but not extravagant or complicated. Less about the menu and more about sharing time with the people you want to share time with. Maybe this year released the pressure valve a tiny bit and broke us out of this system of the ultimate performance, freeing us to make it what we want.

Thanksgiving <u>always</u> feels different for people who work in food media: By the time the day arrives, most of us have made the meal in some version for weeks. In my case, by Thanksgiving Day I had already prepared and performed: turkey schnitzel with all the trimmings, turkey Parmigiano, full turkey breast roulades  with two different stuffings, individual turkey cutlet roulades with spinach and cheese, and my mac daddy that broke the internet for our show, plus a Thanksgiving lasagna that layered homemade ground turkey and cranberry sausage with egg pasta sheets, roast pureed butternut squash or pumpkin, and a creamy ricotta and spinach layer at its center. I also made the Simplest Ever Thanksgiving: roasted beets and carrots, herb-marinated turkey breasts, cracked cranberry sauce. I even did a vegetarian Thanksgiving—red cabbage and walnuts and Jaeger spaetzle (mushroom ragu over German dumplings).

So on actual November 26 of 2020, when I had to once again make roast turkey, stuffing, mashed potatoes and parsnips, cranberry sauce, green beans and shallots, twice-baked stuffed butternut squash, cider gravy . . . I just wasn't feeling it. After weeks and weeks of pregaming, to see game day all packed up in plastic boxes and wiped down to deliver to my nearest and dearest kind of broke me.

I dropped my mom's off because she was too nervous to sit outside and visit with me, since there had been construction workers running around our house site without masks on. My dad sent his driver, our friend Dave, to pick his up. I made John the largest turkey platter of our married life. It looked almost medieval—but I had zero interest in eating any of it myself. I can't say it enough: What a weird year.

I broke everything down and cleaned up methodically. I sent John and Bella to bed at around 10. Then I poured a glass of wine and made garlic and oil pasta with lots of anchovies, one of Grandpa Emmanuel's favorite meals, so I could spend time in my kitchen and in my heart with him. I thought about how much I love sardines, too, because he did. I loved sitting on his lap as a kid and watching him play cards with the Runzo boys, and listening to the stories they shared. I loved the light in his eyes. I think I have his eyes. They're small and almond shaped, but they have a spark, and they're his. I thought of my mom and how I have her nose but not her lovely little head. I have a giant pumpkin head! But my nose, like hers, has a little dimple in it, and I love that. I hope I have her fearlessness and her fierceness, and live up to her work ethic. I thought about my first dog, Boo, and how I'd clear off the coffee table, she'd stand on it, and we'd dance to Ella Fitzgerald or Chet Baker. And if I sang, she'd sing along with me. I thought of Isaboo—how big her tongue was, what her kisses felt like, and how she loved butternut squash. She'd have been all in for that on this day.

I turned off all the lights but the Christmas ones I'd put up early, as I do every year. I sat at the counter, ate my spaghetti, sipped my wine, and remembered all the beauty from all the years past. And while it took me until the very end of the day, it worked. I found Thanksgiving.

Marvelous Mushroom Soup

WITH MARSALA

2 large bulbs garlic, ends cut to expose the cloves

2 tablespoons EVOO, plus more for drizzling

Salt and freshly ground black pepper

6 cups vegetable stock

1 cup dried porcini mushrooms or mixed dried mushrooms

4 tablespoons (½ stick) butter, cut into pieces

1¼ to 1½ pounds fresh mushrooms, wiped clean and sliced

2 tablespoons fresh thyme (a small handful), chopped

2 tablespoons fresh rosemary (a small handful), chopped

1 onion or 3 small shallots, chopped

1 cup Marsala

1 cup heavy cream

Finely chopped fresh chives and/or flat-leaf parsley, for serving

▪ Preheat the oven to 375°F.

▪ Place the garlic bulbs on a sheet of foil. Drizzle with EVOO, season with salt and pepper, and wrap up tightly. Place on a large baking sheet and roast until very soft, about 1 hour. Let cool, then squeeze the garlic from the skins onto a cutting board. Using the flat side of your knife, smear the garlic across the board, creating a paste.

▪ In a large pot, bring the stock and dried mushrooms to a low boil over medium-high heat. Simmer until the mushrooms are soft, about 20 minutes. Using a slotted spoon, transfer the mushrooms to a cutting board, reserving the stock in the pot. Chop the mushrooms.

▪ In a Dutch oven or soup pot, heat 2 tablespoons EVOO (two turns of the pan) over medium-high heat. Melt the butter into the oil, then add the fresh mushrooms, thyme, and rosemary. Cook, stirring often, until the liquid from the mushrooms evaporates and the mushrooms are well browned,

about 20 minutes. Season with salt and pepper.

▪ Add the onion and garlic paste and stir another minute or so. Add the Marsala and cook, stirring, until the liquid is absorbed. Pour in the mushroom stock, leaving behind any grit in the bottom of the pot. Stir in the chopped reconstituted dried mushrooms and the cream. Using an immersion blender, puree the soup. Cover to keep warm. Serve in small bowls topped with chives and/or parsley.

This soup is meal enough for me! You may want to double the recipe and put half in the freezer for a cold day when you don't feel like dealing with dinner.

Pappardelle alla Boscaiola

1 cup dried porcini mushrooms
3 cups bone broth or vegetable stock
⅓ pound pancetta - optional -
3 T EVOO - 1 lb. fresh mushroom
such as crimini, maitake &
shitake - 3 shallots, chopped
4 cloves garlic, chopped, 3 T rosemary, chopped
salt & red pepper flakes, peperoncino
1 cup white wine - 14 oz Italian tomatoes
2 cups passata - ½ c heavy cream
1 pound pappardelle 1 c pecorino or
Parmigiano-Reggiano

Plump porcini by simmering
in stock. Remove, chop &
reserve 1½ c stock. Dice the
pancetta, if using. Heat EVOO over
medium high, brown sliced fresh mushrooms
then add finely chopped shallots, garlic,
rosemary, salt and red pepper.
Soften 2-3 minutes, add wine &
reduce by half. Add canned
tomatoes & 2 c passata, simmer 10
minutes, add cream, reduce heat to
low. Cook pappardelle in salted
water a minute less than package
directions, reserve ½ c water, drain.
Toss pasta, sauce, cheese & pasta liquid.

Serves 4

Pappardelle Boscaiola

SERVES 4

3 cups chicken or beef bone broth

1½ cups dried porcini mushrooms

3 tablespoons EVOO

6 ounces meaty pancetta, finely chopped

3 shallots, finely chopped

4 large cloves garlic, chopped

2 tablespoons finely chopped fresh rosemary

2 tablespoons chopped fresh sage

Salt and freshly ground black pepper

1 cup Tuscan white wine

1 (14.5-ounce) can diced or crushed fire-roasted tomatoes

1½ cups passata or tomato puree

1 pound pappardelle

½ cup heavy cream

¾ cup grated Parmigiano-Reggiano or Pecorino Romano cheese, plus more for serving

▪ In a medium pot, bring the broth and dried mushrooms to a low boil over medium heat. Let simmer until softened, 12 to 15 minutes.

▪ Bring a large pot of water to a boil for the pasta.

▪ In a deep skillet or Dutch oven, heat the EVOO (three turns of the pan) over medium heat. Add the pancetta and cook, stirring, until the fat renders, about 3 minutes. Add the shallots, garlic, rosemary, and sage and season with salt and pepper. Stir until the shallots soften, 2 to 3 minutes. Add the wine and cook until the wine is reduced by half, about 5 minutes.

▪ Using a slotted spoon, transfer the porcini to a work surface and chop them up. Add them to the sauce, then add most of the stock, leaving the last few tablespoons in the pot to avoid any grit that may have settled in the pan. Add the tomatoes and passata to the sauce. Reduce the heat to medium-low and let the sauce simmer.

▪ Salt the boiling water and cook the pasta for 1 minute less than the package directions for al dente. Drain the pasta. Stir the cream into the sauce. Toss the pasta with the sauce. Add the cheese and season with salt and pepper. Divide the pasta among shallow bowls, passing more cheese at the table.

Aka Woodsman's Pasta, this is hearty proof that nothing bad ever happens when mushrooms, cream, pancetta, and Parmigiano are involved.

Pumpkin-Stuffed Pasta or Gnocchi

WITH BROWN BUTTER AND SAGE SAUCE AND WALNUTS

SERVES 4

1 stick (8 tablespoons) butter

6 cloves garlic, chopped or grated

1 cup walnuts or hazelnuts, chopped

Salt

1 pound pumpkin ravioli or tortellini or 1½ pounds gnocchi

24 fresh sage leaves, coarsely chopped

⅛ teaspoon freshly grated nutmeg

1 tablespoon white balsamic or balsamic vinegar

3 cups baby kale, medium spinach, or arugula

¼ cup grated Parmigiano-Reggiano cheese, plus more for topping

■ Bring a large pot of water to a boil for the pasta.

■ In a large skillet, melt the butter over medium heat. When the butter foams, add the garlic and nuts and stir until the garlic softens, about 2 minutes.

■ Salt the boiling water and cook the pasta for 1 minute less than the package directions for al dente.

■ Meanwhile, add the sage to the sauce in the skillet and cook over medium heat until the butter browns and the sage is starting to crisp and brown, about 5 minutes. Stir in the nutmeg and vinegar and remove from the heat.

■ Before draining, ladle out about ½ cup of the starchy pasta cooking water, then drain the pasta. Add the pasta, cooking water, greens, and Parm to the sauce. Gently toss until the sauce coats the pasta and the greens wilt, 1 to 2 minutes. Serve the pasta with more cheese, for topping.

These are two recipes from the popular "mini-Thanksgivings" I made for the show. Add a leafy green salad and some pie and you've got a lovely and festive li'l feast.

Turkey Schnitzel with Cranberry Sauce,

BRUSSELS SPROUTS WITH APPLES, AND STUFFING BALLS

SERVES 4

TURKEY SCHNITZEL WITH CRANBERRY SAUCE

SERVES 4

½ to ¾ cup neutral oil, for frying

6 to 8 turkey breast cutlets

1 cup all-purpose flour

3 large eggs

2 tablespoons Dijon mustard

1 cup fine dried breadcrumbs

1 cup panko breadcrumbs

1 teaspoon ground white pepper

1 teaspoon dried sage or poultry seasoning, such as Bell's

½ teaspoon freshly grated nutmeg

Salt and freshly ground black pepper

Cranberry Sauce (recipe follows) or 1 (14-ounce) jar lingonberry preserves

■ Preheat the oven to 250°F. Line a sheet pan with foil or parchment and place a wire rack in it.

■ Pour about ⅛ inch oil into a large cast-iron skillet and set it on the stovetop.

■ On work surface, pound the cutlets between sheets of parchment to ⅛ to ¼ inch thick.

■ Set up a breading station: Line up three shallow bowls on the counter. Spread the flour out in one. Beat the eggs and mustard in the second. Mix together both the breadcrumbs, the white pepper, sage, and nutmeg in the third.

■ Season the cutlets with salt and pepper. Heat the oil over medium to medium-high heat. Coat the turkey first in the flour, then dip into the egg and finally the breadcrumb mixture. Working in batches of 2 or 3, cook for 2 to 3 minutes on each side in hot oil. Transfer to the sheet pan and keep warm in the oven.

■ Serve the schnitzel with the cranberry sauce on the side.

CRANBERRY SAUCE

MAKES 2¼ CUPS

1 (12-ounce) bag fresh cranberries

⅔ to ¾ cup sugar, to taste

Salt

■ In a pot, combine the cranberries, sugar, and 1 cup water. Bring to a boil, add a pinch of salt, and cook to reduce and thicken, about 20 minutes.

(CONTINUED)

BRUSSELS SPROUTS WITH APPLES

SERVES 4

1¼ pounds medium Brussels sprouts (a rounded pint bucket), trimmed and halved

2 teaspoons honey, preferably acacia

1½ tablespoons olive oil

¼ teaspoon freshly grated nutmeg

Salt and freshly ground black pepper

2 apples

Juice of ½ small lemon

2 tablespoons butter

2 large shallots, chopped

1 tablespoon fresh thyme, chopped

10 to 12 leaves fresh sage, stacked and thinly sliced (about 2 tablespoons)

⅔ to ¾ cup walnuts or blanched hazelnuts, chopped

2 tablespoons sherry vinegar or white balsamic vinegar

Freshly shredded or grated pecorino cheese

■ Set up a large bowl of ice and water. In a pot of boiling salted water, cook the Brussels sprouts for 3 minutes. Drain and cold-shock in the ice bath. Drain again and dry.

■ Heat a cast-iron skillet over medium-high heat. In a bowl, toss the Brussels sprouts with the honey, oil, nutmeg, and salt and pepper to taste. Arrange the sprouts in the skillet cut-side down and reduce the heat a bit. Cook until deeply browned, 4 to 5 minutes. Flip and cook 1 to 2 minutes more and transfer to a platter.

■ Meanwhile, peel, core, and slice or chop the apples. Toss with the lemon juice.

■ Add the butter to the skillet and when the butter foams, add the apples, shallots, thyme, sage, and walnuts. Season with salt and pepper. Cook for a few minutes to soften shallots and apples. Stir in the vinegar and return the Brussels sprouts to the pan. Remove from the heat and top with pecorino.

STUFFING BALLS

SERVES 4

5 to 6 cups cubes (½ inch) stale white bread

2 tablespoons poultry seasoning, such as Bell's

Salt and freshly ground black pepper

4 tablespoons (½ stick) butter

2 ribs celery with leafy tops, finely chopped

1 large onion, finely chopped

1 small apple, finely chopped

¾ to 1 cup chopped mixed fresh herbs: parsley, sage, and thyme

1 large egg

About ½ cup chicken broth

■ Preheat the oven to 325°F.

■ Toss the bread cubes with the poultry seasoning, salt, and pepper. Spread out on a baking sheet and toast to dry out the bread until lightly golden. Let cool. Leave the oven on but increase the temperature to 425°F.

■ In a large skillet, melt the butter over medium to medium-high heat. When it foams, add the celery, onion, and apple. Season with salt and pepper and cook until softened, 7 to 8 minutes. Cool the mixture.

■ In a large bowl, combine the sautéed mixture, cubed bread, herbs, egg, and chicken broth and toss to evenly moisten. Line a sheet pan with parchment paper. Form the stuffing mixture into 12 balls and place on the lined sheet pan. Transfer to the oven and bake until heated through and golden brown on the outside, 20 to 25 minutes.

Healing Our Broken Home

One morning in the fall of 2020, I was interviewing Jenna Bush Hager on Zoom for the show. She'd written a beautiful book about her grandparents Barbara and George H. W. Bush, and was promoting it. As I was prepping for the interview, I started to think about the passing of the elder Bush in 2018. The image that instantly came to me was of service members and others lined up when his funeral procession passed them on its winding road through Texas. Organizers had followed his wishes to have him taken by train across the countryside, where people lined the tracks as his remains passed through their towns. I thought also about John Lewis's funeral procession as he made his final journey across the Edmund Pettus Bridge in Selma, Alabama, with marines saluting, the same bridge where he'd been brutally beaten during a Civil Rights march decades before.

I thought about the statesmen from different parties who found commonalities and compromise with the other side—Tip O'Neill and Ronald Reagan and JFK. I thought of all the ceremonies with the Clintons, Obamas, and Bushes standing together and, whether celebrating or mourning, being there for each other. I miss that America. No matter how staunch or dedicated the Democrat or Republican, for most of my life there has been decorum and a degree of mutual respect among our politicians (Nixon being the glaring exception). And the call to run for government was considered an honorable one that attracted the best among us.

When I was in high school, the first rite of adulthood was getting a driver's license. The second, just as momentous, was registering to vote. I remember getting excited every day to go into Mr. Luce's social studies class. We had a mock city with a mock government and we talked incessantly about current events. I was so thrilled to be engaging in the arena of civics; one of the proudest moments of my young life was becoming the mayor of "Sunshine City." I always thought of politicians as people of service, and that to serve your community or your state or federal government was an honor reserved for the best and brightest. We not only wanted to vote, we daydreamed about one day being one of these folks that we were voting _for_. What I reflected on the most over the last few years and most definitely in 2020 is how we have vilified not only each other, but the integrity of being a person of service. Somehow we universally came to believe there are no good people in politics anymore.

I still study civics every day. I watch probably too much news, and I read a lot of history. I love Jon Meacham, Eddie Glaude Jr., Bob Woodward. I reread <u>Notorious RBG</u> to celebrate Ruth Bader Ginsburg after her death. Madeleine Albright is one of my all-time heroes. Her book <u>Fascism: A Warning</u> was a must reread for me last year. I love books, and reading history and politics helps me put the world in some kind of order. I think it's everyone's civic duty to learn and be aware, and I for one will be absorbing history and current events for as long as I walk the earth.

I want our nation to come back to that time when politics was a noble calling and we revered it. When we respected politicians, from our local superintendents and city council members to the Supreme Court justices, senators, representatives, and president. These jobs deserve admiration and gravitas—both from those holding the office and those of us who put them there. We're a young country and so unique. We're mostly people who were kicked out of other places. We're the leftovers, and we built this amazing thing. We're supposed to be proud of it, and to tend and care for it, not to feel entitled to that freedom we so cherish and to look at our fellow Americans with hate. I terribly miss the time when we could disagree with each other, but still respect each other.

It feels like we we've all living in a broken home, filled with constant contention, constant fighting. I know everything happens in waves, and it's cyclical, but the cycle that we're in right now feels especially dark, with so many wounds exposed, and salt being rubbed into them by bad actors. Racial unrest, economic insecurity, election doubt. We can't even agree who to listen to about our health! The planet is on fire; we're waking up to blood-red skies. The earth is suffering, as are so many of the creatures living on it. I'm overwhelmed with longing for us to come back together and begin the hard work of fixing the many broken parts of our world.

You may have guessed by now that I'm a registered Democrat. My mom voted for McGovern, so it's no big surprise where I landed. But to tell you the truth, I live pretty squarely in the center. Yes, this is an option! I'm a conservative on some issues and a liberal on many others. I respect and admire both Democrats and Republicans. I've interviewed many of both over the years—Cindy and John McCain, Ann and Mitt Romney, Dr. Jill and Joe Biden, when he was vice president. And I've voted for both sides, too. As an American, I have the freedom to do that, for which I am grateful.

A week after I spoke with Jenna, I interviewed Michelle Obama, and we talked about the importance of being heard and feeling heard. And that's at the core of our national problem. Americans are too terrified to hear each other. It's hard to listen when you think someone is attacking the fiber of your being or the fabric of your country. And we're so afraid of our opponents right now that we are crippled by it. When everyone's coming from a place of fear, it's an easy leap from there to hate—especially with the right people exploiting it.

We did this to ourselves. All of us. We <u>let</u> ourselves be divided. We have to take responsibility for that. I feel that in questions we get from viewers and in catching up with friends I've known for a decade or more. It's a fundamental necessity for a functioning democracy that we hear our fellow countrymen, listen without judgment or throwing labels at each other, and try to understand one another's situation. This is every American's country, and if wide swaths of people feel they aren't being heard, we're doing something wrong.

So this is our state of mind and being. Add to it a global pandemic. Add to that social unrest—the murders of Breonna Taylor, George Floyd, Rayshard Brooks, Ahmaud Arbery, and so many other names we should memorize. We're experiencing the kind of economic despair we

haven't seen since the Great Depression, and a tidal wave of food insecurity and evictions. These are our gaping national wounds, and they hurt. And the point of the pain has to be healing.

I saw proof, in the days after the election, of healing beginning. A woman protesting for LGBTQ+ rights and supporting the Biden/Harris ticket became friends in a parking lot in Arizona with a woman in a bright red MAGA mask. They ended up talking about how much they had in common rather than what drove them apart. Inside the Arizona counting center, two men behind Plexiglas cubes were counting votes ten feet apart. One was a Republican, one a Democrat. They'd become friends, too, while hearing people screaming one another down in the parking lot through the doors and cement walls, and beyond the police barrier. They did their job, counting ballots, while making small talk. They didn't necessarily agree more on November 7 than they did on November 3, but they found enough in common over those few days that they could call each other friend.

Americans are great at kindness and empathy, especially face to face. We're at our best when we come together and love each other and work on the really tough stuff together, rather than apart. That's how we'll build back from this, one sympathetic ear at a time.

Our new president knows something about building back from loss. Joe Biden has been kicked down by fate over and over, and what brought him back from all of it was faith. Joe's a Good Man. He thinks about everyone ahead of himself. He worked across the aisle for decades. When the race was finally called, he opened his acceptance speech as president-elect by thanking his Black, first-generation Indian American vice president, and then giving her the floor. To me, she's MVP, not just VP! I saw so many interviews with little girls and young women who were moved to see her take that podium. They were on fire because they finally could see a woman—a Black and Indian woman—rising to the second-highest office for the first time in the country's 240 years, on the centennial anniversary of women's suffrage. I had to stop all of my work (on this book, my Italian homework, and delivering recipes for my show) because I couldn't see through my happy tears that day.

I'm going with a baseball metaphor here (sorry). In the 2020 election, the game went into extra innings. Trouble is, after the election, it's time to move on to the next game—not keep playing the last one. And the opponent shouldn't be the other end of the political spectrum. It should be COVID, and poverty, and racial oppression. And wildfires, foreign adversaries, and dictators around the world hurting their own people. _America, we are on the same team!_ We need to come together on infrastructure. On access to health care and nutrition for hungry children. There are basic human needs we should address together, rather than pushing each other farther and farther apart. If we're gonna keep this team going, we need to take the field together, and make our opponents the challenges we face, not our teammates.

On November 7, for the first time since March 12, I found myself suddenly without the feeling of dread I'd been carrying. The fact is, more Americans voted for Joe Biden and Donald Trump, _each of them_, than had for any candidate in U.S. history. What that says is that we all cared, we're all moved to action. And that fact alone is one small step _toward_ each other rather than away from one another. There is a poetry and a symmetry to that. It could be the first line of an open conversation. We all cared enough to get out there, more than ever.

For this reason, I put my head to the pillow that night for the first time in a long time without dread in my heart, but thoughts of hope and joy. And I slept.

Turkey Breast Roulade

AND SIMPLE GRAVY

SERVES 4 TO 6

TURKEY ROULADE

4 tablespoons (½ stick) butter, plus a little softened butter or EVOO for the turkey skin

1 small bulb fennel, finely chopped

2 Honeycrisp apples, peeled and finely chopped

2 ribs celery with leafy tops, finely chopped

1 large onion, finely chopped

Salt and freshly ground black pepper

½ cup packed chopped mixed fresh herbs: parsley, sage, rosemary, and thyme

¼ cup Calvados or brandy

½ cup white wine

2½ cups seasoned stuffing cubes or breadcrumbs

1 to 1½ cups chicken or turkey stock or broth, plus more for the roasting pan

1 large egg

12 ounces Italian or breakfast sausage (optional), browned and finely crumbled

1 boneless, skin-on turkey breast (4 to 5 pounds)

3 tablespoons Dijon mustard

Poultry seasoning, such as Bell's

GRAVY

3 to 4 tablespoons butter

2 teaspoons coarsely ground black pepper

3 to 4 tablespoons AP flour

1 quart turkey or chicken stock

1 tablespoon Worcestershire sauce

Salt

2 tablespoons Dijon mustard

■ Prepare the roulade: In a large skillet, melt 4 tablespoons butter over medium to medium-high heat. Add the fennel, apples, celery, and onion and season with salt and pepper to taste. Add the fresh herbs and cook until the vegetables soften, 7 to 8 minutes. Stir in the Calvados, then add the white wine and let it absorb. Stir in the stuffing and add enough stock to moisten. Transfer to a large bowl to cool. Add the egg and sausage (if using) to the cooled stuffing and mix together.

■ Place the turkey breast on a work surface and starting at the fattest part of the breast, cut horizontally through the meat, pulling the meat back as you go, like you're opening a book. Keep cutting until you are almost but not all the way through to the other side. You will end up with a roughly heart-shaped piece. Set it skin-side down on the work surface between two sheets of plastic

(CONTINUED)

wrap or parchment paper. With a meat mallet, gently pound into a rectangular shape, getting the thickness as even as possible.

■ Position a rack in the center of the oven and preheat the oven to 425°F.

■ Lay the turkey breast on top of 4 to 6 lengths of kitchen string, spacing the strings evenly apart (these will be used to tie up the roll). Season the flesh side of the turkey breast with salt and pepper, then slather it with the mustard. Spread the stuffing over the turkey, leaving a 1-inch border all around. Starting at the end of the turkey breast that doesn't have any skin on the underside (you want to end up with the skin on the outside of the roll), roll up the breast. Tie it into a compact roulade with the kitchen string. Lightly smear the skin with a little softened butter or EVOO and season with salt, pepper, and poultry seasoning to taste. Place on a rack set in a roasting pan or sheet pan. Pour a little bit of stock into the bottom of the pan to help keep the turkey breast moist.

■ Roast for 30 minutes, then reduce the oven temperature to 350°F and roast for 1 hour more. Remove from the roasting pan and set aside to cool a bit. Reserve the roasting pan and the drippings.

■ Make the gravy: In a skillet or saucepot, melt the butter over medium to medium-high heat. Whisk in the pepper and flour. Whisk in the stock and cook until thickened. Season with the Worcestershire and salt to taste.

■ Add a little water to the drippings in the roasting pan to loosen. Pour the drippings through a fine-mesh sieve into a large measuring cup, then pour the strained drippings into the gravy and whisk to combine. Remove from the heat and stir in the mustard.

■ To serve, cut off the kitchen strings and slice the roulade. Ladle some gravy onto a dinner plate and top with slices of roulade.

Tray Bake Turkey Breast and Roast Veg

WITH WORCESTERSHIRE-CIDER GRAVY AND CRACKED CRANBERRY SAUCE

SERVES 4 TO 6

TURKEY AND MARINADE

1 cup packed mixed fresh herbs: parsley, sage, and thyme

Juice of ½ lemon

1 tablespoon Worcestershire sauce

1 tablespoon soy sauce

1 tablespoon Dijon mustard

1 clove garlic, finely chopped or grated

¼ cup EVOO

1 boneless, skin-on turkey breast (4 to 5 pounds)

Salt and freshly ground black pepper

VEGGIES

3 pounds combined potatoes and root veggies (beets, turnips, carrots, parsnips, parsley root, or large radishes), peeled and cut into wedges or similar shapes and sizes

2 large shallots or small onions, roots attached and sliced into wedges

¼ cup EVOO

2 teaspoons grated lemon zest

2 teaspoons grated orange zest

2 tablespoons fresh rosemary, finely chopped

Salt and freshly ground black pepper

¼ cup white wine

¼ cup turkey or chicken stock

FOR SERVING

Worcestershire-Cider Gravy (recipe follows)

Cracked Cranberry Sauce (recipe follows)

■ Marinate the turkey: In a food processor, combine the herbs, lemon juice, Worcestershire, soy sauce, mustard, garlic, and EVOO and pulse several times to combine. Generously season the turkey breast with salt and pepper. Add the marinade and the turkey to a zip-top bag and coat evenly. Refrigerate for at least 1 hour and up to several hours.

■ Position a rack in the center of the oven and preheat the oven to 350°F.

■ Prepare the veggies: In a large bowl, combine all the vegetables, EVOO, both citrus zests, the rosemary, and salt and pepper to taste. Arrange in a roasting pan or large sheet pan. Sprinkle with the wine and stock. Place the marinated turkey breast on top of the vegetables.

■ Roast until a meat thermometer reads 165°F, 2 to 2½ hours. Increase the heat to high/broil to brown the skin a bit, then remove and let rest 20 minutes.

■ To serve: Slice the turkey, arrange a few slices on a bed of root veg and potatoes, and bathe them in the Worcestershire-cider gravy. Serve the cranberry sauce on the side.

(CONTINUED)

WORCESTERSHIRE-CIDER GRAVY

MAKES ABOUT 2 CUPS

4 tablespoons (½ stick) butter

4 tablespoons AP flour

2 tablespoons Worcestershire sauce

2 teaspoons freshly ground black pepper, or to taste

½ cup cloudy cider

1½ cups turkey or chicken stock

■ In a saucepan or skillet, melt the butter over medium to medium-high heat. Whisk in the flour to combine, then add the Worcestershire, pepper, cider, and stock and cook until thick enough to coat a spoon.

CRACKED CRANBERRY SAUCE

MAKES ABOUT 2¼ CUPS

1 (12-ounce) bag fresh cranberries

Peel from 1 large orange

¾ cup sugar

■ In a small saucepot, combine the cranberries, orange peel, sugar, and 1 cup water. Bring to a boil, then reduce the heat a bit and let the berries bubble away until they burst and form a sauce, 12 to 15 minutes. Remove the orange peel and cool to room temperature or chill.

Giving Thanks Lasagna

TURKEY LAYER
½ cup fresh cranberries
¼ cup sugar
2 tablespoons EVOO
1 pound ground turkey, white and dark meat combined
1 small onion, finely chopped
2 cloves garlic, chopped
1 tablespoon poultry seasoning, such as Bell's
Salt and freshly ground black pepper
1 cup turkey or chicken bone broth or stock
½ cup finely chopped mixed fresh herbs: parsley, sage, thyme, and rosemary

RICOTTA LAYER
3 cups ricotta cheese
2 large eggs
1 cup grated Parmigiano-Reggiano cheese
1 cup cooked kale or spinach, squeezed dry in a kitchen towel and finely chopped
Ground white pepper
⅛ teaspoon freshly grated nutmeg

WHITE SAUCE
3 tablespoons butter
3 tablespoons AP flour
1 teaspoon granulated garlic
Salt and ground white pepper

1 cup turkey or chicken bone broth or vegetable broth
2 cups whole milk or half-and-half
⅛ teaspoon freshly grated nutmeg

FOR ASSEMBLY
1 pound lasagna noodles
Salt
Spiced Butternut or Pumpkin Puree (recipe follows)
2 cups freshly shredded low-moisture mozzarella cheese (use the large holes of a box grater)

■ Make the turkey layer: In a small pot, combine the cranberries, ½ cup water, and the sugar. Bring to a boil, then cook the cranberries until they split open and the sauce thickens. Remove from the heat and let cool.

■ In a large skillet, heat the EVOO (two turns of the pan) over medium-high heat. Add the turkey and brown and crumble it. Add the onion, garlic, poultry seasoning, and salt and black pepper to taste. Cook, stirring, to soften. Add the broth and let it absorb. Let the mixture cool to room temp. Stir in the cranberries and chopped fresh herbs.

■ Make the ricotta layer: In a large bowl, mix together the ricotta, eggs, Parm, kale, white pepper, and nutmeg.

■ Make the white sauce: In a saucepot, melt the butter and whisk in the flour, then add the granulated garlic and season with salt and white pepper. Let it bubble, then add the broth, milk, and nutmeg. Cook until thick enough to coat a spoon.

■ Preheat the oven to 400°F.

■ Assemble the lasagna: Bring a large pot of water to a boil. Salt the water and cook the noodles for 5 minutes. Drain and arrange between layers of kitchen towels or parchment, and cover with a towel to keep moist.

■ In a 9 × 13-inch baking dish, layer in this order: half of the white sauce, one-quarter of the pasta, half of the squash puree, one-quarter of the pasta, all of the ricotta cheese, one-quarter of the pasta, all of the turkey, one-quarter of the pasta, the remaining half of the squash puree, remaining white sauce, and mozzarella.

■ Cover with foil and bake for 1 hour. Uncover and continue baking until browned, another 20 to 30 minutes. Let stand for 20 minutes. Cut and serve.

(CONTINUED)

SPICED BUTTERNUT OR PUMPKIN PUREE

MAKES 3 CUPS

You can make the puree just before assembling the lasagna: After roasting the squash, dial the oven temp down to 425°F for baking the lasagna.

1 medium-large butternut squash or 1 small pumpkin, halved and seeded

Nonaerosol olive oil spray or olive oil

½ teaspoon smoked paprika

¼ teaspoon freshly grated nutmeg

Pinch of ground allspice

Pinch of ground cinnamon or smoked cinnamon

Salt and freshly ground black pepper

1 tablespoon EVOO

1 tablespoon butter

2 large shallots or 1 small onion, finely chopped

1 large clove garlic, finely chopped or grated

1 cup chicken broth or stock

½ cup heavy cream

▪ Position a rack in the center of the oven and preheat the oven to 450°F.

▪ Mist or brush the squash with olive oil. Season with smoked paprika, nutmeg, allspice, cinnamon, and salt and pepper. Roast cut-side down until tender, about 30 minutes. When cool enough to handle, scoop out the flesh into a bowl.

▪ In a medium pot, heat the EVOO (one turn of the pan) and the butter over medium heat. Add the shallots and garlic and season with salt. Cook 2 to 3 minutes to soften. Add the stock and cook at a low boil to reduce by half. Add the squash flesh, puree with an immersion blender, then add the cream.

Pilgrim Sandwich

MAKES 1 SANDWICH

1 piece turkey schnitzel (see page 245) or sliced roast turkey

Chicken or turkey stock (optional)

10-inch length of baguette, halved and hinged

Brown or Dijon mustard

Sliced sharp white cheddar cheese

Thinly sliced cornichons

Thinly sliced shallots

1 or 2 romaine lettuce leaves, shredded

Cranberry sauce

▪ Preheat the oven to 350°F.

▪ If using schnitzel, set it on a small baking pan/sheet and warm in the oven until crisped up. (Leave the oven on.) If using sliced roast turkey, reheat in a little chicken or turkey stock.

▪ To build the sandwich, lightly toast the bread. Spread mustard on the bottom half of the bread. If using schnitzel, halve the cutlet on the diagonal lengthwise so that it will fill the baguette shape more evenly. Set the schnitzel or warm turkey on the baguette and top with cheddar. Set the sandwich on a baking sheet in the oven until cheese is melted.

▪ Remove from the oven and top the cheese with cornichons and shallots, then top that with lettuce. Spread cranberry sauce on the top half of the bread, close up the sandwich, and serve.

John's French 50

MAKES TWO COCKTAILS

2 ounces Cognac or brandy

1 ounce freshly squeezed lemon juice

1 ounce simple syrup

A few dashes orange bitters (optional)

Champagne, for topping

Lemon twists, for garnish

In a cocktail shaker, combine the Cognac, lemon juice, simple syrup, and bitters (if using). Add ice and shake vigorously. Strain into two chilled coupes or champagne flutes. Top with champagne. Garnish each with a lemon twist.

This is John's riff on the French 75, dedicated to our friend (and my own celebrity crush) Curtis "50 Cent" Jackson.

December

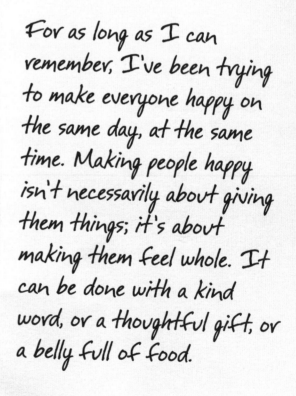

For as long as I can remember, I've been trying to make everyone happy on the same day, at the same time. Making people happy isn't necessarily about giving them things; it's about making them feel whole. It can be done with a kind word, or a thoughtful gift, or a belly full of food.

AGRODOLCE CLAMS WITH RED SAUCE

BAGEL LAB

SIMPLE FISH AND TOMATO STEW

RIB EYES WITH SHERRY-GARLIC MUSHROOMS AND
TWICE-BAKED STUFFED POTATOES

CAVIAR AND CAPELLINI

WINTER CHIMICHURRI FOR FISH (OR STEAK OR CHICKEN)

Hope for the Holidays

HOLIDAY CICCHETTI: EGGPLANT CROQUETTES AND
FRIED STUFFED SAGE LEAVES

BEEF IN BRUNELLO WITH POLENTA

INDIVIDUAL BEEF WELLINGTONS

TORTELLINI IN BRODO

EASIEST BRISKET EVER, ZUCCHINI AND POTATO LATKES,
AND BITTER GREENS SALAD

JOHN'S PEAR SPRITZER

Hope for the Holidays

I walk away from each holiday season scarred. Literally. Because from the day before Thanksgiving through the end of the long weekend, I lean hard into the metal rungs of ladders, sometimes for many hours, to decorate nine Christmas trees for our house and my family members' houses, before driving back to New York City before dawn on Tuesday to tape a long sprint of shows before the holiday break. The resulting bruises, swelling, and breaking of skin from my knees to my ankles is visible for months afterward.

For years I've posted shots of my trees on social media, and inevitably people start debating in the comments whether or not I did them myself. Yes, I did. I am one of _those_ people. Christmas music is fair game from Halloween on. (John makes holiday playlists every year that I run in huge loops—when I'm not playing endless hours of holiday movies, of course.) One of the biggest losses from our fire that's especially haunting me as I write this was my first-edition clothbound <u>The Grinch Who Stole Christmas</u>, which each year I would read aloud to visiting friends.

What was my holiday wish for 2020? On August 10, the morning after the fire, I asked Steve Colletti, our contractor, "So can you rebuild by Christmas?" The ruins of the house were still smoldering and hadn't been cleared from the land yet. I'm sure you can imagine the look on his face. Realistically, maybe we'll be back in our new home in time for my mom's birthday in July, seven months after Christmas.

John and I had so much to be grateful for in 2020. But you might not know it if you looked at it like a laundry list. We lost Isaboo, our dog of fifteen years, and our home of fifteen years. Like most people, we also lost our sense of safety and security, time with our family, our social lives, travel. Still, we gained an understanding of so many things that we didn't have until now.

This year saw a great milestone for the show, our 2,500th episode. To mark it, in November, we hosted a Zoom Cook-Along with ten wonderful viewers and the incredible guests we hosted virtually—a dad who cooks with his son to help him relax and focus

because he has Asperger's Syndrome; a war veteran with PTSD who got a dog to calm him, so he wouldn't hurt his wife, as he so honestly put it; a young woman who cooks up a storm from her wheelchair and watches everything we do on the show; a mother who has no money but finds joy in cooking dinner with her kids. By the end of the show everyone was crying and asking me questions not just about food but about life, and I was overwhelmed with joy. We briefly lost the connection for the last part of taping, and everyone in the control booth back in NYC said they were happy for the break so they could distance from one another and take their masks off and wipe away the tears. Happy tears. Cathartic tears. What all those guests taught us was 2020's most important lesson: The more you lose, if you've lucky, the more you'll see just how much you have left to be really, truly grateful for.

We've normally the inn that harbors six or seven families and their kids at the holidays. And though we couldn't do that in 2020, we couldn't let the holidays come and go without spreading some kind of cheer for ourselves and everyone on our video calls. The trees would not go up, but I wasn't going to skip decorating entirely.

I took to my notebook in the middle of the night
And I doodled sketches both merry and bright
Of garlands that sparkle with ribbons and bows
and tiny Christmas lights like new fallen snow
So yes, it's a year like no other year
But it can still be a year that's full of good cheer!

Sounds like a Christmas poem, doesn't it? So I took these scribbles and doodles and asked my friends Susan and Peter and Susan's sister Sara to come in and consult and HELP! If I'd tried to string yards and yards of garlands with della robbia and ribbons, Bella would've eaten everything and gotten sick all over the furniture. So they took the time and came in with their masks and gloves and worked like elves/specialty electricians to make my crazy holiday visions come true. Thank you, friends!

As I've said before, I miss in-person shopping. And this year's list is hard! No one wants anything except more loungewear and basics. It's ironic that the only thing left of my house post-excavation was a perfectly clean cellar, a giant hole in the ground. And if you could've seen my cellar at the holidays, you'd fall over. Santa and Chanukah Harry have nothing on me. From one end to the other, stacks and stacks and stacks

to be wrapped for all those we love, all the ribbons and bows in apple and pear crates, a huge variety of pens, and tags. Stuff to be wrapped would go on the Ping-Pong table. Stuff to be shipped on the air hockey table. I had a <u>system.</u> So in 2020, it was all online, and somehow we got it done. I still sent gifts to every family and every child, and spent many a night when I should've been asleep working away to make the holidays happen. Shout-out to Cara Jammet and Michelle Boxer, the elves who helped me pull it off. Give and ye shall receive, apparently, because beautiful gifts flowed in our direction, too. In March my friend and colleague Andrew Kaplan sent my belated Christmas gift and it brought me to my knees. I cried for an hour when I opened six boxes filled with new copies of cookbooks that we'd lost to the fire. Jacques Pepin, Yotam Ottolenghi, Samin Nosrat, Michael Solomonov, and Joshua McFadden.

At first I thought, Wow that's so great! He gave me cookbooks! Then I saw that Jacques's had a letter on top. I went through and realized every single one had a beautiful personal note from the author or the giver, and I literally collapsed in tears. Even friends who hadn't written books of their own—Cara and Patrick Jammet, Anne Burrell, Michael Schlow—replaced my set of Phaidon cookbooks, inscribing them with personal notes.

My friends Anne and Harlan gave me a painting of a rooftop in our neighborhood in New York City by Sonya Sklaroff, a famous artist. I wrote a long letter to Sonya, explaining that it reminds me of my view. Every day since, we've texted each other and sent pictures of what we've working on. On my living room wall now is a painting of Bella that she wouldn't let me pay for. When I stand at the stove, I look right and I see Bella, and I look left and I see our NYC neighborhood.

Jack Antonoff and Carlotta Kohl gave John a piece of recording equipment that I don't know the name of, but it's one of his favorite things. Rachel Antonoff sent a weekend bag with a beautiful dress and a jumpsuit she designed (which I was going to order when I had time) packed neatly inside. Our thank-you note was (woefully) late because the box arrived at the site of our old house, and one of the workers there placed it in a shed for safekeeping. When we look all around at our walls, when we get dressed, when we pass through our small new world, we think of our friends, who add so much beauty to our lives.

The holidays are a time for friends, family, grace, and forgiveness. For as long as I can remember, I've been trying to make everyone happy on the same day, at the same time. I'm dancing as fast as I can and it's still nothing I can ever achieve. Making people happy isn't necessarily about giving them things; it's about making them feel whole. It can be done with a kind word, or a thoughtful gift, or a belly full of food. I've learned in fifty-two years that you can't force happiness or wholeness on a person. But it sure feels good to try.

The only gift I've ever wanted to give my mother was for her to have the life she imagined, the fairy tale she must've pictured when she was a little girl. Her life was difficult; she worked so hard at her many jobs and at raising three kids on her own, and was disappointed so many times. And no matter what I do, what I give her, she'll never have what she deserved to have all those years ago. That breaks my heart more than anything 2020 could throw at me.

But what the holidays give us is an annual chance to try again. And if you can't make everyone happy at the same time, you can spread joy to one or two people, or even hundreds, with your actions. There's always someplace where you can make joy happen. I've seen it; it's real; I know it's true. If you believe in the spirit of the season and you try as hard as you can to be a good neighbor, family member, colleague, human, with peace and love and community in your heart, good things will happen.

Agrodolce Clams

WITH RED SAUCE

SERVES 4

3 dozen littleneck clams or 3 pounds cockles

3 tablespoons EVOO

3 small shallots or 1 small onion, finely chopped

6 fat cloves garlic, thinly sliced or chopped

4 tablespoons sun-dried tomato paste or regular tomato paste

1 tablespoon fresh oregano, chopped, or 1 teaspoon dried

1 tablespoon Calabrian chile paste or 1 teaspoon crushed red pepper flakes

1 teaspoon ground fennel, fennel pollen, or fennel seeds

½ cup sweet vermouth

1 (28-ounce) can diced or crushed Italian tomatoes

½ cup drained sweet Peppadew or sweet pickled cherry peppers, chopped, or sweet red pepper relish

Salt and freshly ground black pepper

A fat handful of fresh basil leaves, torn

Ciabatta or other crusty bread, for serving

▪ In a large bowl of ice water, scrub the clams well with a brush to get rid of any dirt and debris.

▪ In a large skillet or Dutch oven, heat the EVOO (three turns of the pan) over medium-high heat. Add the shallots and stir until they begin to soften, a minute or two. Add the garlic, tomato paste, oregano, chile paste, and fennel. Stir until the tomato paste darkens in color, about a minute more. Add the vermouth and cook until the liquid starts to reduce, 30 seconds or so. Stir in the tomatoes and peppers, then let the mixture come to a bubble. Season the sauce with salt and black pepper.

▪ Add the clams and cover the pan. Cook until the clams open, 7 to 8 minutes (discard any that don't open). Stir in the basil. Divide the clams and sauce among shallow bowls. Serve with the bread.

Bagel Lab

Every other Sunday or so I make bagels for 5 or 6 people and I call it bagel lab because I create new cream cheese flavors and mix up the toppings. This one includes a cream cheese with beet horseradish and scallions paired with smoked salmon and beet carpaccio. Other popular

ones this year were ginger, garlic, chive, Sriracha cream cheese with pickled ginger and shiso on top on toasted poppy and sesame bagels and pepperoni (grated) cream cheese with oregano and semi-dried tomatoes, garlic, and scallions on toasted sesame bagels. This Chanukah-Christmas Bagel Lab was colorful and very special!

6 everything bagels, sliced and toasted

Beet Horseradish Cream Cheese (recipe follows)

12 slices smoked salmon

Beet Carpaccio (recipe follows)

3 tablespoons capers, drained

½ English cucumber, seeded and sliced into half-moons

Tufts of dill tops

Schug (optional; page 49)

These are served open-faced. Top each bagel half with a generous and even mound of the cream cheese. Arrange a ruffled slice of salmon on each side of each bagel half. Fill the center of the bagel with the beet carpaccio and add a few capers and bits of cucumber and dill. If desired, dot with schug.

(CONTINUED)

BEET CARPACCIO

MAKES 2 CUPS

4 or 5 baby beets or 2 small red beets, scrubbed and very thinly sliced on a mandoline or wide single-blade slot of a box grater

¼ red onion, very thinly sliced

1 large radish, red or purple, cut into matchsticks

A handful of fresh parsley, chopped

Juice of 1 small lemon

2 tablespoons EVOO

1 teaspoon sugar

Salt and freshly ground black pepper

■ In a bowl, combine the beets, red onion, radish, parsley, lemon juice, EVOO, sugar, and salt and pepper to taste. Let stand for a minimum of 30 minutes or chill until ready to serve.

BEET HORSERADISH CREAM CHEESE

MAKES ABOUT 1 POUND

2 (8-ounce) bricks cream cheese

1 clove garlic, grated

3 tablespoons prepared beet horseradish

¼ cup finely chopped fresh dill

4 scallions, finely chopped

Salt

■ Set the cream cheese in a bowl and let sit for 20 to 30 minutes at room temperature to soften a bit. Combine all ingredients in a bowl with a rubber spatula and add a pinch of salt to taste.

Simple Fish and Tomato Stew

SERVES 4 TO 6

½ lemon

2 pounds sustainable cod, cut into 2- to 3-inch chunks

¼ cup EVOO

1 bulb fennel, quartered, cored, and finely chopped

1 large onion, quartered and thinly sliced, or 3 shallots, finely chopped

1 rib celery, finely chopped

5 to 6 cloves garlic, thinly sliced or chopped

2 bay leaves

Herb bundle: a few sprigs of thyme and handful of parsley sprigs

1 teaspoon crushed red pepper flakes

Salt and freshly ground black pepper

1 teaspoon fennel pollen or 1 shot of Pernod or other anise liquor (optional)

1 cup white wine

2 cups chicken bone broth or seafood stock

1 (28-ounce) can Italian crushed tomatoes

A handful of basil, torn

1½ to 2 pounds mussels, scrubbed

½ cup chopped mixed herbs: celery tops, parsley, and chives,

Crusty bread, such as warm ciabatta, for serving

■ Squeeze the lemon over the cod to dress.

■ In a large pot with a lid, heat the EVOO (four turns of the pan) over medium to medium-high heat. Add the fresh fennel, onion, celery, garlic, bay leaves, herb bundle, pepper flakes, and salt and black pepper to taste. If using fennel pollen, add it now. Cook for 5 minutes to soften. If using Pernod, add it now and let it absorb. Add the wine and cook until reduced by half. Add the broth, tomatoes, and basil and simmer a few minutes to combine the flavors. Adjust the seasoning.

■ Add the cod and mussels, cover the pan, and cook to open the mussels (discard those that do not open), then continue cooking if needed until the cod is firm and opaque.

■ Serve topped with the chopped mixed herbs. Pass crusty bread at the table.

This dish is a simplified alternative to a cioppino. I made it for Christmas Eve 2020, but it's a solid, comforting meal all winter long.

Rib Eyes with Sherry-Garlic Mushrooms

AND TWICE-BAKED STUFFED POTATOES

SERVES 4

RIB EYES WITH SHERRY-GARLIC MUSHROOMS

SERVES 4

STEAKS

4 boneless rib-eye steaks (1½ inches thick) or 4 beef filet steaks (2½ inches thick) or a combo

2 large cloves garlic, smashed and halved

A few sprigs of rosemary and thyme

Nonaerosol canola spray or neutral oil

Kosher salt and freshly ground black pepper

4 tablespoons (½ stick) butter

MUSHROOMS

4 tablespoons (½ stick) butter

1 pound cremini mushrooms, wiped clean, trimmed, and sliced

2 tablespoons fresh thyme, chopped

Salt and freshly ground black pepper

2 large shallots, finely chopped

4 cloves garlic, finely chopped

½ cup dry sherry

¼ cup finely chopped fresh flat-leaf parsley

■ Prepare the steaks: At least 1 hour (and up to several hours) before cooking, pat the steaks dry, rub with the garlic, and place in a bag with the herbs. Allow to come to room temperature. Remove the steaks from the bag and reserve the garlic and herbs.

■ Position a rack in the center of the oven and preheat the oven to 375°F.

■ Heat a cast-iron skillet over medium-high heat. Mist or add a thin layer of oil to the pan. Working in batches, brown the steaks on both sides to caramelize the sugars, seasoning liberally with salt and pepper after turning. Transfer the steaks to a sheet pan.

■ Roast the steaks for 6 minutes for pink centers. Remove from the oven. Set the skillet on the stovetop again and heat the butter, garlic, and herbs until they bubble together. Working in batches, add the steaks and baste with the herb butter. Let the steaks rest a bit before serving.

■ Meanwhile, cook the mushrooms: In a large skillet, melt the butter over medium-high heat. When the butter bubbles, add the mushrooms and thyme and brown them. Season with salt and pepper, add the shallots and garlic, and stir 1 to 2 minutes. Add the sherry and swirl, then remove from the heat.

■ Top the steaks with the mushrooms and garnish with parsley.

A steakhouse classic reimagined, this meal is full of flavor and big and hearty. Tell everyone to eat a light lunch!

TWICE-BAKED STUFFED POTATOES

SERVES 4

4 large russet potatoes

4 tablespoons (½ stick) butter

¾ cup sour cream

3 tablespoons prepared horseradish

¼ cup finely chopped fresh chives

Salt and freshly ground black pepper

2 cups grated or shredded sharp white cheddar cheese

▪ Preheat the oven to 400°F.

▪ Wrap the potatoes individually in foil. Bake until just tender, 45 minutes to 1 hour. (Leave the oven on if serving right away.)

▪ Let the potatoes cool just enough to handle. Take a slice off the tops and gently scoop all the flesh into a bowl, leaving a shell or boat. Add the butter to the potato flesh and mash to melt. Add the sour cream, horseradish, chives, salt and pepper to taste, and 1 cup of the cheddar. Stir to combine and refill the potatoes with the mixture. Top with the remaining 1 cup cheddar.

▪ When ready to serve, return the stuffed potatoes to the oven and brown.

Caviar and Capellini

SERVES 4

3 tablespoons butter

2 shallots, minced

2 large cloves garlic, finely chopped or grated

Grated zest of 1 lemon

Salt and ground white pepper

1 cup vodka

1 cup heavy cream

1 (8.8-ounce) package capellini

4 ounces caviar (125 g tin)

Finely chopped dill and chives, for serving

■ Bring a large pot of water to a boil for the pasta.

■ In a large skillet, heat the butter over medium heat. When it melts and just begins to foam, add the shallots, garlic, and lemon zest and season with salt and white pepper. Stir a minute or so, add the vodka, and reduce to ¼ cup. Add the cream and bring to a bubble, then reduce the heat to low.

■ Salt the boiling water and cook the pasta to just shy of the package directions for al dente, about

4½ minutes. Before draining, scoop out about ½ cup of the pasta cooking water and add to the cream sauce. Drain the pasta and toss with the sauce and half the caviar.

■ Serve in shallow bowls and top with dill and chives and dollops of the remaining caviar.

This dish is about celebration, a special occasion, so, yes, it's a splurge. I make it in Italy when we gather with friends to celebrate our anniversary, and we made it at midnight on this New Year's Eve. Hello, 2021!

Serve this with a salad of romaine, celery, fennel, red onion, and toasted hazelnuts with some EVOO and lemon juice.

Winter Chimichurri for Fish

(OR STEAK OR CHICKEN)

SERVES 4 TO 6

CHIMICHURRI

1 cup packed baby kale or medium spinach leaves

1 bunch flat-leaf parsley, stemmed (about 1 cup)

¼ cup mixed fresh oregano and thyme

2 large cloves garlic, smashed and peeled

¼ cup roughly chopped fennel fronds

1 teaspoon ground fennel or fennel pollen

1 teaspoon crushed red pepper flakes

Salt and freshly ground black pepper

½ cup EVOO

⅓ cup sherry vinegar or white wine vinegar

PROTEIN

4 to 6 boneless sirloin strip or rib-eye steaks (¾ inch thick, 6 to 8 ounces each), or 4 to 6 boneless, skinless chicken breasts (6 to 8 ounces each), or 4 to 6 halibut or cod fillets (6 to 8 ounces each)

Salt and freshly ground black pepper

Nonaerosol olive oil spray

■ Make the chimichurri: In a food processor, combine the kale, parsley, mixed herbs, garlic, fennel fronds, ground fennel, pepper flakes, and salt and black pepper to taste and pulse until the kale and herbs are finely chopped. Add the EVOO and vinegar and process again until the chimichurri is fairly smooth. Adjust the seasoning and transfer to a small bowl.

■ Cook the protein: Preheat a large cast-iron or other nonstick skillet over medium-high heat. Using paper towels, pat the beef, chicken, or fish dry and season with salt and black pepper. Mist the pan with olive oil spray. Add the protein, then mist the tops with more oil.

■ For beef: Cook, turning occasionally, for 7 to 8 minutes for medium-rare. For chicken: Cook, turning occasionally, until cooked through, 9 to 10 minutes. For fish: Cook, turning once, until opaque in the center, 6 to 8 minutes. Let the beef or chicken rest for 5 minutes before serving. The fish can be served immediately.

■ Transfer to plates or a platter and top with the chimichurri.

Cicchetti are small snacks to serve alongside cocktails, olives, nuts, chips, and other small bar bites. There are endless recipes for *cicchetti*, but these are a couple of my favorites to make.

Holiday Cicchetti:

EGGPLANT CROQUETTES AND FRIED STUFFED SAGE LEAVES

EGGPLANT CROQUETTES

YIELDS 24 CROQUETTES

2-pound firm eggplant, peeled and finely diced

Salt

3 tablespoons currants

3 tablespoons EVOO

1 teaspoon crushed red pepper flakes

1 tablespoon fresh oregano, finely chopped, or 1 teaspoon dried

3 cloves garlic, finely chopped or grated

3 tablespoons toasted pine nuts, chopped

1 cup grated pecorino and/ or Parmigiano-Reggiano cheese

3 egg whites, lightly beaten

Frying oil, such as safflower or peanut

1 cup AP flour

2 large eggs

1 cup fine dried breadcrumbs

⅛ teaspoon freshly grated nutmeg

1 tablespoon grated lemon zest

Lemon wedges or warm tomato sauce, for serving

■ Toss the eggplant with some salt and set aside on paper towels for 30 minutes to remove excess liquid. In a small bowl, soak the currants in warm water to plump them.

■ In a large skillet, heat the EVOO (three turns of the pan) over medium heat. Add the eggplant and sauté 7 to 8 minutes. Add the pepper flakes, oregano, and garlic and stir another minute or so. Remove from the heat. Drain the currants and add to the pan along with the pine nuts. Let cool and combine with ½ cup of the pecorino and two-thirds of the beaten egg whites.

■ Pour 1 inch of frying oil into a Dutch oven and heat over medium to medium-high heat.

■ Set up a breading station: Line up three shallow bowls on the counter. Spread the flour out in one, beat the whole eggs and remaining egg white in the second, and mix together the breadcrumbs, nutmeg, lemon zest, and remaining ½ cup pecorino in the third.

■ Form 24 croquettes (about 1½ tablespoons each) or small eggplant patties and coat in the flour, then the egg, and finally the breadcrumbs. Working in batches, fry the croquettes to a deep golden, flipping halfway through. Drain on paper towels and serve with lemon wedges or warm tomato sauce.

(CONTINUED)

FRIED STUFFED SAGE LEAVES

▪ This is a method more than a recipe.

▪ Match up large sage leaves and sandwich a small piece of ripe Taleggio, soft Fontina, or Gorgonzola dolce between 2 leaves, pinching them together into a packet. Toss the stuffed leaves lightly in flour, coat both sides in beaten egg, and bread them in seasoned breadcrumbs (for every 1 cup breadcrumbs, season with ⅛ teaspoon grated nutmeg, 1 teaspoon grated lemon zest, and ½ cup pecorino or Parm). Fry in 1 inch of safflower or peanut oil over medium to medium-high heat to golden. Drain and serve with lemon wedges.

Beef in Brunello

WITH POLENTA

BEEF AND MARINADE

1 chuck roast or round roast (3 to 4 pounds)

2 carrots, sliced on an angle

2 ribs celery with leafy tops, sliced on an angle

1 large or 2 medium onions, chopped

4 large cloves garlic, smashed

2 large bay leaves

1 teaspoon juniper berries

4 sprigs rosemary

A small handful of thyme

1 (750 ml) bottle Brunello di Montalcino

TO FINISH

2 tablespoons olive oil

4 tablespoons (½ stick) butter

Salt and freshly ground black pepper

Finely chopped rosemary and thyme, for garnish

Polenta (recipe follows)

▪ Marinate the beef: Pat the meat dry and place in a large container with the carrots, celery, onion, garlic, bay leaves, juniper berries, rosemary, thyme, and wine. Marinate the beef in the refrigerator for 24 hours. Remove the meat from the marinade, reserving it, and pat the meat dry.

▪ In a large Dutch oven, heat the olive oil (two turns of the pan) over medium-high heat. Melt in 2 tablespoons of the butter. Add the beef and brown well and evenly. Season the beef generously with salt and pepper. Stir in the reserved marinade and vegetables. Set over very low heat, cover, and cook for 2 hours, turning occasionally.

▪ Remove the meat to a carving board and let rest. Strain the sauce and return to the pot. Set over medium heat and cook, whisking, to reduce it a bit. Whisk in the remaining 2 tablespoons butter.

▪ Slice the roast (removing strings if the roast was tied), sprinkle with chopped rosemary and thyme, and serve a few slices on each plate, draped in rich wine sauce, over or alongside polenta.

Note: You can also make this in the oven. Marinate the beef as directed. When ready to cook, preheat the oven to 325°F. Brown the beef and add the marinade and vegetables and bake for 2 hours.

Serve the beef and polenta with a simple salad of mixed bitter greens or a celery and raw portobello mushroom salad with celery tops and parsley.

POLENTA

SERVES 6

3 cups chicken broth or stock

2 cups whole milk

1½ cups coarse polenta

1 tablespoon coarsely ground black pepper

Salt

3 tablespoons butter, cut in small pieces

1 tablespoon acacia honey or other light-colored, mild-flavored honey

1 cup grated Parmigiano-Reggiano cheese (a couple of handfuls)

■ In a saucepan, combine the chicken broth and milk and bring to a low boil. Add the polenta, pepper, and a good pinch of salt. Cook, stirring frequently, for 25 to 30 minutes. Add water to thin the polenta if it gets too thick to stir before it is tender. To finish the polenta, stir in the butter, honey, and Parm. The polenta should be pourable from a ladle.

Individual Beef Wellingtons

SERVES 4

DUXELLES

- 1½ pounds mushrooms: hen of the woods (maitake) and cremini or any mix you prefer
- 6 tablespoons (¾ stick) butter
- 2 large shallots, finely chopped
- 4 cloves garlic, finely chopped
- 1 tablespoon fresh thyme, finely chopped
- Salt and freshly ground black pepper
- ¼ cup dry sherry

INDIVIDUAL BEEF WELLINGTONS

- 4 center-cut filet mignon steaks, 2½ inches thick
- Salt and medium-grind black pepper
- 1 tablespoon neutral oil or nonaerosol neutral oil spray
- ¼ cup brandy
- 4 teaspoons Dijon mustard
- 1 (8-ounce) terrine of peppercorn mousse pâté or truffle mousse pâté
- A small handful or scoop of flour, for rolling the dough
- 1 (14-ounce) package all-butter puff pastry, thawed for 2 hours in the fridge before using
- Egg wash: 1 egg beaten with 2 teaspoons water

■ Make the duxelles: Clean the mushrooms, stem, and cut into ¼-inch pieces.

■ In a large skillet, melt the butter over medium-high heat. When it foams, add the mushrooms and brown until fragrant and the volume reduces by about half. Add the shallots, garlic, and thyme and season with salt and pepper. Stir for 3 minutes to soften the shallots. Add the sherry and let it absorb fully. Remove from the heat and cool.

■ Make the Wellingtons: Bring the meat to room temp and pat dry. Gently press down on each steak to spread it and increase the surface area a bit, leaving steaks about 2 inches thick. Season with salt and pepper.

■ Heat a cast-iron skillet or griddle over high heat. Brush the oil all around the pan or mist with cooking spray. Add the meat to the pan, reduce the heat to medium-high, and cook the meat to develop a crust but not to cook through; it should remain very rare, 1½ to 2 minutes on the first side, 1 minute on the second side. Remove from the heat, add the brandy, and let it absorb, turning the meat in it. Set the steaks aside on a plate to cool completely, 15 to 20 minutes at room temp or 10 minutes in the fridge.

■ Position a rack in the center of the oven and preheat the oven to 400°F. Line a baking sheet with parchment paper.

■ Spread the top side of each steak with 1 teaspoon mustard. Cut the terrine into four equal portions.

■ Lightly flour a work surface and roll out the puff pastry dough a bit, then cut into 4 equal rectangles. Set a portion of terrine in the center of each rectangle and press gently to spread it out a bit, leaving a border. Top each with one-quarter of the cooled duxelles and a steak, mustard-side down. Pull the edges of the pastry up and around the beef, pleating it in the center and pressing so there are no open seams. Brush with some egg wash to help seal. Flip the bundles over, seam-side down, and brush the tops and sides with egg wash.

■ Arrange the Wellingtons seam-side down on the lined baking sheet and bake until golden, 12 to 15 minutes.

Tortellini in Brodo

SERVES 4 TO 6

FILLING

2 tablespoons EVOO

½ pound ground turkey

¼ pound ground veal

½ cup minced onion

2 cloves garlic, grated or minced

⅛ teaspoon freshly grated nutmeg

Salt and ground white pepper

1 ounce sliced mortadella with pistachio (2 to 3 slices)

1 ounce sliced Prosciutto di Parma (2 to 3 slices) or a small piece of an end, chopped

2 tablespoons chopped flat-leaf parsley

¼ cup grated Parmigiano-Reggiano cheese

1 large egg

TORTELLINI

Food Processor Easy Egg Pasta Dough (recipe follows)

2 tablespoons semolina

4 quarts brodo (bone broth or stock), store-bought or homemade (see Note)

■ Make the filling: In a medium skillet, heat the EVOO (two turns of the pan) over medium heat. Add the turkey and veal and lightly brown. Add the onion, garlic, and nutmeg and season with salt and white pepper. Cook to soften the onion. Add ½ cup water and let it fully absorb. Cool the mixture completely and transfer to a food processor.

■ To the food processor, add the mortadella, prosciutto, and parsley and pulse to fully combine and mince. Transfer the filling to a bowl, add the Parm and egg, and combine thoroughly. Cover and set aside.

■ Make the tortellini: Cut the dough into 3 sections and pass each through a pasta machine three times on the thickest setting, then twice on each subsequent setting to form thin sheets (I stop one away from the thinnest setting).

■ Lay the pasta sheets on a work surface and cut into 2½-inch squares. Dot each square with filling. Fold corner to corner to form a triangle and use a dab of water on a fingertip to seal. Push out air pockets and bring the bottom two corners of the filled triangles together and pinch tightly to seal. Roll each tortellini forward to set the filling into a firm ring inside the pasta. As you work, set the tortellini on a tray dusted with the semolina.

■ When ready to serve, bring the brodo to a low boil. Add the tortellini and gently simmer until the pasta is al dente and the filling is cooked through, 3 to 5 minutes. Ladle the brodo and tortellini into bowls.

Note: You can make bone broth by roasting chicken, turkey, and beef bones and combining in a large pot of water with root vegetables (like carrots, turnips, and/or parsnips), onion, celery, and garlic. Boil to extract all the flavor, then strain. Or buy store-bought chicken, veal, turkey, and/or beef bone stock and combine in one pot.

FOOD PROCESSOR EASY EGG PASTA

MAKES 1 POUND

2 cups AP flour
1 tablespoon semolina
1 teaspoon salt
⅛ teaspoon freshly grated
   nutmeg
3 large eggs
About 1 tablespoon EVOO

■ In a food processor, combine the AP flour, semolina, salt, and nutmeg and pulse together. Add the eggs and pulse on a long burst to combine the eggs. Stream in the EVOO to combine into a dough. Remove to a work surface and knead to form a smooth surface on the dough, about 10 minutes. Wrap in plastic and let rest for 30 minutes before rolling out.

This is a traditional Christmas dish, except when our friend Tommy requests it for his autumn birthday.

Easiest Brisket Ever,

ZUCCHINI AND POTATO LATKES, AND BITTER GREENS SALAD

SERVES 4 TO 6

EASIEST BRISKET EVER

SERVES 4 TO 6

- 4 pounds well-trimmed brisket
- Kosher salt and freshly ground black pepper
- 4 tablespoons (½ stick) butter
- 4 medium onions, chopped or quartered and thinly sliced
- 2 bay leaves
- 1 teaspoon ground thyme or small bundle fresh
- 1 teaspoon ground white pepper
- 2 to 3 tablespoons dry sherry (optional)
- 2 tablespoons olive or canola oil
- 2 cups beef bone broth or low-sodium beef stock
- 2 tablespoons demi-glace or 1 bouillon cube
- 2 tablespoons Worcestershire sauce

▪ Remove the brisket from its packaging, place on a cutting board or plate, and season with salt and black pepper. Allow to come to room temperature.

▪ Meanwhile, in a large, deep cast-iron skillet or large Dutch oven, melt the butter over medium-low to medium heat. Add the onions, bay leaves, thyme, and white pepper. Season with salt and cook until golden brown and soft, 25 to 30 minutes. Add the sherry (if using) and let it absorb. Transfer the caramelized onions to a bowl.

▪ Position a rack in the center of the oven and preheat the oven to 325°F.

▪ In the same pan, heat the olive oil (two turns of the pan) over medium-high heat. Add the brisket and brown for about 5 minutes on each side. Reduce the heat and top the brisket with the caramelized onions and add the broth. Melt in the demi-glace or bouillon and add the Worcestershire. Cover the pot with heavy foil or a lid and place in the oven to braise until very tender, 3½ to 4 hours. Slice and serve.

(CONTINUED)

(CONTINUED)

> Shallow-fry or, if you'd prefer less oil and drier latkes, bake them (see Note).

ZUCCHINI AND POTATO LATKES WITH ZA'ATAR

SERVES 4 TO 6

APPLESAUCE

3 apples, peeled and cut into small dice

1 cup cloudy apple cider

2 tablespoons fresh thyme, chopped

½ teaspoon salt

LATKES

2 zucchini, halved, seeded, and shredded on the large holes of a box grater

2 potatoes, peeled and shredded on the large holes of a box grater

Kosher salt

2 medium or 1 large egg, lightly beaten

3 tablespoons za'atar, store-bought or homemade (recipe follows)

¼ cup whole wheat flour, matzo meal, or AP flour

½ teaspoon baking powder

Frying oil (olive or grapeseed) or nonaerosol cooking spray

YOGURT SAUCE

1 cup yogurt or sour cream

1 clove garlic, grated

½ cup finely chopped mixed fresh herbs: dill, parsley or cilantro, and chives

1 tablespoon prepared horseradish (optional)

Juice of ½ lemon

■ Make the applesauce: In a small pot, combine the apples, cider, thyme, and salt and cook over medium-high heat until a slightly chunky sauce forms, about 20 minutes.

■ Make the latkes: Place shredded zucchini and potatoes in a large bowl or colander lined with a clean kitchen towel. Add 3 generous pinches of salt. Mix well and let sit for 5 minutes to let the salt draw out the water, then squeeze out excess liquid from the vegetables by twisting the kitchen towel. Place the wrung-out zucchini and potatoes in a dry bowl and add the eggs, za'atar, flour, and baking powder and mix to combine.

■ Pour a shallow layer of frying oil into a large skillet and heat over medium-high heat until the oil starts to shimmer (or reaches about 375°F).

■ Meanwhile, use your hands to form 12 equal-size zucchini/potato patties and place on a plate.

■ Working in two batches, add the latkes to the hot oil and cook until golden and crispy on the outside, about 3 minutes on each side. Drain latkes on paper towels. You can keep the latkes warm on a baking sheet in a low oven if necessary.

■ Make the yogurt sauce: In a small bowl, stir together the yogurt, garlic, herbs, horseradish (if using), and lemon juice.

■ Serve the latkes with both sauces on the side for topping.

> Note: To bake latkes, preheat the oven to 425°F. Mist a parchment-lined sheet pan with cooking spray. Add small mounds of the latke mixture to the lined sheet pan and flatten with a fork or the palm of your hand. Mist the top side of the latkes with the cooking spray and bake until crisp and golden, about 15 minutes, flipping halfway through.

ZA'ATAR SPICE

MAKES A GENEROUS ¼ CUP

2 tablespoons toasted
  sesame seeds

1 tablespoon sumac

1½ teaspoons ground cumin

1½ teaspoons ground
  coriander

1 teaspoon dried oregano
  or thyme

1 teaspoon Aleppo pepper
  or other ground chiles of
  choice

▪ In a small bowl, stir
together the sesame
seeds and all the
seasonings.

BITTER GREENS SALAD

SERVES 4 TO 6

1 head escarole, chopped

1 head Treviso or radicchio,
  thinly sliced

1 cup parsley tops

1 cup celery tops plus 2 ribs
  thinly sliced on an angle

½ red onion, very thinly
  sliced

2 or 3 baby beets (optional),
  shaved on a mandoline

DRESSING

1 tablespoon prepared
  horseradish or
  horseradish with beets

2 teaspoons Dijon mustard

Juice of ½ lemon

2 tablespoons wine vinegar
  or apple cider vinegar

⅓ cup EVOO

Salt and freshly ground
  black pepper

▪ Combine the salad ingredients
in a large bowl. Whisk up the
dressing or shake in a mason jar.
Adjust the seasoning. Dress the
salad and toss to serve.

John's Pear Spritzer

MAKES ONE COCKTAIL

1½ ounces pear brandy

3 to 4 ounces champagne

Thin slice of pear, for garnish

Fresh rosemary sprig, for garnish

Fresh thyme sprig, for garnish

■ Add the brandy and champagne to an ice-filled wine goblet. Stir gently and garnish with a pear slice, rosemary sprig, and thyme sprig.

Full Circle

The annoying little wheel that spins on the computer—as I write this, it feels like our world is that wheel, as the hours, days, weeks, and months pass, and we remain in a holding pattern, waiting for things to go back to normal. This year has had me spinning and thinking about circles, things happening and then happening again, over and over. Pandemic spikes. Businesses gone or reinventing, then reinventing again. Congress spinning its wheels on nearly everything the country needs done. The election being called. Being uncalled. Being called again. But at the same time, so many new things and ideas were born. What we thought we needed to survive and to be happy changed, our lives changed, as we watched the wheel spin and waited for the host to let us into the Zoom.

I'm religious, in my own way. And I believe that the longer you've lived, the more things start to make sense. Patterns start to form and reveal themselves. And this year has certainly proven this idea.

My greatest fear as a person on TV every day was crossing the line between my private life and public life. I worked hard to keep the two separated. Then, in shooting a daily national television show inside my

house, I was forced to overcome this fear. Then, in overcoming it, I arrived at a really good place. I was finally comfortable letting people into my home, I finally learned that lesson. And I lost my home.

When you've blown wide open and become hyperaware, as we all were this year, you start to see patterns. Here's one of mine: For years I've been obsessed with first responders. I've always been a passionate advocate for them. I'd even suited up and charged into a controlled fire to help raise awareness about how brave and how underfunded fire departments are. That's why when my home caught fire, I knew what to do. I supported them, and then those guys supported me. And I likely survived the fire at my home because of them. If God or the universe or whatever you believe in only gives us what we can handle, it gave me something I'd literally been _trained_ to handle.

Another pattern I saw was Isaboo. She came into my life on 07/05/2005. She left us on 05/20/2020.

Al Roker! For the first show we tried to shoot for CBS in the guesthouse in August, our first big test after the fire, I interviewed Al . . . who happened to be the first person to put me on television twenty years earlier. Full circle.

Maybe this one's less a circle and more just perfect dramatic irony: After we came upstate, New York City became the world's top COVID hotspot and one of the main locations for the country's Black Lives Matter protests. We watched it all with horror and awe, respectively. The marches were mostly peaceful, but not always. The day after a car fire on our apartment block, near Union Square, our friend Cara offered to go to our apartment and send some important things to our place upstate, for safekeeping. She shipped our passports and most of our other important documents, some favorite clothes and jewelry, and anything precious we'd kept in the city. It all arrived safely, we were relieved to see. Days later, it all burned in the house fire.

Then there's my car. John and I were going to take a drive on the afternoon of our anniversary in September, about a month and a half after the fire. We'd planned to go in the car John bought me for my fortieth birthday, a beautiful '68 Mercedes, born the same year I was. That morning, our friend and contractor Steve decided to take it for its inspection and to get it cleaned, as a surprise to me. Somebody slammed into it in the parking lot at Jiffy Lube, wrecking it. So while I was sitting in the garage we'd converted into an office for

me in our new life, working, the car that should've been where I was got destroyed, on the very day I'd planned a special drive in it.

My purpose in sharing my thoughts about this year, the purpose behind this collection of stories and recipes from the hardest year of my adult life (and almost everyone else's), was to reach out and share some of the things that I've learned. We've all been, the world over, through a collective experience together. It's not often you can say that. Anyone paying attention felt the same fear, heartsickness, worry, and sadness—but because of the nature of the virus, it was harder for us to connect with each other. I wanted to share my stories and recipes to reconnect.

For me, 2020 was a bunch of patterns and circles. Circles of life and death, loss and gain, dark and light. As so many people have said, the year was its own lifetime. But the more it heaped on us, the more small

discoveries we made about ourselves, our abilities, our loved ones, our endurance. Americans had to learn so many new tricks, at every age, young and old. Some had to grow up too fast; others had to master, at an advanced age, whole new routines and disciplines (Zoom comes to mind). It was a year of starting out and being brave in new ways. And a year of starting over or just staying motivated enough to get up and try again in our Groundhog Day existence. The year brought many of us back to our humanity, in a weird paradox, like when a dream of falling turns into flying.

Over the course of one year, I lost my dog, my house, and like many, access to my workplace. I didn't see my New York City apartment

after leaving it in March, or my friends, my colleagues, or my community there. But I gained strengthened relationships with my readers, viewers, friends, family, and others. Everything was done with intent and planning this year, and it was stripped right down to the bone. On my show I wore less makeup, had no blowouts, adopted a minimalist wardrobe, had no flattering lighting, scripting, producing. . . . I became on TV who I authentically am in life.

This happened to so many people: The high heels stayed in the closet. The roots grew out. Mascara seemed like overkill for a video call at the dining room table or kitchen counter. We all got real. We kept working, watching our kids, cleaning our homes (which were also our offices and our schools . . .), and all of this through these cycles of loss.

Even in the absolute worst of times, we look for what we've learned. So many of us came together as families. Spent more time together—cooking, reading, commiserating, celebrating, feeling sad, feeling scared, feeling grateful. And from far apart so many of us grew closer. Sadly, our country also grew farther apart in some ways. The year brought so many people not only to cooking but to conversations they might not have had. In many ways, the ugliest year of our lives also brought us closer together.

What I've learned this year is that maybe our show should've <u>always</u> been smaller, more intimate. I received countless letters from people saying what "Rachael at Home" meant to them, that watching me cook in my kitchen, they felt like we were going through this together. The intimacy we created this year inspired long, beautiful, poignant expressions of thought. Through those letters I often felt a deeper connection than I would have even from in-person contact with them—that's how deeply they poured themselves onto page after page. And the gifts! Sometimes I just literally burst into tears. One woman, an artist with a shop on Etsy, made a framed needlepoint showing John with his flying V guitar, me in the necklace John gave me that I always wear, Bella and a bag of Nutrish, and Boo and Isaboo with halos over their heads. Another jaw-dropper came from a group of women in Vermont. After my house burned down, they got together and made a quilt over months, and stitched the words "May this quilt protect you." It went right on the bed and we call it our superhero cape. Another crocheted me a giant owl blanket—because I love owls—and you can button the feet! It is so beautiful.

A potter made me gorgeous pottery, and after I sent her a thank-you note, she made me more stuff. It becomes a circle of thank-yous, of infinite, self-regenerating gratitude! It's beautiful and life-affirming. In spite—or because—of the heartache of 2020, I saw a beautiful outpouring of love and emotion and grace. I spent a lot of my time, two to three times a week, trying to answer as many of those letters as possible by hand, to connect the circle. I call them my "gratitude days."

The year also taught me that we can do anything that we put our minds to. John and I had to work harder than ever. But it brought us a deeper appreciation of every single job on the show, because we've had to learn how to do many of those from home with nothing but advice, a computer, an iPhone, and a bunch of cables. And prayers—both ours and those of the producers and crew who watch us from afar.

The year was losses and gifts. Every time something bad happened, something happened almost immediately afterward to give me renewed hope. That messaging was there the whole year without question. Plain as day, as the nose on my face and the circles under my eyes. More circles! Those circles went deep this year, too.

The world spins in circles, as it takes another trip around the sun. I'm sending this book off to my publisher during the 2020 holiday season. I believe in the power of the collective of a Mass. In the twinkle of Santa's eye, the hope of the menorah, and the light of a New Year's dawn. Most important, I believe in us. I believe in humanity. I hope the gains we've made personally and spiritually will create new bonds and new pathways in years and decades to come. I feel that 2020 built a wave, one that's not going to crash down on us but instead carry us along and lift us up. I know it will take hope, faith, and charity—that awesome threesome—to get us through what lies ahead. And a lot of hard work. But this is America, where we have all of those things in spades. And plenty of delicious food to fuel the fight.

ACKNOWLEDGMENTS

I hate to say this was a girls' club, but it was. I wrote this book in a very different way from the twenty-six previous ones, and it started with intense conversations with my friend and editor Lauren Iannotti. I couldn't just sit and write these stories in a notebook as I usually do. These stories started as discussions, because they were so much about me and my life, and it made me so uncomfortable to focus on myself that I would get lost, start writing about other people and their suffering, lose the point, and go sideways. Lauren, thank you for keeping me between the lines on the page and on the road.

To Celeste Fine: I have fired so many agents in my life. I don't even consider you an agent; I consider you a friend who came in and said, "Man, I get you. Let me do this one project and we'll see how goes." I'd say it went pretty well! But can we figure out another title for you? I hate the word "agent."

To Pamela Cannon at Ballantine: Pamela, you suffered through the pain of my first memoir/mashup, *Rachael Ray 50*, when we cried and poured buckets of wine together. I can't imagine an editor going through worse than what I put you through. You're patient; you never placate; you're a pro. And you are the walking, talking personification of New York. Just texting with you makes me miss the city, because somehow you even text like a New Yorker.

Thanks to photographer Silja Magg and her team, who shot the cover of this book and many of the inside photographs. I hate having my photo taken and Bella—my wild, enormous, goofy, suspicious-of-strangers dog—wasn't much better. My husband wouldn't have you in the house, and all I cared about was whether the dinner I cooked for you and the crew came out right. But we all survived. Thank you for the beautiful work. I hope the curry was yummy.

Thanks to Kate Mathis, Megan Hedgpeth, and Barrett Washburne, the dream team who shot the food photos and then some. To creative director Phoebe Flynn Rich for helping steer the ship visually, and to Debbie Glasserman at Ballantine for bringing it all home. To Minnie Kim, Nicole Jones, Paige Landsem, and Alexandra Wozniczka: Thank you for letting us hassle you for images!

I talk a lot in this book about the process of John and me working alone, and frankly that's the only thing I can report from the home front in my dispatches—because we're the only ones here. But I know my friends in New York have worked tirelessly to take our recordings—our nonsense, our goings-on, my "let's make seven different pizzas today" fifteen hours of footage—and turn them into actual programming suitable for television. Thank you to everyone in the control room, the editing suites, and the kitchen. Special thanks to Rich Cervini, Janet Annino, Scott Preston, Robbie Vilchez, Leslie Williams, Chad Carter, Andrew Goldman, Meredith Weintraub, Emily Reiger, Tommy Crudup. They're not colleagues; they're friends who get me and direct me. Thank you to Jorge "Papi" Andrango, kitchen steward and backbone of the food team, who kept things rolling at the studio throughout lockdown.

A special thank-you to Michelle Boxer for helping me sort so many ingredients–not a normal gig for a director of communications. In those early days you *were* the kitchen. In later ones you helped me piece my life back together.

The first thing I did in 2020 after my house burned to the ground was our remote kids' cooking camp, the brainchild of my colleagues Jo Gryfe and Andrew Kaplan. The camp helped me come back to myself, and I'm grateful to them and to Lee Shraeger and his entire team for making it the success that it was–not to mention the chefs who joined us: Bobby Flay, Maneet Chauhan, Carla Hall, Jet Tila, Anne Burrell, and so many others.

Thank you to Cara Jammet for trying to dress me as you'd like me to dress in the country, but I said no so you sent me a bunch of sweatpants and turtlenecks. Thank you to Patty Mocarski for the hair color and the scissors to cut John's hair, and to Joe J. Simon for the makeup. I hope I didn't embarrass you guys–I did the best I could.

To my sister, Maria Betar, and our friends up here in the woods–Amy Colomb and Melanie Older–who drove miles and miles to secure COVID-safe ingredients and supplies we needed to record a food show from our home, and an endless supply of Lysol wipes for John. We could not have made the show or this book without you. Thank you for the early mornings, the patience, and all the road running you did.

Most of all, I have to acknowledge my husband, John Cusimano. Alongside John Hall and his trusted team, my husband runs our company, Watch Entertainment. He is a lawyer and his specialty is entertainment contracts and licensing. He knew nothing about TV production other than what he'd picked up from popping into the studio for the last fifteen years as a guest. He is now everything from gaffer to lighting director to director of photography to any number of jobs I don't even know the name of. Neither of us is patient; it's why we make great partners–we understand that about each other. But in 2020 he was the most patient I've seen him in the twenty years I've known him. He deserves a crown, but I couldn't buy one big enough to fit on his head after Janet gave him the director's chair. Thank you, I love you, my John-of-all-trades.

RACHAEL RAY is a multi-Emmy Award-winning syndicated television star, an iconic Food Network personality, a bestselling cookbook author, founder and editorial director of her own lifestyle magazine, *Rachael Ray In Season,* and founder of the Yum-o! organization and The Rachael Ray Foundation. She splits her time between New York City and the Adirondacks with her husband, John; her family; and her beloved pit bull, Bella Boo Blue.

rachaelrayshow.com